D1295934

Pound/Zukofsky

Louis Zukofsky, May 1929

THE CORRESPONDENCE OF EZRA POUND

Pound/Zukofsky

Selected Letters of Ezra Pound and Louis Zukofsky

EDITED BY BARRY AHEARN

A NEW DIRECTIONS BOOK

Some of the letters in this volume were previously published in *Montemora 8*.

The frontispiece and passport photograph on page 2 are both used courtesy of Paul Zukofsky.

Manufactured in the United States of America
First published clothbound in 1987
Published simultaneously in Canada by Penguin Books Canada Ltd.

Library of Congress Cataloging-in-Publication Data

Pound, Ezra, 1885–1972.
Pound/Zukofsky : selected letters of Ezra Pound and Louis Zukofsky.
(A New Directions Book)
(The Correspondence of Ezra Pound)
Includes index.
1. Pound, Ezra, 1885–1972—Correspondence.
2. Zukofsky, Louis, 1904–1978—Correspondence.
3. Poets, American—20th century—Correspondence.
I. Zukofsky, Louis, 1904–1978. Correspondence.
Selections. 1987. II. Ahearn, Barry. III. Title.
IV. Series: Pound, Ezra, 1885–1972. Correspondence.
PS3531.082Z4985 1987 811'.52 [B] 86–19181

ISBN 8112–1013–8

New Directions Books are published for James Laughlin
by New Directions Publishing Corporation,
80 Eighth Avenue, New York 10011

Contents

Editorial Practice

Most of the letters that passed between Ezra Pound and Louis Zukofsky have survived, but not all. There are occasional references on both sides to matters which must have been mentioned in correspondence now missing. My estimate is that we have about 90 to 95 percent of the letters. The total number amounts to 430, of which 222 are by Pound and 208 by Zukofsky. This last figure, however, is somewhat misleading. Pound's letters tended to be shorter than Zukofsky's. Zukofsky wrote more total pages than Pound, so that the breakdown of pages is approximately 55 percent by Zukofsky and 45 percent by Pound. The letters are housed primarily in two locations, at Yale University's Beinecke Library (Zukofsky to Pound) and at the Humanities Research Center of the University of Texas at Austin (Pound to Zukofsky). A handful (7) of letters from Pound to Zukofsky are in the collection of the library of the University of Victoria, British Columbia, Canada. Another handful (5) of Zukofsky letters to Ezra and Dorothy Pound can be found at Indiana University's Lilly Library. This edition includes one letter each from these latter two collections: Pound's letter of February 1928 (University of Victoria) and Zukofsky's letter of 7 May 1951 (Lilly). An interesting anomaly in the Beinecke collection is that some of Pound's letters to Zukofsky are housed there. In 1956, Zukofsky offered these to Charles Hamilton, who bought them and sold them to the Beinecke. One aspect of the transaction is puzzling: Zukofsky seems to have selected pages of Pound's letter at random. As a result, some of Pound's letters exist as a page or two at the Humanities Research Center, with the missing pages to be found at the Beinecke, and vice versa. In addition, some pages of the Pound originals are missing. Where possible, these have been replaced in this edition with Pound's carbon copies at the Beinecke. Almost all of the enclosures that Pound and Zukofsky mention are no longer with the letters, though a few of them survive in other portions of the Pound and Zukofsky archives.

This edition prints 96 of the letters, 44 by Pound and 52 by Zukofsky. I gave the edge to Zukofsky because Pound's letters for the most part tell us more about a man of whom much is already known, but Zukofsky is still relatively little known. In an ideal world all the letters would be printed, but the economics of publishing makes that impossible at present. It was decided by the editor and the publisher that the wiser course would be to keep the edition within the price range of the average scholarly book buyer; it is this constraint that has dictated the publication of only a quarter of the letters. The first criterion for selection was the degree to which a letter sheds light on the literary activities of the poets. The second was the extent to which a letter tells us about their personal relationship, their personal lives, and their political and economic views. Fourteen of these letters (nos. 6, 7, 12–15, 17, 21, 27, 28, 31–34) have been previously printed, in the eighth and final number of the literary magazine *Montemora.* They were presented there, however, with only minimal annotation. I have also made some minor corrections in the texts. Five other letters that appeared in *Montemora* are not reprinted here.

Pound's letters have been edited to look as much like the originals as possible. His misspellings have not been corrected. When Pound took care with his text he could spell perfectly. His misspellings, therefore, may be taken as one indication of the degree to which he felt his correspondence deserved careful attention. Pound's punctuation has also been left untouched. Where the editor has felt it necessary to intrude with an explanation, amplification, or correction, such intrusions are placed within square brackets. Some of the dates of the letters have been supplied from postmarks or internal evidence. These too are placed between square brackets. Pound's own afterthoughts and additions are placed within angle brackets. All of the above rules hold true for Zukofsky's letters, with the single exception that his salutations, which are placed above the first line in the holographs, are here moved down to begin the first line. Zukofsky never seemed to emphasize spacing as much as Pound did. Perhaps the major reason for this is that all of Zukofsky's letters were handwritten, whereas almost all of Pound's were typed. There are a few omissions. In Letter 58, a list of corrections to *The Exile* printing of "Poem Beginning 'The' " has been deleted. Paul Zukofsky requested that a few, minor deletions be made in Letters 43 and 88. These omissions have been indicated by ellipses enclosed in square brackets. All other ellipses are reproduced as in the originals.

The form and number of pages of the letters are indicated at the head of each. For example, TLS-3 indicates a typed letter signed by the author, consisting of three pages. Other abbreviations used are: ALS–autograph letter signed; and TCS–typed card signed. Signatures are located on the page as closely as possible to the same position in the originals.

Wherever possible, notations at the end of each letter inform the reader about people, books, journals (including Pound and Zukofsky's own works), organizations and the like that Pound and Zukofsky refer to. In a few cases, the references remain unidentified. Readers wanting further information about many of the people named should refer to the Biographical Notes.

This volume would not have been possible without the assistance of a number of indispensable books. Biographies of Pound by Charles Norman, Noel Stock, and James Wilhelm were often open on my desk, as was Celia Zukofsky's *A Bibliography of Louis Zukofsky* (Los Angeles: Black Sparrow Press, 1969). Donald Gallup's *Ezra Pound: A Bibliography* (Charlottesville, Virgina: The University Press of Virginia, 1983) helped me with almost every letter and is cited in the notes as "Gallup." Three other books cited frequently in the notes are: Louis Zukofsky, *"A"* (Berkeley, California: The University of California Press, 1978); Louis Zukofsky, *All: The Collected Short Poems 1923–1964* (New York: W. W. Norton, 1965); D. D. Paige, *The Selected Letters of Ezra Pound 1907–1941* (New York: New Directions, 1971).

I am deeply grateful to all the research librarians who helped me. Special thanks go to Donald Gallup, former Curator of the Collection of American Literature at the Beinecke Rare Book and Manuscript Library, and to his successor, David Schoonover. Ellen S. Dunlap, former Research Librarian at the Humanities Research Center of the University of Texas, went out of her way to help with the project and was invariably gracious. Both Saundra Taylor of the Lilly Library and C. G. Petter of the University of Victoria Library were extremely helpful.

Others who made the edition possible were: Massimo Bacigalupo, Philip Bollier, Gene Brucker, the late Basil Bunting, Joseph Cohen, Guy Davenport, L. S. Dembo, William di Canzio, Jill Farmer, Richard Finneran, Peter Green, Eva Hesse, Hugh Kenner, Paul Mariani, Timothy Materer, Samuel Moore, Charles Norman, Mary Oppen, Mary de Rachewiltz, Olga Rudge, Maaja Stewart, Sidonia Taupin, Carroll F. Terrell (who first conceived of a Pound/Zukofsky volume), Emily Mitchell Wallace, John and Patricia Walsh, James Wilhelm, Jonathan Williams, and Paul Zukofsky. I am especially indebted to Peter Glassgold, whose efforts in the editorial offices of New Directions were all-important.

At a crucial stage in the research for this volume, Tulane University's Senate Committee on Research provided me with a Summer Fellowship. For that I am most grateful.

Finally, deepest thanks to my wife, Pamela, who pitched in on many occasions with singular success.

Introduction

Ezra Pound (1885–1972) and Louis Zukofsky (1904–1978) met only three times: in Rapallo in 1933; in New York in 1939; at St. Elizabeths in 1954. At Rapallo they spent several weeks together. The other encounters lasted for a few hours. Yet by the time of their first meeting they had already exchanged 272 letters, over half the total of their entire correspondence. The significance of all this is simply that Pound and Zukofsky knew each other quite literally as men of letters. Pound wrote perhaps more to Zukofsky than to anyone else with whom he had such slight personal acquaintance. The same can probably be said of Zukofsky's letters to Pound, though he may have written as many to Lorine Niedecker.[1]

Zukofsky wrote so frequently to Pound because he considered Pound the foremost poet writing in English. His dedication of *An "Objectivists" Anthology* to Pound, reprinted here as he sent it to Pound on 12 October 1931 (Letter 40), makes that clear. Zukofsky began a transatlantic acquaintance by submitting "Poem Beginning 'The' " for *The Exile.* The letter accompanying the manuscript has not survived, though Charles Norman quotes a fragment from it in his *Ezra Pound.* As Norman indicated to me, he does not actually remember seeing such a letter. He may have been shown a draft of the letter by Zukofsky, or simply heard Zukofsky recall the substance of the letter. Whatever the message by which Zukofsky announced himself to Pound, it was probably cursory. The poem itself was the crucial introduction.

The editor of *The Exile* had opened up his journal to names that were completely unknown to the literary world at the time. Zukofsky had published in *Poetry* and a few small magazines in New York, but his reputation was no greater than that of scores of other young contemporaries who have long since been forgotten. We should note that when he wrote Pound, Zukofsky seemed to think of Cummings as the other great poet from whom

[1] Zukofsky's friendship with Niedecker was also conducted largely through the mail. We will probably never know if he did write more letters to her than to Pound, since Niedecker sliced up the letters and mounted bits of them on cardboard. Though useful as a system for isolating critical *obiter dicta,* it reduced Zukofsky's letters to shreds.

he could learn. He had already written Cummings, with the hope of arranging a meeting, but nothing had come of it. One is reminded somewhat of James Boswell's casting about for a great man to biographize, a journey which took him to Hume and Rousseau as well as to Doctor Johnson.

Zukofsky read Pound's critical pronouncements–*How to Read, ABC of Reading,* essays in *The Little Review, The Criterion, The Dial*–carefully and repeatedly. Sometimes the state of his finances compelled him to read them while standing in the bookstores that stocked foreign periodicals, especially ones that carried Italian journals, such as Brentano's. He also spent a lot of time in the New York Public Library. So for the most part, he did not query Pound about poetry, except when he had a question that ranged beyond subjects Pound had addressed. In his letter of 5 November 1930 (Letter 28), Zukofsky asks Pound about the relation between word accent and musical accent. He was following in Pound's footsteps by taking courses in Provençal, but by 1930 studies in that language were no longer at the cutting edge of literary scholarship, as they had been at the turn of the century. At the same time, he reports on the state of scholarship in the University of Wisconsin's English Department, finding that it falls short of the standards he has learned to expect from his reading of Pound. All of Zukofsky's criticisms of the faculty at Wisconsin seem to add up to the never-stated conclusion that what was wrong with them was that they were not Ezra Pound. Zukofsky finally got his chance at the "Ezuversity" in Rapallo, three years later.

Pound did not consider his letters to Zukofsky to be a correspondence course in creative writing. Just as Zukofsky's requests for help were rare, so Pound's strictures were few and far between. In March 1940 (Letter 85), Zukofsky's submission of a translation of a poem by Catullus prompted Pound into some brief remarks about Catullus and Sappho, but the relevance of Pound's linkage of Sappho and Catullus seems tenuous at best. The letters on the whole are not rewarding to the reader seeking literary criticism, though in one of his last letters to Pound (3 August 1960), Zukofsky spoke of digging the "nuggets of literary criticism" out of their correspondence. For the most part, the "nuggets" are not there. What Pound felt was important for young poets to know had already been said in his critical essays, or could be found by the serious student in his poems.

The letters begin with Pound in the middle of changing the personnel who ran *The Exile.* He was trying to ease John Price out of the picture and put Pascal Covici in charge. Pound probably had as one of his aims in founding *The Exile* the providing of a center around which a group of younger poets and novelists could gather. Since *The Exile* was an American production (after the first issue), Pound began to think in terms of a group based in the United States. He let the magazine expire after the fourth issue, trusting that new magazines on the scene, such as *Hound & Horn,* would take up the slack. Pound did not want to put all his poets into one basket, however, and prodded any of his American correspondents who he thought had the wherewithal to get into action. On 12 August 1928 (Letter 6), he wrote Zukofsky urging him to form a literary group in New York that he hoped would be characterized by some of the energy that had shone in the *Others* crowd. The extent to which Pound was out of touch with the New York literary scene is underscored by the list of luminaries he urged Zukofsky to seek out. Some of them, such as Jeanne Foster, had long since left Manhattan. Pound was unsure of the whereabouts of others; he tells Zukofsky to seek out Jane Heap, "if she is in N.Y." Zukofsky was quite willing to be directed by Pound. It meant, among other things, an introduction to William Carlos Williams, another attempt to get in touch with Cummings (this time with the added authority of Pound's name behind the request for a meeting), and the chance to make contact with the new authors who had appeared in *The Exile.*

Of course, the potent literary salon that Pound had hoped would appear in New York was never to be, but this did not stop him from trying to resuscitate American writing. And, in the long run, some of the friendships Zukofsky made through Pound's mediation were important, especially the friendship with Williams. Almost as soon as Zukofsky and Williams met, Zukofsky was editing the senior poet's work and sending it on to Pound. Pound, whose talents as an editor were extraordinary, began to notice that Zukofsky also had talent in that direction. He suggested to Harriet Monroe that Zukofsky be given charge of one issue of *Poetry.* The result was the "Objectivists" number of February 1931. Pound's most massive epistolary bombardment of Zukofsky occurred in October 1930, when he sent many pages of advice about editing the issue to his protégé. Pound saw an opportunity to start a new revolution in American poetry, as he indicated in his letter of 24 October 1930 (Letter 24), "The thing is to get out something as good as Des Imagistes by any bloody means at yr. disposal." *Des Imagistes* had been a powerful influence when it appeared in 1914, but as far as Pound was concerned Imagism had long since become outmoded. Zukofsky naturally reacted by adopting some of Pound's suggestions while resisting others. Between the lines of his replies to Pound one can detect some resentment that his issue was being so minutely fashioned from Rapallo. This was, after all, his issue to edit, no matter how much he respected his mentor. Pound had thought of this opportunity with *Poetry* as a chance to make the magazine vital once again. If the "Objectivists" number was a success, then Basil Bunting and René Taupin could be brought in to edit other issues. Miss Monroe was not getting any younger. Eventually, perhaps, Pound's followers in America could take over the magazine. Pound had hopes that Morton Dauwen Zabel, already an associate editor, could be brought into the fold. Unfortunately, Zukofsky's editorship of the "Objectivists" number proved to be the high-water mark of his early career. It did not spark the revolution in poetry that he and Pound had hoped for.

Pound continued, for the time being, to believe in Zukofsky's talents. On 23 February 1933 (Letter 56) Pound asked him to select American contributors to *Active Anthology*. Again, he was depending on the young poet's editorial instincts. Nor was Pound reluctant to enlist Zukofsky in battles for worthy causes. A letter of January 1931 (Letter 35) finds Pound calling for an attack on an unnamed individual at Random House for blocking any chance that Random House might publish Pound. Zukofsky is instructed to make the charge, but without any mention of the fact that Pound has put him up to it. Pound exulted in literary warfare. As he said on 8 November 1932 (Letter 52), "Our anthologies do seem to annoy, which is the best possible sign." Zukofsky, however, did not relish fighting the good fight as much as Pound did. Early in his career he was willing to take up the cudgels for all that was good and beautiful in poetry. But decades of rejection left him discouraged. Late in his life, he participated in a panel discussion about poetry. The question was put to the panelists: "What is the duty of the poet in the contemporary world?" Zukofsky answered that it was the duty of the poet to survive.

Writing to Zukofsky on 10 July 1933 (letter not included in this edition), Pound suggested he might want to extend his first European tour into a permanent stay. He wonders if Zukofsky has an interest in "constructing vicariously a salon," and even mentions a certain young lady—left nameless—to whom he is willing to introduce Zukofsky, and who might be of help in forming the salon. But Zukofsky, for whom Wisconsin had been his "hell hole," and who talked idly of moving to the Soviet Union, only felt at home in and around Manhattan. He may have made this clear to Pound when they finally got to see each other in August of 1933, or perhaps Pound saw Zukofsky's bias toward New York as provincialism. Though Pound and Zukofsky, according to all reports, got along well in Rapallo that summer, 1933 happens to mark a turning point in their relationship. Pound seems to have lost a good deal of his enthusiasm for his young friend's work. When *Active Anthology* finally appeared, Pound remarked in his afterword that, "A whole school or shoal of young American writers seems to me to have lost contact with language as language. . . . in particular Mr Zukofsky's Objectivists seems prone to this error, just as Mr Eliot's followers tend toward neo-Gongorism." Two years later, in 1935, Zukofsky and his younger friend Jerry Reisman wrote a screenplay of Joyce's *Ulysses.* They hoped that Joyce would approve it, and Zukofsky sent the typescript to Pound, asking him to put in a good word for them with Joyce. Pound's letter of 6 March 1935 (Letter 67) expresses his adamant refusal to do so. He goes on to accuse Zukofsky of being artistically backward, of being stuck in 1927—the year he first came to Pound's notice. Part of the reason for the growing rift between the two poets can be traced to their differing positions on political and economic issues, a rift which I cover in more detail below.

One aspect of Zukofsky's work Pound often singled out for criticism was its obscurity, its "Xcessive complicity" and lack of lucidity, as Pound noted on 14 December 1931 (Letter 45). It was a theme to which Pound kept returning, even when Zukofsky sent him prose, such as a copy of the manuscript for *The Writings of Guillaume Apollinaire.* Pound leapt to his typewriter on 6 December 1932 (Letter 53) and urged Zukofsky to begin studying the "technique of FLOW." He was upset by what seemed to him a lack of clarity, though by 1954 (Letter 89) he was not quite so taken aback by his friend's tendency to be "not ALWAYS comprehensible." Like Zukofsky, however, Pound was not afraid of the difficult, and applauded when the difficulties appeared to be necessary. After receiving the formidably complex "A"–8, the most ambitious single work that Zukofsky had yet produced, Pound was able to report on 7 January 1936 (Letter 72), that he had "read with pleasure A.8." Furthermore, he was going to urge T. S. Eliot to print it. But it was evidently too much for "the Possum." None of it appeared in *The Criterion.*

It was particularly gratifying to Zukofsky that Pound had liked "A"–8. The ongoing *"A"* was the project nearest to his heart, and it is clear from his letters that Zukofsky was most upset when Pound showed doubts about it. This is particularly evident in his letter of 12 December 1930 (Letter 33), composed under the stress of editing the "Objectivists" number of *Poetry.* Zukofsky denies the charge that *"A"* is an imitation of *The Cantos,* and strenuously disputes the allegation that he is too much under Pound's influence. Another letter, of 7 December 1930 (Letter 43), finds Zukofsky seeking to remove Pound's doubts about the poem by telling him that the musician Tibor Serly finds "A"–7 to be like music in its logical development. One interesting point about *"A"* that is not mentioned in the letters is that Pound had done some editing on early versions of "A"–1 and

"A"–2. The manuscripts are now in the Pound Archive at the Beinecke Library. Before Zukofsky got much further with the poem, however, he stopped asking Pound for such detailed advice. In contrast with Zukofsky's defense of *"A,"* Pound has almost nothing to say about his *Cantos*. Most of what he does say is simply concerned with his desire to place them in publications that will pay for them. Nevertheless, the letters are often a good index to what was on Pound's mind in the 1930s, and inevitably some of the concerns he expresses to Zukofsky appear later in *The Cantos*. For example, the assertion Pound found in William Dudley Pelley's magazine, *Liberation*–that the Rothschilds used the American Civil War for their own nefarious ends–shows up in Canto 48.

Pound's letters are a curious mixture of forthrightness and reticence. He was always ready to air his views on matters of public concern, but rarely talked about personal matters. In this respect, these letters contain no surprises; they are much like the Pound letters already in print. So quiet is he about his private life that when he mentions "Olga" (Rudge) for the first time, in December 1931, the mystified Zukofsky asks, "Who's Olga?"

For the most part, Zukofsky and Pound saw eye to eye on literary matters. Both men agreed almost completely on the value or lack of it in their contemporaries. Both were keenly interested in providing an outlet for the works of their friends. So, when Zukofsky would write of plans he and others had formulated to start a publishing house, whether it be To Publishers, the Objectivist Press, or schemes that fell through, Pound was quick to reply with lengthy letters of advice about who should be published and in what order, what sort of press equipment and financial backing would be required, and so forth. Occasionally, when Pound's exacting standards were not met, he could be blunt with his partners. After receiving the Objectivist Press edition of William Carlos Williams's *Collected Poems 1921–1931,* Pound wrote to Zukofsky on 6 February 1934 (letter not included here) that he was highly dissatisfied with the selection of poems. Williams, he wrote, "has putt in, I shd. think ALL the mos' grdm sentimental diabetis he ever had." For the most part, however, such Poundian complaints were the exception rather than the rule.

Perhaps the greatest literary disagreement between Pound and Zukofsky came in the 1930s. As the decade progressed, Zukofsky's respect for Cummings waned, while Pound's seemed to increase. On 15 March 1935 (Letter 68), Zukofsky was moved to contrast the "solipsistic daze-maze of Mr. Kummings" with the "spark of energy" he detected in Lorine Niedecker. Zukofsky probably felt that he himself was a better poet than Cummings, and that Pound had backed the wrong horse.

Pound's regard for Cummings was partly based on attitudes about the

Soviet Union that Cummings had expressed in *Eimi.* Cummings's characterization of his trip through Russia as a journey through hell agreed with Pound's growing conviction in the mid-1930's that the Marxist experiment was a failure. In the early part of the decade, Pound had seen the Soviet Union as a promising arena. He even suggested in 1931 that Zukofsky might want to spend some time there. Zukofsky's reply of 25 April 1931 (Letter 38) agrees that "Rhoosia" is the place for the young to be, but not himself. During the mid-1930s, Pound's letters increasingly reflected his admiration for the economic policies of Benito Mussolini. When *Il Duce* spoke in Milan on 6 October 1934, announcing that the problems of economic production had been solved and that the next step was to solve the problems of distribution, Pound was delighted. He wrote to Zukofsky on 16 October (letter not included here) to announce, "The boss BURIED scarcity economics ten days ago. NO flowers." Zukofsky was quite upset by his friend's support of Mussolini, especially when Pound spoke out in public. In a letter to Pound of 25 May 1935 (not printed here) he exploded, "I believe that the writer of certain correspondence re Mussolini in the Criterion and American notes in N[ew].E[nglish].W[eekly]. is not even fit to judge even one 'fahrt's worth of Work,' as you put it."[2] Many of the letters Pound and Zukofsky exchanged for the rest of the decade are marked by tedious wrangling over economic questions. Much of the time they argued over the definition of "commodity," with neither man convincing the other to change his mind about it. All this contention almost drowned out literary discussion.

While pointing out the benefits that Mussolini had conferred on Italy, Pound was even more concerned that Zukofsky be won over to the side of Social Credit. When his pupil proved recalcitrant, the instructor got angry. He wrote to Zukofsky on 13 May 1935 (letter not included here):

> Like all god damn inhabitants of the lost continent, you maintain yr/ ignorance/ and take no notice of let us say Hargrave's[3] work with british MASSES, to produce mass resistance. It is disgusting to see a bloke that once was intelligent SIT DOWN on a given date–yours 1919)

[2] See Pound's "American Notes," *New English Weekly* 6:25 (4 April 1935). "The howls about 'Fascist danger' in America are mostly nothing but hypocrisy. A few men really fear fascism. A vast mass of slimy and ignorant editors fill their columns with false dangers to hide the real progress of absolutely irresponsible and de facto tyranny (laws against 'criminal syndicalism,' etc., and grabs at real power, untempered by ANY organization or principle whatsoever)."

[3] John Hargrave was one of the most important leaders of the British Social Credit movement. Pound corresponded with him extensively.

But Zukofsky remained unconvinced of Social Credit's value. As he wrote to Pound on 11 May 1935 (letter not included here), "I will not take up with Social Credit because like Pres. Roosevelt etc., it is still trying to save *Capital.*" The cure for economic ailments, said Zukofsky, was communism. Writing about the American scene to Pound on 18 January 1936 (letter not included here), he expressed the wish that Pound would come and see for himself. "It's very simple. Any intelligence worth anything can see that communism is the only way out–whatever he thinks of the present control of the Party." Later that year, Zukofsky found himself defending the government of the U.S.S.R. to Pound. Letter 75 is one of many in which Pound's advocacy of Fascism for Italy–and Social Credit for Britain and America–collides with Zukofsky's praise of Soviet Communism. It is worth noting that once Zukofsky cast his praise in the form of poetry, in "A"–8, Pound did not object to it. Ultimately, both men were poets rather than politicians.

Though Pound's biography–the details of his day-to-day life–are only meagerly scattered through his letters, Zukofsky was accustomed to venting his frustrations about life during the Depression. The difficulties of making ends meet during these years made all the more acute Zukofsky's bitterness about not being paid for his poems and essays, a bitterness evident in his letter of 15 December 1932 (Letter 54). On 7 December 1931 (Letter 43), he gives a vivid description of his hand-to-mouth existence, during which he spends 15 cents on breakfast and skips the subsequent two meals. In a letter of 14 December 1931 (Letter 45), he laments the penuriousness of his brother Morris, who seems to have employed Louis at starvation wages. A year later, during the last months of the Hoover administration, Zukofsky complains that Samuel Putnam owes him 11 dollars, money badly needed to pay the rent. Zukofsky periodically reminds Pound, too, that various family members are dependent on him for their survival. Pound was touched by this distress, though perhaps not surprised. Pound himself had been no stranger to poverty, and had moved in circles where many worthy artists did not know where to find their next meal. Yet Pound did send Zukofsky small sums for the purchase of books to be sent to Rapallo, and often allowed Zukofsky to keep anything left over. Pound showed his generosity in an ampler way when he helped finance Zukofsky's passage to Europe. He even provided Zukofsky with his favorite room in the Paris hotel where he always stayed, and gave him tips about where to find good, cheap meals.

Pound's characteristic generosity is often evident in the correspondence. In one of his earliest letters to Zukofsky, that of 5 March 1928 (Letter 4),

Pound urges him to make the acquaintance of his parents in Philadelphia. Zukofsky did so, and kept up his contact with both father and son. (In the mid-1930s, Zukofsky wrote a letter to Homer Pound that questioned whether Social Credit had as clear-cut a program for disposing of private banks as the Communists did. Ezra replied angrily, charging that Zukofsky's letter was so much "puke.") In the 1950s, the Zukofskys were able to repay some of the help Pound had given to the young Zukofsky. They kept sending packages of cookies, cakes, and candies to St. Elizabeths. Much of Pound's correspondence to Zukofsky in the late 1950s is a series of thank you notes. Two of them appear in "A"–13, pp. 264 and 288.

These expressions of gratitude sometimes came to the Zukofsky home after a letter in which Pound berated Louis for some intellectual or political failing. In a 1957 letter not included here, Pound explodes, "If you are capable of encouraging or consoling Possum for tolerating Niebuhr[,] our correspondence had better draw to a close."[4] One month later, Pound writes again: "Thank yu for one frUIT cake at least I spose its a frUIT cake & that I ought to let it ripen before breaking into it TO find out."

Pound's asperity is certainly one of the hallmarks of his correspondence. He petulantly asks in one of his last letters to Zukofsky, that of 23 June 1959 (Letter 93), whether his Brooklyn friend has "shown any interest in life of the mind, for the past 20 years?" The anger is directed at someone whom Pound respected. He had at last come around to believing that Zukofsky's art outshone that of Cummings. Pound berated Zukofsky now because he thought that the intellectual life of the nation needed the services of the Brooklyn poet, but the poet was keeping quiet. Pound did not fully understand that Zukofsky's silence in the critical world was not altogether voluntary. In the 1950s, Zukofsky was still having the same trouble getting published that he had had in the 1930s. He still had no publisher, though Pound did. When Zukofsky was unable to find a publisher for *Bottom: On Shakespeare,* the letters he had received from Pound were given to the University of Texas in exchange for their publication of that volume. It was not until 1966 that Zukofsky saw one of his books released by a trade publisher. Were it not for Zukofsky's failure to find a publisher

[4] The "encouragement" of Possum (T. S. Eliot) turned out to be a mystery to Zukofsky. His reply to Pound pointed out that he had met Eliot only once, in London in 1957, and that "As for my 'encouraging' T.S.E., my gawd, do you really believe that would be possible even if I had tried, you knowing about his vices and my inability to say anything I can't possibly feel, let alone think,–whatever expression I used by way of polite courtesy in meeting him that one time in my life? I dropped in to say hello, because I was in London & he was human enough to let me do so. And that was the end of that."

for another of his projects, this edition of the Pound/Zukofsky letters might not have been necessary. In a letter of 15 October 1960, not included here, Zukofsky announced to Pound that "the University of Texas Press has asked me to edit a volume of letters." The volume would have consisted of letters to Zukofsky from various correspondents, including Pound. Accordingly, he wrote to ask Pound's "permission to select and print from whatever of your letters I have." No letter from Pound giving or withholding permission has survived, but the book never appeared, in any case.

One of the most fascinating aspects of the correspondence is the way in which both men could come to verbal blows, yet continue their dialogue. From time to time, for example, Pound threatens to cease writing to Zukofsky, but he never does ring down the curtain. The great hiatus in their correspondence (1940–1948) was caused by the interruption of postal service during World War II. What kept them talking was a special relationship they established, a relationship partly serious and partly facetious: that of father and son. In his letter of 28 October 1930 (Letter 27), Pound takes a paternal role in advising Zukofsky how to behave in Madison. He remembers his own, comparable experiences in Crawfordsville, Indiana, and speaks of himself as the "aged parent." Zukofsky was not slow to take up his role. In a letter of 6 March 1931 (not included here), he refers to himself as "sonny" and to Pound as "papa." A few months later, on 28 October 1931 (Letter 41), Pound salutes Zukofsky as his "Deerly beloved son." This exchange of domestic pleasantries continues into December 1932, with Pound beginning a letter, "Delectus mihi filius," and Zukofsky replying with, "Our Favver Who Art on Earth." By the late 1930s, when relations had grown strained, Zukofsky still referred to himself as "yr. erst. son." By taking the roles of father and son both men showed themselves thinking in terms of literary tradition, with Pound handing down a portion of his art to Zukofsky, just as he himself had found a poetic father in Browning. In one letter, Zukofsky even refers to Browning as "your papa." Playing the son was at first a comfortable persona for Zukofsky. The role suggested a close relationship and a willingness to listen with pious respect to the teachings of Pound. For Pound, acting as papa was a role he relished from a very early stage in his career–at least as far back as his London years. Later on, he dubbed himself "grampaw" of the young writers who came to St. Elizabeths. To be a father, as Pound saw it, meant to be a teacher, to guide the young in the proper paths.

Another side of the father/son bond also proved useful, but more so to Zukofsky. It is the son's privilege–even a necessity–to rebel against the father. So long as the rebellion is not absolute secession, the son can stay in close contact with the father yet still point out parental failings. As the 1930s wore on, this aspect of the father/son tie became more and more important. When Zukofsky wanted to "bawl out" (as he phrased it) his literary father, he could do so with all the privileges of immunity enjoyed by a well-intentioned but stubborn son. Finally, however, when the two resumed corresponding in the 1950s, the relationship had changed. It was no longer a dialogue between "papa" and "sonny." Zukofsky had become his own man.

It has become a commonplace for defenders of Pound to point to his friendship with Zukofsky as one major indication that he was not anti-Semitic. Had they known of the father/son dialogue between the two their case would have been strengthened. But what do the letters tell us about the relationship between Pound and Zukofsky insofar as this question is concerned? What did it mean to Pound (and Zukofsky) that the man with whom he carried on such a lengthy exchange was also a Jew?

To begin with, we should note that although Zukofsky's father was, according to Zukofsky, a pious and practicing Jew, Zukofsky himself was not. As early as "Poem Beginning 'The,' " Zukofsky was calling himself a *shagetz,* a term which he uses again in his letter of 15 April 1940 (Letter 86).[5] According to his own admission in letters to Pound, Zukofsky lost his religious beliefs when still a teenager. His early letters to Pound also indicate that Zukofsky had little sense of himself as part of the Jewish community. At times, he could sound a bit anti-Semitic himself, as in his letter of 19 December 1929 (Letter 13): "Do I luf my peepul? The only good Jew I know is my father: a coincidence." In the 1920s, it seems, Zukofsky's allegiance was entirely to his family–not to his "peepul." Zukofsky's descriptions of his few dealings with Jewish organizations, such as the *Menorah Journal,* are characterized by disgust at their backwardness and benightedness. As he says on 12 January 1930 (Letter 16) about one visit he made to their offices, "my seeing the Sanhedrin a few weeks ago was only a temporary fall to the plea of 'thoughtful' heads." On the other hand, when Zukofsky encounters anti-Semitism he is resigned. His letter of 15 April 1933 (Letter 58) finds him taking it for granted that he can't teach at Columbia University because he is a Jew.

Nevertheless, as virulent anti-Semitism increased in Europe during the 1930s, Zukofsky grew more and more alarmed and angry. He began to

[5] Leo Rosten's *The Joy of Yiddish* defines a "Shaygets" as a young, male Gentile. Zukofsky's use of the word, however, suggests he understood it to mean an anti-Semitic Jew.

point out to Pound the foolishness and danger of linking economic reform with animus against Jews. On 12 April 1934 (Letter 63), he wrote to Pound, objecting to Major Douglas's anti-Semitism, as expressed in the journal *Social Credit.* At this point Zukofsky is still showing traces of anti-Semitism himself, probably to demonstrate to Pound that his objections are not based on a sense of racial superiority or defensiveness. After expressing his unhappiness with the Major, he goes on to say that he would "betray and immolate most of my people for 1 Serly." From the standpoint of the post-Holocaust era, Zukofsky's choice of the word "immolate" becomes sadly prophetic and extremely unfortunate. Of course he was probably thinking of the Jews burned alive in East European pogroms, memories still strong in the Lower East Side of his childhood and youth.

Zukofsky's warnings to Pound do seem to have had some effect. On the 6th and 7th of May 1934 (Letter 64), Pound urged Zukofsky to join the side of economic truth or he might suffer at the hands of the Ku Klux Klan. Pound was sure that if the righteous Jews did not turn against the economic crimes of their cousins, the usurers, then the resulting massacre would lump together the guilty and the innocent. Pound assured Zukofsky that he was doing his best to drive home this distinction between the just and the unjust to the minds of such people as William Dudley Pelley. "I shall tell Pelley," writes Pound, "there haz been non-yitt bankers and financiers." Even so, Zukofsky never seemed to be able to convince Pound that his tirades against Jewish bankers were playing into the hands of those who didn't care so much for economic justice as for the opportunity to kill Jews. On 10 July 1938 (Letter 81), Pound queried Zukofsky about the Khazars. Someone had written him to the effect that the Jews of ancient Israel no longer existed, that in fact modern Jews were descended from this Middle Eastern people. Pound may have been thinking of this new perspective on anti-Semitism as a way of avoiding altogether the problem of lumping the just with the unjust. If there were no such people as Jews, then the problem of indiscriminate anti-Semitism would disappear. One could focus one's attention on usurers of whatever description.

The Khazar theory, however, has not been used to reduce or eliminate anti-Semitism but to exacerbate it. Pound's attention was brought to it once more in 1955 as he mentions in his letter of 24/25 September 1955 (Letter 90), "Bro/ Freedman has dug up a few savory morsels." As Benjamin Freedman, in his booklet *Facts Are Facts,* delves into the question of Jewish origins, he too comes up with the "fact" that modern Jews are descended from the Khazars. He goes on to suggest that the latter-day Khazars are out to gain world domination, and that something should be done to stop them. Pound's characterization of this hate-mongering as "savory morsels," and this after the history of Nazi atrocities had long been a matter of public record, is immensely disheartening.[6]

Toward the end of the first part of their correspondence, just before it was interrupted by war, Zukofsky had this to say about his friend's views. "As for yr. anti-semitism I believe you're no more anti- than Marx himself, tho' the cluttered mess of the rest of yr. economic and political thinking makes it appear so" (18 January 1939, Letter 84). Zukofsky's opinion about this aspect of Pound never really changed. His mentor, he believed, had been mistaken about who was responsible for the world's miseries, but did not hate any race. When called on to say something about Pound for Charles Norman's *The Case of Ezra Pound* (1948), Zukofsky responded when he could have remained silent. As he says in his remarks, "a preference for silence might be misinterpreted."

> I never felt the least trace of anti-Semitism in his presence. Nothing he ever said to me made me feel the embarrassment I always have for the "Goy" in whom a residue of antagonism to "Jew" remains. If we had occasion to use the words "Jew" and "Goy" they were no more or less ethnological in their sense than "Chinese" and "Italian."

Zukofsky thought his remarks important enough to reprint in his collected critical essays, *Prepositions*. Earlier in the volume comes his 1929 essay on Pound. Here was where Zukofsky felt the attention should be focused, on Pound the poet, not on the Pound who erred. Zukofsky was still patient with his friend's mistakes even toward the end of their correspondence. In a 1958 letter not printed here, Pound called on Zukofsky to speak out against Emmanuel Celler, then a United States Representative from Brooklyn: "A thing like Celler does no good to the jews OR to the communist party. Some jew ought to say so." Zukofsky's reply was short and negative, explaining that he was "not in politics."

The correspondence of the late 1950s was only fitful. A few years later, Pound entered his silent period and stopped writing to Zukofsky altogether. It seems unlikely that he replied to the last few letters he received from his former student and "son." At least no answers have survived. But

[6] The Khazar theory is still useful to anti-Semites. In New York City, in the summer of 1985, I found—on a seat in the waiting room of the Long Island Railroad's Brooklyn station—a leaflet distributed by the "Christian Revolutionary Brotherhood." The Brotherhood charged that "the Judaic group of today does not descend from the Jews of the Bible, but rather from various early Medieval convert groups, chiefly Khazar. . . ." After sundry complaints about the "militant atheism" of the "Judaics," the Brotherhood concludes by referring to the modern state of Israel as "this abhorrent afterbirth of the Synagogue of Satan."

Zukofsky continued to express to others his gratitude for Pound's early encouragement, and he continued to insist that Pound was a supremely great poet. His presence at the 1975 Ezra Pound Conference in Orono, Maine, was his last public acknowledgment of the esteem in which he held his literary "papa." Finally, as Celia Zukofsky tells us, before his death her husband left in his study a copy of *Prepositions* open face down on the desk. It was open to a page of his own essay on Pound.

A Note on Pound's Stationery

At the time Pound began corresponding with Zukofsky, his stationery featured a printed letterhead. In the upper left-hand corner was his name in boldface. On the right, also in boldface was his address. Centered at the top of the page, in small italic type, was the motto "res publica, the public convenience."

In March 1932, Pound made a change. The motto was discarded and replaced by a Gaudier-Brzeska profile drawing of Pound. Two letters of 1934 (8 and 10 February) lack the Gaudier-Brzeska. Instead, in the upper left-hand corner, we find a Wyndham Lewis drawing of Pound. For the next two years Pound did without artwork, but in January 1936 the Gaudier-Brzeska returned to the letterhead, this time on the right. There it remained. Pound's letters for 1937 (Anno XV) have a printed motto in the upper left-hand corner: "A tax is not a share[.] A nation need not and should not pay rent for its credit."

From year to year, Pound shifted his name and address around on the sheet, never seeming quite satisfied with their position. At least his correspondents always knew where to write him.

Pound's admiration for Mussolini and for Italian Fascism is reflected on his stationery. Beginning on 16 June 1932, his letters to Zukofsky note the date according to the Fascist calendar (which dated events from 28 October 1922, when Mussolini and his fellow marchers arrived in Rome). From 1935 to 1937, the printed letterhead noted both the Christian year and the Fascist. Starting in 1938, however, only the Fascist year was given. That same year saw the introduction of a new motto, a quotation from Mussolini: "Liberty is not a right but a duty."

None of Pound's postwar letters to Zukofsky feature printed letterheads.

Pound/Zukofsky

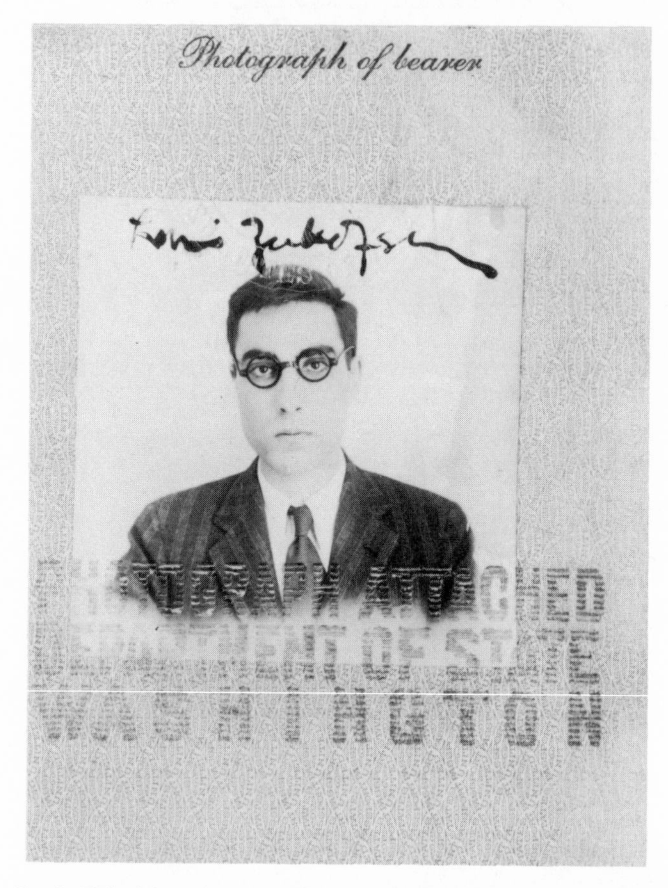

Louis Zukofsky, photograph for passport, issued June 17, 1933

The Letters

1. TLS–3.

18 Aug. 1927 Rapallo

My Dear Zukofsky:

Thanks. First cheering mss. I have recd. in weeks, or months, or something or other.

In the present anarchic state of the Exile's management I hesitate to say that anything will positively be printed; though I understand that No. 2. is actually about to see daylight INSIDE the burning cordon of our Custom's vigilantes.

BUT the new publisher and the original murkn agent are (at the moment, and let us hope but in transient gustiness) forming so complex an equation of x plus or minus x to the fourth.

that . . . .

HOWEVER, as far as the editorial office is concerned; that being so far as the formation of No. 3. as a pile of typescript in this desk is concerned "WE" (singular) are pleased etc. to accept Poem beginning "The"

In return for which will you (singular) please look through it again and see whether or not there is a drag at the beginning of the second movement; or whether it is only in the edtr's middle aged consciousness.

I found tendency to skip somewhere about there, and look forward to what might or mighnt be coming. She picks up again later.

///

The Antheil is not so good. In any case I want to use "Poem beg. The" FIRST, and before I touch the Antheil.

If I print 'em together our detractors wd. say you broke in by boosting young George [Antheil] or wd. suspect me of being influenced by gang feeling. Which I am not. (at least in this case)

NEXT MORNING

In the unlikely event of actual crisis of printing occurring, will you please consider minor data. (Of course I will ASK the printer to send you a proof; but in the interim.)

24. is it bought or brought
    (no objection to commercial ravens if intentional)
    in fact one about as likely as other.
59. punctuation?? "Rabbaisi",
76. frero (roumanian or rheto-romansch?)
    hermano
    fratello, frate,
    (I forget the portogoose of it)
    or perhaps Whitmanian, like Comerado.
123. bear or bears
140. do you want the "ghost". if it was an after thought, I am inclined to think first thought better.

5th movement. Do you want the transposition actually made, or merely fac/simile's. If you actually want 218–223, put in at 205, do you want the line numbers changed, or left scholastically as iz.?

226. brutes or brute ones.
    (the ones don't strike me as partic. felicitous. but it's your pome.

I like it better on second reading. I mean the whole thing, not that one line.

I suppose the address on the envelope, and not the P.O. box, is the one your now use??

Heaven know whether anyone will get PAID anything.

I can't guarantee there will be an Exile No. 3. But when you have enough suff for a volume, as good as this, I will, if it then be necessary, give you a hand.

yours

EP

new publisher: Pascal Covici. The first number of *The Exile* had been imported into the United States. The duty on the imported copies, however, had been too high. Pound therefore arranged for it to be printed by Covici in the United States. The full story of this affair is told in Barry Alpert's "Ezra Pound, John Price and *The Exile*," *Paideuma,* 2:3 (Winter 1973), pp. 427–448.

agent: John Price.

The Antheil: Zukofsky's poem, "Critique of Antheil," appeared in *The Exile,* number 4.

2. ALS–2.

6 Sept. 1927. 57 East 111 Street, New York.

To Mr Ezra Pound, edtr of The Exile.

Sir,

It seems then if I work and pray I may yet eat more than pie. Tho nothing less than guerdon is your letter of one night and next morning.

As for that other π, I wish I could grasp its literary equivalent and so find the ratio that would amputate the squares from the possibly there circle of the beginning of "The's" second movement. (Pardon the bathematics, and the astrologer's illusion that a circle is perfection.) But doesn't the movement begin with a natural slowness of tempo rather than drag? For myself, I was at the time of writing too pleased, however shyly, with Peter Out and too distraught with Lion heart to notice such drag, and now am embarked on new seas, so I remain undisturbed tho perhaps wall-eyed. Fact is I fear for not so much the second movement, as for the too precipitous end. Its chanted faith hardly begins to be buttressed, id est I feel it might have been, may still be, the beginning of something else and s[omething]. e[lse]. and s.e. What? Who knows? Hope it comes.

Corrections:
In the Dedication the reference to Bach is 309, to J. Erskine 184, 185, to James Joyce 13, 20, 28, 29, to the Bolsheviki 203, to Werfel 68, to Yehoash 110–129, 205–223, 318–330 (These may or may not agree with your copy.)

23. Read: Have not the lambs become more sapient drinking of the spring.
24. Read: brought the prophet bread
59. No quotes for Rabbaisi; commas, however, indicating direct address.
76. frero – Whitmanian, I am afraid
123. read: The Bedouin bears the Desert Night
128. read: All the stars in dowry his meed
140. omit ghost

5th movement–yes, please place 218–223 at 205, and change the line numbers.
226. read brutes for brute ones. Thanks.

And now le loup a son secret, actually 5 volumes by L.Z. exist, none typed. When they are, will you at that dim time indicate what should not see the light of day? And shall I ⟨then⟩ write you at Paris or Genova or where?

Yours
Louis Zukofsky.

Peter Out: "Poem Beginning 'The'," l. 62. *All,* p. 14.
Lion heart: "Poem Beginning 'The'," l. 76. *All,* p. 14.

3. TLS–1.

[February 1928] Rapallo

[Pound pasted the following extract from *The Dial*'s letter at the top of the sheet.]
Some time ago, Louis Zukofsky offered us work–prose and verse–neither being quite ready for publication.

Dear Z:

The above was position of Dial on Feb. 9th.

I told [Pascal] Covici to send you proofs. Dunno if he will. He tells me Exile 3, will be out in March. I suggest you try Dial on any stuff they haven't yet seen, (at once) and that if you feel so disposed you then ship along any further unvendible matter you possess, My schedule being that I send off mss. of future no. of Xile when I receive copies of number current.

Also any of your contemporaries with whom you care to associate. Somebody OUGHT to form a group in the U.S. to make use of the damn thing now that I have got it in motion. Failing development of some such cluster I shall stop with No. 6.

Length doesnt matter. I shall prob. use your Antheil. not yet sure it is advisable, but in any case it wdnt. prevent use of something else as well. If you have spare copy you might look thru it again. If I use the present version it wd. be mainly for sake of last line. Have another look at the beginning and middle. Aht iss long.

Whether you like any of yr. own generation, or want to meet any of 'em. or wd. be any use trying to concentrate mss. must be manifest by yr. own overt act. I cant be xpected to know.

EP

your Antheil: See Pound's letter of 18 August 1927.

4. TLS–3.

5 March 1928 Rapallo

Dear Zukofsky:

Mss. recd. this a,m,: First impression: No hesitation in accepting the prose, both the Cummings and the Preface.

Preface appears to me NOT pref. to poems enclosed but to poems as yet unwritten. You postulate a new sensibility or a new state of mind, but the verse still boggles along with the CADENCE and diction of 1890: obviously this is botch.

(all except the Lennin, which I am ready to print, if you care to detach from the rest; though even that (saved by contents and drive) is not wholly in language of post-1917.)

C. S. Wood has been writing intelligent stuff on mass-consciousness. One cant fall back merely into mediaeval habit of allegorical utterance: Everyman speaking, and speaking old fashioned pre-unanimiste english.

Cadence of this stuff ⟨is its⟩ weakest component. Not by any means up to level of Poem begining THE.

Jah, art iss long.

Gertie [Stein] and Jimmie [Joyce] both hunting for new langwitch, but hunting, I think, in wrong ash-pile.

Re/ private life:

Do go down an' stir up ole Bill Willyums, 9 Ridge Rd. Rutherford (W. C. Williams M.D.) and tell him I tole you. He is still the best human value on my murkn. visiting list.

(If ever you are in Phila. go see my dad. H[omer]. L[oomis]. P[ound].; assay dept. U.S. Mint.)

//

Cummings I have met. Dont know his address. Believe he regards me as gentle bore and relique, sort of Kris Kingle, very bearded. I find it healthy to meet his conviction on this point, but imagine he finds me merely blanketing fog. All of which is probably as it shd. be.

I "can sympathize"; Yeats has been next door for a fortnight, and we lunch daily, and have dined almost daily during that period. Makes one believe, if not in progress, at any rate in motion———or at least in sequential alteration of mental modalities.

Also a stimulus. Am about ready to take up residence, day and night shift in a razor factory.

///

Re language: poets since Adam's uncle Joe, have been trying to speak "for humanity", for NOT merely themselves but for "everyone" :::: considered probably AS a series of detached individs. capable of sym-pathy or of looking out from same central point as author.
Suggest you look up ALL Jules Romains Unanimiste stuff (vide my Instigations, in pub. lib. if not obtainable elsewhere) :: that was an attempt, J. R. found something but not enough. That was 1911 and 12.

Cant lie down on it. Your prose on Cummings much further along, also the preface.

//

Les'see wot else you've got. I can't run Exile without at least three people who want to drive thru. Shd. be delighted to have Cummings, but he seems to be in the popular magerzines. AND he'd probably think he was carrying me on his back. (Not that I care a damn what he thinks . . . but . . . complicates editorial function.)

Antheil is ill, god damn it. And his last attempt at a manifesto no use to Exile, and I can't believe of any use to himself.

I shd. be inclied to print anything of Bill W[illia]m's that you picked out. Editing ought really to be done by the young (?? what age are you) not by the senile or even by the mature. –eh–same for purposes of commerce, Condé etc.

Problem: shall I take last number of Mr Bert. D. Wolfe's magazine, down to lunch with the senator?

///

Not sure one can write TO the future. IF a man can manage to write IN the present it is about the apogee of human potential.

EP

the Cummings: "Mr. Cummings and the Delectable Mountains" appeared in *The Exile,* number 4.
the Preface: "A Preface" appeared in *The Exile,* number 4.
the Lennin: Zukofsky's poem, "Memory of V. I. Ulianov." *All,* pp. 23–24.
C. S. Wood: Charles Wesley Wood, author of *The Myth of the Individual* (New York: The John Day Company, 1927).
pre-unanimiste: Pound had written approvingly of Jules Romains' belief in the existence of group consciousness. See "Unanimism," *The Little Review,* 4:12 (April 1918), pp. 26–32. Gallup C345.
Romains: Pound's essay on Romains also appeared in *Instigations,* as part of "A Study of French Poets."
magazine: Communist, edited by Bertram Wolfe. His *A Life in Two Centuries* (New York: Stein and Day, 1981) is an account of his activities as an American Communist in the years between the World Wars.
the senator: Wiliam Butler Yeats. His visit to Rapallo is recalled in "A Packet for Ezra Pound," part of *A Vision.*
TO the future: Pound refers to the collection, "18 Poems to the Future," which Zukofsky had sent to Pound on 20 February 1928.

5. ALS–4.

Mar. 20 '28. 57 East 111 St., New York.

Dear Pound: Re- A Preface and 18 Poems to the Future thet wuz: Thee is right and thee isn't. After your judgment what seems wrong with these poems is not so much the utterance but a state of mind (responsible for it) which has not yet become the new sensibility postulated in the preface. No wonder. Since it is obvious that the mentality which in these poems discovered for itself Marxian economics is instinctively bound to Spinoza's natura naturans. The resultant 'ebrew humility (there is such a strain in the chosen, at least in some of 'em) does not make for an immediate realization of proletarian triumph. Obviously my day is still that of imperialism. As you say 'if a man can manage to write in the present'–and that is all I do, if I do–recognize the proletarian slough of despond. Rather a chick's cry in the wilderness, not even a proletariat's, let alone proletarian. Yet a feeling for mass-consciousness, not found in Romains' worship of groups, soulless as he admits and troubled with a kind of radio static.

Accordingly I have done some trepanning. In the first place, I change the caption to read merely A Preface and Seven Poems–thus retaining only numbers 5, 6, 10, 11, 12, 14, 18. And introduce changes as follows:

No 5. Quotation from Bunyan to read—the night was as troublesome as the day.
Stanzas 3 and 5, enclose in parenthesis instead of dashes.

No 6. Omit quotation from B[unyan]'s. P[ilgrim's]. P[rogress].
Line 1 – omit Come
Line 6 – omit
Line 9 – omit See
Line 10 to 16 inclusive – omit
Line 17 – Read: I do not see the ground for the light
of the furnace leaps etc.
Line 28 – Read: Ah even in our night
the flunkey
motors off

No. 12. Omit quotation from Bunyan.
Stanza 4 – Line 1. Read: So that men might stand.
Stanza 5 – Lines 2–4 Read: And men's hearts of caresses
For new sharers of burden
As they rest and no time presses.

No. 14. Quotation from Bunyan—read: Your wages such as a man could not live on (omitting I was born indeed in your dominions etc)

Leaves 7 to which, I think, the charge of "1890" does not apply. At any rate, these poems strike me as valid and new, cadence and all, though they were written three years ago. As for the mere decorative accompaniment of the quotations, as well as their malicious intent towards Respectable idolators of Bunyan of the last 240 years, no literature writes Trotsky (née Bronstein) is proletarian. With the beatific seven on my side I again submit these poems to you. And if still you say botch, then, of course, you print only the Lenin and the Preface, making changes in the latter as follows:

¶2. read: it becomes clear why the . . . accompanying my poem

¶4. "Behind this poem, then, the pessimistic philosophy" etc.

What on mass-consciousness has C. S. Wood written, besides Heavenly Discourse which reads like The Truth Seeker? —There is noos value in Bert Wolfe's Communist (tho' I guess one must be careful to discriminate—p-ss-t—treason).

No Kiddin', are you going to take up residence day and night shift in a razor factory? My question isn't funny. I once told my communist friend, Whittaker Chambers, (I am not a Party member by the way) to announce his coming visit to M[ark]. V[an]. D[oren]. of the Nation with "Dear

Mark, I am coming with a bomb soon.["] Chambers did, and The Nation or at least its mark was more than mildly disturbed for a week.

I have written Cummings and Williams (it is not merely coincidence that my written wish to meet W.C.W. should cross your suggestion that I do so). If they see me, or forward their work to exile, bless them for it, and Antheil (is he better?) and H[omer]. L[oomis]. P[ound]. (thanks for inviting me to see him, and yourself) and me, too.

Yours,
Z.

natura naturans: Zukofsky refers to a passage in Spinoza's *Ethics* (Part 1, Proposition 29, note). The passage defines "active nature" (*natura naturans*) and "passive nature" (*natura naturata*). Zukofsky quotes the same passage in "A"–6 (pp. 22–23).

6. TLS–7.

12 Aug. 1928 Rapallo

Dear Z:

As my suggestion that you see Bill W[illia]ms. seems to have done no harm, but rather to have afforded some pleasure and consolation to both, I further suggest that you make an effort toward restarting some sort of life in N.Y.; sfar as I know there has been none in this sense since old [Alfred] Steiglitz organized (mainly foreign group) to start art.

At any rate will you send me FULL reply to these presents, and if the idea dont move you, pass on this note to Bill.

I suggest that you form some sort of gang to INSIST on interesting stuff (books) ⟨1.⟩ being pubd. promptly, and distributed properly.

2. simultaneous attacks in as many papers as poss. on abuses definitely damaging la vie intellectuelle.

//

Whether you can meet at Bills, or whether you can find some cheap restaurant and dine together once a week as we have done at various times in London, is obviously an affair to be decided by local taste.

But there are now several enlightened members of yr. body impolitic that might learn the val. of group action.

At any rate send me yr. opinion on the availability of the following:
Herman Spector, 1101 East 7th, Brooklyn
John Price, 7 Chauncey St. Astoria, N.Y. (who worked hard to start Exile, possibly sunk in childbearing.)
his friend Wadsworth.
Pauline Leader.
that rough diamond (professdely) Joe Gould.
Hotel Bradford 65 E. 11th St, N.Y.
Joseph Vogel, 478 Cherry St., N.Y.
(Hamilton man) travels by cattle boat.
///
I dont know how much magnetism is needed. Bill ought to be able to get 'em together once.
Of the earlier possible lights, there was once a certain Lola Ridge.
///
A group of this sort must have some access to journals. Not a solid journalist group but someone who can get into print. Price and Wadsworth both can . . . without being in position to high-hat those who cant. Besides I dont think they are high-hatists.
////
Question of whether such a group cd. include someone higher hup in choinulism, like Mark Van Doren, or Frieda Kirchwey of the Nation. (F. K. is I believe the Nations private bolchevik.)

Prob. imposs to include definite party men (like Mike Gold) ⟨If you succeed in forming group–ought to invite him from time to time–⟩ ⟨His memoirs have lit. val.⟩

At any rate you ought to look round you and see who would or could be possible. You cant have people tainted with the murkn equivalent of n[ouvelle], r[evue], f[rançaise]ism.

In the new masses list I see only Rorty who dont, I believe, live in N.Y. (and Gold himself, IF he is not absolutely wrapped up in N. M. and party.

But YOU folk on the spot must guide me.
///
There is also Marianne [Moore], if Bill thinks it poss. no harm for her to meet let us say J. Gould.

////
There is also, though hardly for same evening ⟨as M. M.⟩, ole Jane Heap if she is in N.Y.; no rudder, but certain available energy, ballyhoo.

///

There is difficulty of meeting place; i,e, to choose a restaurant the indigent can afford, and that wont too greatly disgust the opulent.

One used to be able to eat in N.Y. and in London for 45 cents. Speak me frankly the cost of livink in Manhattan.

I can even subsidize the first meal or two, or some of the fiscally weaker members now and again. As I shd. prob. do if present coram populo.

To keep the group pure in heart, I think one must avoid tired and out worn personalities. I wont invidiously give a list. But some of my contemporaries have so institutionalized themselves, and make ⟨dignity⟩ rather than their mental activity ⟨etc _________⟩. Fill in the blanks to suit yourself.

Must make a NEW grouping. and the older elements must be the uncompromised (either toward mediocrity or popularity.) also the mugs the y,m,c,a, types, the gorddam seerryous neo-Lippmans etc.

If in doubt and ignorant of past records, you might consult me re/ proposed affiliations.

////
As objectives, the sort of thing I mean IS that it is a damn nuissance, Adolphe not being in print YET. Same re Bill[Williams]'s novel. same re my bother about "How to Read", a 45 page condensation and summary of my critical conclusions, destined to blow the top off university bunk system in teaching lit. etc.

///

e,g, the delay "Poem beg. 'The' " wd. have suffered but from transpontine intervention.

The delay you will all of you (everyone on this list) encounter WHEN you have volume ready for printing.

To say nothing of very real val. of honest verbal crit. ⟨viva voce⟩ mutual of mss. before they are pubd.

Fer gard zake keep this letter, if you dont want to act on it, pass it on to Bill or to Vogel and see if they can, or want to. and let me know

1. on receipt of it what you think.
2. after fortnight what further results or reactions.

I am holding this down to people actually in N.Y. and suburbs; IF you form a group, it will be easy enough to direct people from other outlying parts of the khuntry to it.

These cenacoli in Paris and London have been effective. In fak peepul now come from the outlying gehennae to "study" the results.

Such wuz fer ezampl the Academie Goncourt at the start, or the Mercure de France group. Got to look ahead. Several of you will still be men of letters in 1952.

NOT too many women, and if possible no wives at assembly. If some insist on accompanying their mariti, make sure they are bored and dont repeat offense. Also mariti shd. ignore, and remain unblandished by, other females during presence of legal consort. Cf. Cosimo Medici on government.

//

By the way, Aldington has made a damn good job of his "Gourmont" (Covici). Ought to be boomed, so'z to sell out expensive edtn. and go into a cheap one that you cd. afford. By far best Ald. has done. Unhampered by Brit. assininity. (i mean on part of pubshers, publik etc.)

///

Group is very useful, for gathering information, etc. both enlightenment, and stimulus to action.

always 60% of group duds, but it dont matter. Or perhaps it isn't "always."

Two not enough; four or five real lives, and it moves.

You and Bill cant swing it on yr. own. Bill magnificent patriarchal elm. Got to have more active mechanism somewhere in the concourse.

Dont feel tied to my nominations; but you haven't in past year suggested any new people.

Harlod Weeks is a live wire, but dont know where he is. was in Cleveland.

Keep free of THEATRES and people interested in staging, stage decoration, and the Drawma.

Whats to be done can be done on one side of a page. Meaning that IF its not there it wont be in ⟨any⟩ dilutation or spread.

(Cummings prob. and exception, but he is hardly likely to enter present combine). ⟨Besides he existed before he wrote a sort of play⟩

restaurant is best, better than studio where complication of host-guest relation arises. Nacherly O.K. to go down to Bill's once or twice if he'll have you..

as also the gordam marital ammosphere of N.Y. Poesy Socierty ! ! ! ! ! ! ! ! ! ! ! ! ! ! ! ! ! Dont be a society. Dont have officers and by laws. (not that I think this exhortation necessary . . .)

You've got to have a busy man; lacking one busy by nature, some more contemplative spirit has to take on the functions.

Gould ought to supply necessary grouch and debunking. Vogel may have the requisite restlessness. Price used to be busy; question of family life now . . . also whether he is fed up with me cause Covici treated him a bit rough.

///

Idea literature to be dissociated from idea Fifth Ave., idea profit, idea communism. (none of these being any more evil than plain, mountain, river, but are all different concepts, to be kept in relation and not to impinge. What group shd. mean is: convenience of literature, i,e, faculty for printing and distributing without too damnd much bother, secondly, as accessory, fight against impingements on vie literaire.

e basta per oggi.

EP

Spector: American proletarian poet whose work had appeared in *The Exile,* number 3. His poem "Sadly They Perish (A Dirge for the Objectivist Poets.)" charges that "objectivists stuff cotton into ears, / disdain the clear emphatic voices of revolt." See *Social Poetry of the 1930s: A Selection,* ed. Jack Salzman and Leo Zanders (Burt Franklin & Co., 1978), pp. 287–289.

Wadsworth: P. Beaumont Wadsworth, a British journalist and would-be novelist. He visited Pound in Rapallo in February 1928.

Leader: American poet and fiction writer. Her work appeared in *Transition.*

Gould: A portion of his "Oral History of the World" appeared in *The Exile,* number 2.

Vogel: American proletarian novelist.

Ridge: American poet. Her volume of poems, *Red Flag,* had been published by Viking in 1927.

Kirchwey: Freda Kirchwey. An editor with *The Nation* throughout the Twenties and Thirties.

Gold: Editor of *The New Masses.*

memoirs: "Jews Without Money (From a Book of East Side Memoirs)," *The New Masses* 4:1 (June 1928), pp. 11–12.

Rorty: James Rorty. American poet, political writer, and sociologist.
Heap: She and Margaret Anderson co-edited *The Little Review.*
Adolphe: Adolphe 1920, a novel by John Rodker, had been serialized in *The Exile.*
Bill[Williams]'s novel: A Voyage to Pagany was published by The Macaulay Company in September 1928.
How to Read: First published in *The New York Herald-Tribune* in January 1929. Gallup C735, C736, C737.
Goncourt: Endowed by the estate of Edmond de Goncourt, this society is composed of ten members, each of whom receives an annuity.
Mercure: The *Mercure de France* had been founded in 1890 by a group of writers that included Stéphane Mallarmé, Remy de Gourmont, Albert Samain, Laurent Tailhade, and Villiers de l'Lisle-Adam.
Cosimo Medici: I have been unable to find any remarks by Cosimo de' Medici (1389–1464) on the role of women in government.
Gourmont: Remy de Gourmont. Selections from All His Works Chosen and Translated by Richard Aldington (Chicago: Pascal Covici, 1928). Pound reviewed this in the January 1929 issue of *The Dial.*
Weeks: Howard Weeks. Pound had published his poem "Stunt Piece" in *The Exile,* number 3.
sort of play: Him.

7. ALS–3.

Aug 12/28. [*sic*] 57 E. 111 St. New York.

Dear Pound— re—yours of the twelfth Aug: It all depends on Bill [Williams], and as soon as he's thru vacationing, I'll let you know.

Meanwhile I'll write Vogel, Price, Gould and co. As I have already intimated Bill thinks he wants a group, but probably doesn't. I myself think more than five "real lives" would be too much. At least, for me, one is enough. I'd like Cummings—so would Bill (he had him out once). Both shy, they wd. take long to thaw. Marianne [Moore], yes, but would she? I'll ask Bill. Add myself—and you have four—three arrived, and one to keep in touch with the younger generation, I mean, such people as I know—Whittaker Chambers, T. S. Hecht, Henry Zolinsky (whose stuff you recently rejected), John Gassner and maybe one or two others. Whittaker Chambers is on the Daily Worker and has access to C. P. Fadiman reviewer on The Nation and of Simon and Schuster. Also a friend of M.V.D. Mark Van Doren, by the way, was once my prof at Columbia. He used to be interested and still is, probably, but I'm afraid I shall always be a mystery to him. Writing of his Jewish students in the Menorah J[our-na]l. 1927, he said this with reference to somebody I am quite sure me—"tho no less intelligent and certainly no less interesting, I shall skip a pale and subtle poet who was not in fact lazy, but the memory of whose painfully inarticulate soul forbids me to use him for any purpose however respectful." I don't think he likes my verse, but is somehow afraid of me. Which is as it should be. But Mark's what you call higher up—mebbe I'll get in touch with 'im agen.

You once met Meyer Schapiro—at least—he told me you did—a fine head if he hasn't been submerged by the bizness of getting a job at Columbia. I think a group including him and Whittaker Chambers (and also Fadiman) would be brilliant, but what n hell you can't get these people to stop being interested in the wrong things. Will try again.

It's too bad that all the worthwhile Goyim and Juice I know are bothered by 1) We gotta make money or 2) Comrade, that ees a bourgeoizification an' decadent. Twud be OK if one didn't have to live ⟨with⟩ them, and they didn't take it to heart that such good material like Zuk, E.P.[,] W.C.W.[,] E.E.C[,] M.M. were just blind "on the imminent problems of the day"—Writes Chambers: I prefer mad Zukofsky to sober Ellis (the Daily Worker cartoonist)—yes but for that reason he won't submit mss to Xile and continues to work, in spite of himself, with Ellis. What dese comoonists dun't know aboot logick eez surrprizink.

All this personal goo—so as you can form an idear of the situation. (Mike Gold, for instance, a fine fellow no doubt but probably impossible—we were brought up together on Chrystie St., tho' I never met him down there and have seen him only once. Spector, too, maybe more consistent but younger (about 21 and probably not congenial to most people), an intellectual Communist whatever that is, wants to kill Gertrude Stein and show everybody up—O well I'd rather read Trotsky's Literature and Revolution.

Point is you've got to get people as will work together—and one or two with business "pull." I'll remember that and write again when there's really something to say.

Z.

O yes you can eat a meal in New York for about a $1 if you have it. Luncheon 55¢. Tip Add'l. ⟨However, I suppose those who haven't the money wud be able to borrow it.⟩

Hecht: S. Theodore Hecht, a young poet who had been a classmate of Zukofsky's at Columbia University.

Zolinsky: Henry Saul Zolinsky, a friend of Zukofsky, whose poems appeared in three issues of *Poetry,* including the "Objectivists" issue.

Gassner: A friend from Zukofsky's Columbia University days, he became an important drama critic and historian of the theater.

Fadiman: Clifton Fadiman (b. 1904). Critic, editor, and essayist.

Menorah Journal: Mark Van Doren's "Jewish Students I Have Known" appeared in the June 1927 issue.

Schapiro: Meyer Schapiro, who became one of America's most eminent art historians.

Ellis: Frederick Ellis. Whittaker Chambers served as his "idea man" at *The Daily Worker.*

Literature and Revolution: The edition Zukofsky used was probably that translated by Rose Strunsky (New York: International Publishers, 1925).

8. TLS–5. Enclosure.

2 Nov. [1928] Rapallo

Cher Z:

De looks bookz iz O.K. fer sellin US to others. There remains the problem of printing, as in france, so that WE can afford each other's work.

///

There iz a man called Curwen, who may be a sonoffabeech or not; he sez he worked with Bruce Rogers. He is a printer with no capital, he may be the usual sort of leech who lives off rich dilletante suckers.

No harm in your, or in you an young John Price, looking him over. IF I can still find his address.

////

A nuther ijee, wd. be fer us to—really—decide on six or ten or 12 books that are FIT to print. and fer us to constitoot ourselves a bloody sight BETTER book of the month, or quarter, better "book of the quarter club." preferably in cahoots with some decent pubshr, say Liveright IF he wd. rise to it.

I think on 4 books a year I cd. rake in Eliot, Marianne [Moore], Bill W[illia]ms. even possibly Yeats, who might be more bother than he is worth. at any rate it is not utterly out of the question.

Joyce one can't tell about, he wdnt. do any of the work, neither wd. Yeats, but you might find out what their figureheading is rated at. (also inside opinyum re/ value of [Ford Madox] Ford in such a scheme.). ⟨Hell, make it all American— me— Bill— Marianne— Eliot.⟩

Seeriously I think THE BOOK OF THE QUARTER is a paying proposition. do you want to work it with Price, or alone. at any rate, you (single or plural) wd. have to be the secretary, an working staff.

Bill's Collected Poems.
A wad of Gould's History.
some bloody work of mine, to be announced, and
possibly delayed, or not as the need were.
The poems of L. Z.
(when ready. The "A" and the as yet unprojected at.
Adolphe, (where are we), Adolphe to start off with.
McAlmon, selected tales for unselected readers.
Wotterbout Marianne's collected, I spose there iz 32 pages by now.

I shd. think 3 buck vols. wd. be a better bet than 6 but wont interfere with the detail.

Cockburn wd. have something in time. so also Stokes.
/////
If Liv[eright]. wont rise, perhaps McCauley, Bill's pubshrs. wd. take it on.

This is much solider than the damn Lit. Guild that dont know where it is going.
////
Of course there is my Cavalcanti, on which brit. pubshrs. are now getting active, promising sample pages by next post etc.

the thing is that the list is NOT limited to genre, simply best prose or verse, or crit, or novel, we see.

As Book of the Quarter, there is a two years run already in sight. It is rather too good a scheme to waste.

I dont at the moment see why you shdnt. draw a minuscule salary from it IF you can put it over.

The How to read is hardly thick enough for such a series. If, of course, McCauley took on the scheme they cd. take the "How to Read" as GUIDE to the principles of cri'zism which govern our choice of books.

That I think wd. be THE place to fit it.

Get Bill to take you to see McCauley, IF they aint fed up wiff him. Take along my beeyewteeful Dial article on Bill's early life. Just to show he [*sic*] we mould publick opinyum. ⟨Better call en masse of 2.⟩

///

It wd. be an Xcuse for a 50 cent edtn. of "how to read" which is what I want. I dont want to tie the little lesson up in a fancy vol. that the pore cant buy.

//

If some decent pubshr. (uncontaminated by Mr Friede's presence) wd. take it on as publicity stunt fer the rest of his books, that wd, suit farver right away down.

///

This Poetry Caln bizniz, all come from a suggestion of farvers that the Lit. Guild wuz neglektin' potes. Nacherly they do nothing interesting, but the princiPPl seems to work. But the sob they put up when I suggested it wd. have rent the heart of a stone.

It "the clan" not much use to me, as there is about one vol. of poems a year, and 3 vols. of prose that I want to see printed, ... also my choice wdnt be likely to suit [H]Arriet[Monroe]'s circle.

wot ells.

It ⟨the enc. page⟩ is merely another piece of ad. matter that you cd. show to McCauley, as indice that poppa is not wholly impracticl.

ALSO HELL; who got Joyce Printed, who got Prufrock Printed, who got ole Bill's first, (with bill's aid) who sent [Rabindranath] Tagore's first into america, who first sent Frost to Poetry??? etc. . .

JheeZUSS: some god damn pubshr ought

ultimately to git wise to the fak that farver is SOMETIMES RIGHT. (even if the butter an eggs men want dull pronography with beardsley ⟨eye⟩lustrations.)

///

I spose Bill and Marianne, and some other members of the kommy TEE

might occasionally want to vote on what was printed. I might even permit THAT, if they agreed to the start off.
I think the Book of the Quarter is the asset. however dont yell it too loud. It ⟨ought⟩ to be patented as soon as uttered aloud.

yrs.
E

[Enclosure. The following is Pound's typed comment on an advertisement for "the Poetry Clan" torn from *Poetry*.]

When I suggested this, they all yelled murder it is impossible. In 3 or 4 months, they got going and still are.

De looks: In a letter of 22 October 1928, Zukofsky had proposed expensive, limited editions of the works of Pound, Williams, Zukofsky, *et al.*, as the best method of publication.
Curwen: Unidentified.
Bruce Rogers: American book designer.
Cockburn: Claud Cockburn, British journalist.
Stokes: Adrian Stokes, British art historian.
McCauley: The Macaulay Company, the publisher of *A Voyage to Pagany* (published September 1928).
Cavalcanti: The Aquila Press failed before they could publish it. See Gallup B27 for the troubled history of the publication of *Guido Cavalcanti Rime*.
Dial article: "Dr. Williams' Position," *The Dial* 85:5 (November 1928), pp. 395–404. Gallup C727. It is reprinted in Pound's *Literary Essays*.
Friede: Donald S. Friede. He and Pascal Covici had formed the publishing house of Covici-Friede in the spring of 1928.
Poetry Clan: A poetry book club organized by *Poetry*.
enc. page: An advertisement for The Poetry Clan.

9. ALS–2.

Dec. 5, 1928 57 EAST 111 St., New York

Dear Pound: Your Main Points for any group of "young writers especially in America" has been forwarded to Munson.

Finally, after much instigation, this note from Bill: "If, when, as soon as—we can see Macaulay, I'll do my part—but I am hopeless of fruits." Perhaps better so—Matthew Josephson is with Macaulay's.

I have written to Fadiman of Simon and Schuster. No answer yet.

There are still Coward-McCann, Macy-Masius and several acquaintances composing The Elf Pub. Co., to try in proper order. —No advice from you on Liveright.

No one seems especially enthusiastic—especially your enemies. . . I guess they need friendly enemas. . .

Visited Joe Gould again. He never got your letter, but appreciates your notice of him in "The Dial," and promised to write you. Cummings told him of your thoughtful attention in the matter, and seemed to find the praise enviable coming as it does from an "honest man" . . . He (Gould) is very poor. That thought is universal. Repos eternal, donne à cil— and for the rest, it's literature.

Yours,
Louis Zukofsky

Main Points: In a letter of 28 November 1928, Zukofsky informed Pound that the New School for Social Research would sponsor a "dinner for young writers" on 8 December. He went on, "Krutch, Bill and others have been invited to speak. Don't know whether they've accepted. Enyho, [Gorham] Munson invites you to issue whatever program or attack (re. young writers, abuse of our native flowers) you think fit for the occasion. I was asked to read it, but if you don't mind I'd rather leave that part of it to the Chairman." In a letter of 26 November 1928, Pound complied by listing a number of issues (the "Main Points") that young writers should fight for (issues on which they all agreed, freedom from government interference) and fight against (Article 211, the passport system, antiquated copyright laws).

Josephson: American critic, biographer and historian. His essay, "Open Letter to Mr. Ezra Pound and the Other Exiles," *Transition,* number 13 (summer 1928), called on Pound and those others to return to America.

your notice: In Pound's "Dr. Williams' Position," he said of Gould, "But the concrete example of this literary process, whether by Williams or by that still more unreceived and uncomprehended native hickory Mr. Joseph Gould, seems an unrelated and inexplicable incident to our populace. . . . Gould is no less New England, but parts of his writing cd. have proceeded equally well from a Russian, a German, or an exceptional Frenchman. . . ." *The Dial* 85:4 (November 1928), pp. 395–404. The essay is reprinted in *Literary Essays of Ezra Pound.*

Repos eternal, donne à cil: Line 1892 of François Villon's *Le Testament* is "Repos eternel donne a cil."

10. ALS–3.

Dec. 12–28. 57 E. 111 St., New York

Dear Pound: Two enclosures from Mr. Clifton P. Fadiman, the head of Simoon and Shoosters Edtrl dep't. You may tear them up.

The New School Dinner came off—I was not there, but Bill [Williams] tells me they read your letter. Among other things: an intelligent gentleman from Scribner's who had been in touch with you by mail. Who is he? Bill didn't remember his name. Also the usual "intelligent" crap from Mark Van Doren and Gorham B. Moonson who, by the way, has discovered that there are 115 precise forms of literary expression and that it behooves or behives the young American to practice them all quite consciously—in addition to being aware—ful-ly so—of the red hair under his armpits. In retort to someone saying "Isn't Wyndham Lewis right in saying that Pound is interested in the past and outmoded["] (or something of that sort) Bill said yes, Pound was once interested in Wyndham Lewis. . . Bill's darn good! Spent a fine evening with him here in Rutherford last Sunday, and Florence stayed [*sic*] off all the telephone calls.

A magazine called Blues is coming out in Columbus, Miss. Herman Spector and Bill have been asked to act as Contributing edtrs. Bill will give them his name for the first issue, pending trial of the magazine's merits. The edtr, has a patron, and Bill's interested in seducing her for our purposes. But maybe that's a temporary enthusiasm.

The Elf Pub. Co.: merely two old chums (?) of mine Jo Felshin and Sam Samuels. They used to respect (?) your tastes, and I'll soon talk business to them. But the first book they published was A Book of Drinks—How to Make Them. Rather hopeless, I believe—they made their money as may be guessed, and think Robinson Jeffers is just the billiards. The trouble with all bizniz is the effect it has ⟨on⟩ one—now that ees pr-rofound!—but je veux dire, around the arse the wind trembles colder after visits of this sort.

What the devil—I'll see ⟨Rich of⟩ Curtis Brown, in any event. Early next week. I return his letter.

Joe Gould's address is still the Hotel Bradford, 65 E. 11 St N.Y. I think he'd appreciate your getting in touch with Contact for him. He said he'd write you. Lord knows.

The Book League of Am. does it, after all—Damn—As for rake off for yrs. truly—rake off or nothing, if I manage to get something across, I won't feel eleemosynary about it. No, nor mossy in any sense.

- - - - -

I guess I do believe in names, or something of the kind: The Nation's Wood Krutch. . . A good friend of M[ark]. V[an]. D[oren]. and one of the selectors, of the better grade as things go. But whasa to us—or to me, if you don't—

Marianne Moore returned the first two movements of "A" which I send herewith. As being inappropriate for The Dial.
I sent a more appropriate draft which was also returned. The second shipment was accompanied by this note: "The erasures are the very erasures which the intention and art of the poem will deal with in Movements 5 and 6—the deletions to be made in the process of the poem itself, and as poetry. That is, I shall have no excuse for the distemper of the first two movements but the later realization of them in even temper as fugue and polyphony." I'll retain the typescript ⟨of Movements 1 & 2⟩ as is.

So far I've planned 24 movements. I hope that will be all. If it's not too indecent of me to ask you, how do you like the first two?

Wot else? I guess this'll do.

As it is, I've merely taken advantage of your: "I think my philanthropic schemes shd. stop on Dec. 31, 1928," and tried to say everything before the end of the year.

Yours
L.Z.

enclosures: Enclosures lacking.
New School Dinner: See Zukofsky's letter of 5 December 1928.
Moonson: Gorham Munson, American literary critic.
Lewis: Lewis belittled Pound in *Time and Western Man,* first published in the United States in 1928. He said Pound was "full of his old love of the Past. . . ." Wyndham Lewis, *Time and Western Man* (Boston: Beacon Press, 1957), p. 43.
Florence: Florence Williams, the wife of William Carlos Williams.
Blues: Edited by Charles Henri Ford, *Blues* lasted from February 1929 until the fall of 1930.
Jeffers: American poet. In 1928 Jeffers published *Cawdor, and Other Poems.*
Rich: Edwin G. Rich, general manager of the New York office of Curtis Brown, Ltd., a London literary agency that represented Pound.
his letter: Enclosure lacking.
Krutch: Joseph Wood Krutch, drama critic for *The Nation.*
two movements: These are now in the Ezra Pound Archive of the Beinecke Library.
schemes: In a letter of 3 December 1928, Pound expressed his intention to make 1929 a year of "elegant leisure on my own affairs."

11. TLS–2.

24 Dec. [1928] Rapallo

Thurr are sevrul techniques: one is getting OFF the mark at the start.

IF you want the pome "A" to be read, you'll have to sweat like hell on the first three pages.

After that I reckon she'll go " "Greece her knees—" again, Theodore, an' mebbe she'll go."

Second suggestion, re/ following pages. Where accusation possibly false, that reminiscence of E.P. (or in less degree T.S.E[liot]. and still less W.C.W[illiams] might lie) alter, when possible.

This is mere matter of surface changes.

////

That is the main bizniz.

///

S. Schuster: pub. Trader 'Orn

Mr Faddiman, writes in Nation. the youth of those without talent, who write as if they were fifty and very judicious! (calls for no comment)

///

Can't imagine who the "intelligent" from Scribners can be.
Which shade of irony do you emply in use of the word?

Yr. letter valoob. doc. on hist. contempor. murkn intel. life.

//

Does yr. further rmrk. imply that H. Spector is female or androgyne?

Elf sounds more promisin'. If they do 100 books on cocktails, and one of licherchoor, it might keep 'em solvent.

///

I doubt if pop. pbsh. can be . . . oh well . . . if say Price starts collecting NAMES, if several people collect names of the by "Kip" alledged 1500; it might in ten years time . . . .

Elf. cd. use names in SEPARATE compartment from their pop. stuff.

///

You may have to sacrifice the first lines and the "A" to get that pome moving.

There's already Tailhade's "Sortant de chez Erard"

///

(Be aisy, I once reminded W.B.Y[eats]. that Longfellow had written a pome "Life is reel, life iz ernest".) These remarks are not for the prophane.

///

Too bad the Bill incident re/ Wyndham isn't known to some choinulist wif a sense of humour.

etc. yrs. E.P.

Trader 'Orn: Trader Horn (1927), by Alfred Aloysius Horn and Ethelrede Lewis, was one of Simon & Schuster's first best sellers.
Fadiman: Clifton Fadiman regularly reviewed fiction in *The Nation.* Pound may have been displeased by Fadiman's "The Continental Book Flood" (*The Nation,* 5 November 1928), in which he deplored the large number of foreign books being published in the United States.
"Kip": Fadiman, who in his article says, "The result of all this is that a great many books are translated which simply do not deserve it. Not only are they of mediocre quality but they are entirely devoid of sales pull. They merely crowd an already overcrowded market, confuse booksellers, drive reviewers mad–and never reach an audience anyway. Most of them are fortunate to achieve a total sale of fifteen hundred copies."
Tailhade's: Laurent Tailhade. French poet, essayist and translator.
"Sortant": Tailhade's poem, "Place des Victoires," which begins, "Les femmes laides qui déchiffrent des sonates / Sortent de chez Erard. . . ."
a pome: Henry Wadsworth Longfellow's "A Psalm of Life."

12. TLS–1.

9 Dec. 1929 Rapallo

Dear Z.

The Reznikof prose very good as far as I've got at breakfast. BUTT if the blighter has a press and can set type why the hell is it up to me to find a printer fer all the etc. . . . . . .

////

Capital in idea that next wave of literature is jewish (obviously) Bloom casting shadow before, prophetic Jim. [Joyce] etc.

also lack of prose in German due to all idiomatic energy being drawn off into yiddish.

(not concerned with the "truth" of these suggestions but only with the dynamic.)

yrs
EP

Idiotic if there is a press in N.Y/ and a man who can set (hence supervise) that there shdnt. be a movement, a centre. (anybody can compose type; technique is in working press, paper etc.

Reznikof: Charles Reznikoff, American poet. Zukofsky had sent Pound (in a letter of 22 November 1929) *Rashi, Coral, Meriwether Lewis* (plays), "Editing and Glosses" (poems), other poems selected from *5 Groups of Verse,* and a selection of memoirs ("Early History of a Seamstress") by Reznikoff's mother, translated and adapted from her Yiddish. The memoir was later published in *By the Waters of Manhattan* (1929) and in Reznikoff's *Family Chronicle* (New York: privately published, 1963).
Bloom: Leopold Bloom, hero of Joyce's *Ulysses.*

13. ALS–6.

12-19-29 57 E 111 N.Y.

Dear E: Re—Reznikoff: Yah—the blighter has a press, but lord knows in what forsaken town upstate: the 5 W 4 St address is his maternal uncle's—or what—and a matter of "trade" convenience. Besides, the fellow has to spend the years remaining to him, past 35, in a law office, working on definitions. What with this, his own work, and his daily consummation of Bible, Homer and Dante, why shd he sink in 200 or 300 dollars on ginks like myself—. It's enough he has to give his own works away. However, some time ago he said something about going back to part time work and shipping his press to N.Y. so as he might get occasional recreation from it—also something about printing other people's brochures, if he had the capital. He wouldn't think of "asking them" for it—that's the kind of guy he is.

More anon—as soon as my article on him for the Menorah Jl. is completed. If "they" take it. Do I luf my peepul? The only good Jew I know is my father: a coincidence.

Re– this article: may I quote you as a footnote, if I can squeeze it in—i.e. "The Reznikoff prose very good—Capital in idea that next wave of literature is jewish (obviously) Bloom casting shadow before, prophetic Jim, etc.

"also lack of prose in German due to all idiomatic energy being drawn off into Yiddish.

(not concerned with the "truth" of these suggestions but only in the dynamic.)"

Incidentally, your first postulate has already been put by ⟨Mrs.⟩ Kate R. Hecht (who appreciated your lupo)—she is skulping my nut and maybe she'll get done with it sometime—but it wouldn't have been the likes of an antisemite like myself to disseminate suzh malinformation: however, with your kosher label on it . . . I hope you don't feel the Jews are roping you in.

Here's the Reznikoff Razo if you want it: born Brooklyn, N.Y., 1894; educated at the Univ. of Mo. and N.Y.U. Travelling salesman, lawyer, etc. Single. Address: 1379 Union St., Brooklyn, N.Y.

Too bad the man makes mistakes in the writing—pg 269 of Editing & Glosses for instance—David & Michal, which he'd give anything to have omitted now. But that is the price of isolation. So maybe you'd better write to him yourself and play up business: I'll send him your letter on my own hook.

N.B. Since the Menorah won't (??) print my review of Max Brod's Three Loves, panning the Choimans, and if they won't I won't let 'em have the Reznikoff article, maybe you'd better let me know that your scouting of the Lunnon Times Supp. in Engelond brings no fruits eyether.

Eh—wut?

Z

my article: Not published in *The Menorah Journal,* but truncated and published as "Sincerity and Objectification: With Special References to the Work of Charles Reznikoff," *Poetry,* 37:5 (February 1931) pp. 272–285. It is reprinted (with alterations) in *Prepositions.*

Kate R. Hecht: Wife of S. Theodore Hecht.

lupo: Probably a drawing by Pound. It does not appear to have survived.

David and Michal: "David and Michal" in *Poems 1918–1936, Volume I of The Complete Poems of Charles Reznikoff,* ed. Seamus Cooney (Santa Barbara: Black Sparrow, 1976), p. 102. What the "mistakes" were is unclear.

Three Loves: Trans. Jacob Wittmer Hartmann (New York: Knopf, 1929). Zukofsky's review was never published.

14. TLS–2.

25 Dec. [1929] Rapallo

Dear Z.

How far have you run over that ten bucks. Recd. [Henry Adams's] Educatn and Chartres. Shall be interested in latter. I spose he got caught in gothiche because he had never seen anything good???? say St Hilaire in Poictiers; S. Zeno, St Trophime, romanesque????
ow ever we shall see wot we shall see.

///

Mr. Vogel seems in trying shoot the boil orf his i;e; his own boil orf his . . . . to have come dangerously near to hitting his . . . or in other words the irritation at not having been hailed as THE geenuz etc. as has appened to other's before him. Be not worried (not that you are) it is all in the day zwork?

One of old [Ford Madox] Ford's merits is his repetition of: It is folly to seek for the person of the sacred emperor in a low tea house.

In this case the exercise of reason.

///

As for exploring the caves of the vatican etc. The precious memories of scenery carefully observed may be useful to you later in life. I wdnt. for worlds have missed seeing Mr. Hamilton Mabie. and Sam McClure is very likeable. He gimme one damn good piece of advice. I admit I am now advising you to do something contrary to it . . . . but still.

Sam said: Do you want to these articles? I said: Hell no, I want some money. Sam said: Don't do it. Dont ever do anything you dont want to. I never do.

I dont suppose Mr. Rosenfeld wd. say anything as illuminating. Perhaps you'd better see Sam. It wd. be more fun if he is still alive. Tell him I told you to.

Enc. came while I was away. zno importance, but I return it to you. soz you lll know the post did its duty.

EP

Educatn and Chartres: The Education of Henry Adams and *Mont St. Michel and Chartres.*

St Hilaire: Pound praises this church's "proportion" in Canto 51.
S. Zeno: A church in Verona. Pound notes its signed column in Canto 45.
St. Trophime: A church in Arles, France. Pound cites it as a standard of beauty in Cantos 45 and 51.
Vogel: Joseph Vogel. How Vogel expressed his irritation is unclear.
Mabie: Hamilton Wright Mabie. American essayist and literary critic.
McClure: Samuel Sidney McClure (1857–1949). American magazine editor and publisher.
Rosenfeld: Paul Rosenfeld. American essayist and novelist. He was one of the co-founders of the *American Caravan* series.
Enc.: Enclosure lacking.

15. ALS–2.

1/8/30 1051 Tiffany St., New York

Dear E: Note change of address and accept my thanks for the trouble. The fambly decided on an exodus. There are wooden houses on raised foundations across the street: preparation for a real change of scene (??) maybe Ooorope?

Nothing new just yet.

Re– the Chartres: Of course, Henry [Adams] sure did want the Virgin. But he mastered his distinctions. See pg 55 on Flaubert the last lines of pg 10 and pg 11—end zo ford.

Anyhow—don't worry about my running over the ten bucks. How could I?

You've seen Pagany? Or shall I send you a copy? So, so. But speaking of the faerie queene—

There is McClure Newspaper Syndicate 373 4th Av. and McClures publishers 221 W 57. Is Sam both? I'm innocent. And it's rather dangerous to ask people whether they're alive or not. Not by telephone, no.

The telephone: air you there?

—Air? Are, you mean??!

—No, air! and why don't you.

Etc.

Z

O yes it was a good thing to inclose the Return Receipt for the Chartres in an envelop. Now I know that even the return rcpt can get "lost." Which explains Titus' silence and failure to return the MSS. If I were the Am. council in Paris, or is the Baron English?

Chartres: Mont St. Michel and Chartres, by Henry Adams. Zukofsky's remarks about the page references indicate that he sent Pound the Houghton Mifflin edition.
Pagany: Richard Johns' little magazine had just released its first issue. It included a poem by Zukofsky (poem 22 of "29 Poems" in *55 Poems*). *All,* p. 36.
Titus: Edward W. Titus, publisher of the Paris-based little magazine, *This Quarter.*
MSS.: One of these (see the following letter) was Zukofsky's essay on Pound.

16. ALS–3. Enclosure.

Jan 12, 1930 1051 Tiffany St. New York

Dear E: Eliot writes: "I should very much like to see your essay on Pound's cantos, and I think I might be able to publish it: the chief doubt being that their circulation has been of necessity of price and form very small; so that I hope your paper contains numerous quotations to make it more intelligible to anyone who has never see the Cantos themselves."

Will you then please send him your copy of the MS, the other two being in the hands of Titus and the Gug[genheim Foundation]. I have already written telling him ⟨(TSE)⟩ that you would do so, tho' you had refused in the first place because you were Kung's avatar. A "barstud" trick, I know, but what can one do with modest people. —I have got the Post Office authorities after Titus, so that I'll probably send you another typescript. Or the Gug may return the one in their vaults. Or Eliot etc. Or if you're loath to let the thing go, I can send you the original MS. Not that you're loath anything . . . ono . . . i.e.

[Here Zukofsky attached a clipping announcing that Richard Aldington would give a prize of $200 to "the ablest young American poet whose work has appeared in 'This Quarter.' "]

I am seeing Reznikoff in an hour or so, and I shall try to talk bizness. Perhaps we can all chip in and rent a room or cellar for the press. I'm sure he'd be willing to help. We'll see. —By the way he's a Jewish replica of Bill: if you can make it out.— If anything happens, certainly Yussef Fogel can come in. Arter all, the bile weren't next to my nuts! And if we are taught to use the press, he can work all he wants to if he isn't afraid of working next to corpses.

More in a few days.

Don't barther about The Lunnon Times. When Dick gets to Lunnon all by his—

Kate Hecht is no ex-anything. She's merried, has two arfspring. So it's, "whatcheveryou Freudians call it," hell!—I'm a feelossophor.

Bill[Williams]'s regards.

Wot else? The Menorah just sent me a printed rejection slip with the beginning of Asch's Die Mutter which I had not submitted to them, but merely left as an example ⟨of⟩ the kind of translation I could do from the Yiddish. Which is all balm to my righteous see: I'd hate to be wrong about my notice of these people in A–4. I've always avoided them, wished to avoid them, and things seem to be turning out the way I wanted them to: since my seeing the Sanhedrin a few weeks ago was only a temporary fall to the plea of "thoughtful" heads.

I'm still working on the Reznikoff, having got stuck in the process of defining two woids: sincerity and objectification—but I suppose I'll squeeze out of it. Maybe Saturday.

So you're a Shandyist on praenomens. Now if my cognomen were Zhukovsky, then—

but

Z

your essay: "The Cantos of Ezra Pound (one section of a long essay)," *The Criterion* 10:40 (April 1931), pp. 424–440.

Fogel: Joseph Vogel.

Dick: Zukofsky seems to be comparing himself to Dick Whittington.

Hecht: Pound to Zukofsky, 31 December 1929, "Is Kate Hecht the ex-Mrs. Ben??"

Die Mutter: A novel by Sholem Asch, Yiddish novelist. *Die Mutter* (Berlin, Wien, Leipzig: Paul Zsolnay, 1929).

notice: "A"–4, pp. 12–13.

Sanhedrin: Probably the editors of *The Menorah Journal.*

Shandyist: In Laurence Sterne's *Tristram Shandy,* Walter Shandy believes that one's name has a crucial influence on one's character and fortunes.

17. TLS–2.

9 Feb. [1930] Rapallo

Dear Z/

Brace yourself for the shock, but I think it is time I had Mr. E.E. Cumming's works, or at least that copies of them shd. exist in Italy. (Not the Enormous Room, which I have read.

Begin on the Poetry. (am dubious re/ the play). Get a dinner for yourself and guest out of the enclosed if it is poss. to do so in N.Y.

///

Have just read Hemingway's Farewell to Arms. A good deal of it is First Class and deserves serious attention, not merely a pop. novel. I had nothing to say re/ Sun also Rises.

The Farewell is WRITTEN (not perfect throughout; nobody can do that with novel before they are 60)

Did I write you that Rene Taupin had done a vol. on Influence du Symbolisme Francias sur la Poesie Americaine. guess he'll send copy to Bill [Williams]. very good chapter on Bill in it.

//

Oh yes. Shall not take any action re yr. essay on me until you hear from Mockel. If he returns you the French version please let me know at once, and I will send the english version to Eliot. Also send me back the french and I can insert it elsewhere.

It wd. be much more useful both for you and for me to have it in the Mercure than anywhere else it cd. get. After that the Criterion for the english.

I haven't seen Bifur; but shd. prefer Varieties. I think you'll prob. hear something one way or other from Mockel fairly soon.

Hound [and Horn] might give you Taupin to review, but might also be better not to look too chapelle, and to let some less suspicious character tackle the job. You'll soon get branded as a member of the gang if you arent careful.

Hope we can guide Van Hecke, and make the Am. number of Varieties something wiff a punch.

EP

Taupin: French literary critic and professor.
Mockel: Albert Mockel, Belgian-French poet and literary critic.
Bifur: A little magazine published in Paris, 1929–1930. Edited by Georges Ribemont-Dessaignes.
Varietes: Variétés, a little magazine published in Brussels, 1928–1930.
Van Hecke: P. G. van Hecke, editor of *Variétés.*
Am. number: On 17 February 1930, Pound wrote to E.E. Cummings, "Dear Cummings: Van Hecke is asking me to help him make up an American number of *Variétés.*" Paige, *Letters,* p. 227. On 6 February 1930, Pound sent a letter (now in the Poetry Collection at the State University of New York at Buffalo) to Zukofsky which he was to pass on to Williams and McAlmon. Pound listed a number of items he wanted for the American number: tabloids, newspaper headlines, and photographs of representative Americans, machines, and architecture. Zukofsky enclosed the desired items in a letter to Pound of 6 March 1930.

18. ALS-3.

Wed J[un]e 18/30 1051 Tiffany St NY

Dear E: Here's Joonyr's lessons. Probably too long for L'Indice—but when Joonyr starts turn-of-the-screwing you can't keep him away wif a water pistul. If it's bad policy or no indication of normal relaxation to speak of himself at the same time as of the very Great, he has gracefully slipped to the notes and you can cut 'em if you want to.

Am sending my other typescript of the thing to H[ound]&H[orn]—But why should they want it?

No noos from Eliot (wrote him)
No noos from Hours (didn't write them)
No noos from you re- Geo. Oppen's poems. Shd.
have mentioned his contribution (?) of "everything
brightly not there" in all his poems, in the
essay enclosed—but then he's not been published.

Reznikoff's reworking of his Waters of Man. & his mummie's autobiography to appear in Paper Books (50¢ the copy) pub. by Chas. Boni—June 25. You've probably read about the enclosure in the Paris ed. of The Herald

---

R'cd the Ulmann Photos—Also scenes of Los Angeles, Calif, Football Games & "To the Illustrious Obscure" (!) all of which beginning with Also I did not send—who gets them?

As far as I know I am leaving N.Y. for Berkeley, Calif., July 12, or 19, or 26 depending as to how fast I can complete the screwy Einstein trans. and get paid for it. (I have spent all of my energy cursing it for the last two wks between sleep brought on from exhaustion—Ef one could only leave out a sentence, two sentences, but all of it seems never to have been reconsidered by the author). Will spend my summer in Kaigh's attic and try to do my own work for a change—. Sept 17 will find me (it's quite certain) a two-thirds assistant at the Univ. of Wisconsin (Madison)—$1000 the yr. of 9 mos. So you needn't worry about Jr. going the professor's path of difficult peeing. —O well, 6 hrs or even 10 hrs a week of teaching shd. leave plenty of time to work on the Jefferson (on which I haven't had the time to begin).

Assume, since I haven't heard from you that you don't want any other books now, and will return yr tenspot as soon as I get some money—July 1. Broke now.

Shd. also have a typescript of the Reznikoff essay by that time.

Will notify you of change of address as soon as it's changed.

Yrs
Z

lessons: "American Poetry 1920–1930," first published in *The Symposium,* 2:1 (January 1931).

L'Indice: Pound to Zukofsky, 14 April 1930, "I think L'Indice the new eyetalyan paper cd. use but NOT PAY for a brief summary on the state of licherchoor in America."

Hours: Nancy Cunard's Hours Press. Pound had tried to persuade her to publish Zukofsky and Williams.

Oppen's poems: It is not clear which poems Zukofsky sent. By this time he had known George Oppen for two years.

essay: Enclosure lacking.

enclosure: Enclosure lacking.

Ulmann photos: Zukofsky had sent Pound two photographs by Doris Ulmann (enclosed in a letter of 6 March 1930).

Einstein: Zukofsky translated Anton Reiser's biography of Albert Einstein. At Zukofsky's request, he was not credited. *Albert Einstein* (New York: Albert & Charles Boni, 1930).

Kaigh: Irving Kaplan, a friend of Zukofsky.

the Jefferson: A projected essay on Thomas Jefferson that never materialized. See the note to Pound's letter of 22 March 1940.

19. ALS-3.

June 27/30 1051 Tiffany St N.Y.

Dear E: No need to terminate correspondence. You can destroy money order when you get it! However, I'm not sending it.

You will rc've a second copy of Pavannes and one of Instigations under separate cover.

If I see anything you could read, I'll send it: that's if—and how will I know—Read How to Read.

Oi

Eliot wants to publish my paper on you "If I had it set up and sent to you in Galley-proof, would you be willing to abbreviate it as much as is necessary"—i.e. so it'll be short enough for Criterion.

Maybe you want to do the job. I'll ask him to induce you, since you probably have an idea as to what the English publick shd read about you. Of course, my new sweet style will suffer.

Abbreviate—i.e. not revision (not that you wd.)

T.S.E. also wants an unpublished Canto—that's not my affair but "I rather want to get from Pound an unpublished canto to print in The Criterion first"

Thanks a great deal for writing to Wisconsin—Didn't think they'd bother you—why don't they look for my credentials on top of the old apple tree. They're just where they used to be.

Yours
Z

terminate: Pound to Zukofsky, 10 June 1930, "God damn it/ no/ Dont send a money order./ & international stamp coupon would terminate correspondence–/ God damn money orders."

Pavannes: Pound to Zukofsky, [May] 1930, "Enc. $10. please buy & send me registered post one copy of my Pavannes & Divisions." When Zukofsky reported in a letter of 27 May 1930 that he had not used all the money Pound had sent, Pound wrote back (10 June 1930), "If you haven't sense enough to use the chq. send it back. or wait till you see books I could read, or get me an extra Instigations or Pavannes." *Pavannes and Divisions* (New York: Alfred A. Knopf, 1918). Gallup A15.

Instigations: Pound's *Instigations of Ezra Pound Together with an Essay on the Chinese Written Character by Ernest Fenollosa* (New York: Boni and Liveright, 1920). Gallup A18.

Wisconsin: Pound had written a letter recommending Zukofsky to the University of Wisconsin's English Department.

20. TLS–2

3 Aug. [1930] Rapallo

To the respected Zukofsky, seein' his own country foist.

Recd. Adams Letters. supposedly on loan. Glad to have em as dilletante readin but they dont bear on what I want. At least I dont expect em to.

I enc. 11 bucks for the ⟨H. Adams on⟩ Jeff, Madison 4 vols. A.C. Boni edtn. to cover postage etc.

I spose "Echanges" has sent you copy containing your polished French essay. I didn't know you wrote French Monsieur Zeukeufski. You neednt tell your educative confreres that you don't.

"Indice" "suspended for summer". Will send your "Am. Poesy since." to Criterion as soon as Possum Eliot gets the E.P. into print.

Shd. like copy of Freeman rev. of Taup[in].

/////

Have you ever heard of ? or kan you git me copies of The Midland; The Frontier; and (gordelpuss) Folk's Say. In lieu of specimens opinion, if any, wd. serve.

I hear via Lunnon that Mr. Buntin' left them parts wearin the full regalia of the reignin' house of Assam. He'd been sleepin on the Embankment for a time previous.

E

Adams letters: Worthington Chauncey Ford, ed., *A Cycle of Adams Letters 1861–1865* (Boston: Houghton Mifflin, 1920). Zukofsky to Pound, 19 July 1930, "I'm sending you a Cycle of Adams letters 1861–1865. Mebbe the family's attempt at diplomacy and action will interest you."

H. Adams on: Adams's *History of the United States During the Administrations of Jefferson and Madison* (New York: Albert and Charles Boni, 1930).

French essay: "Ezra Pound: Ses Cantos," *Échanges* 1:3 (1930). The translation was by René Taupin.

Freeman: The New Freeman, a political and cultural periodical published in New York from March 1930 until May 1931. Zukofsky sent them a review of Taupin's *L'Influence du symbolisme,* but it was not printed.

The Midland: A regional little magazine extant 1915–1933; published in Iowa City, Iowa.

The Frontier: A regional little magazine extant 1920–1933; published in Missoula, Montana. In 1933 it merged with *The Midland* and became *Frontier and Midland.*

Folk's Say: Unidentified. Perhaps *Folk-say,* published by the Oklahoma folklore society between 1929 and 1932.

Buntin': Basil Bunting was noted for his extensive travels. He had first met Zukofsky in New York the previous month.

21. ALS–5.

Tues, Aug 19/30 1110 Miller Av. Berkeley Calif

Dear E: This paper is a legacy of a professor of ekonomiks—departed to Urope and comes with his house 1000 feet above sea level.

Completed "A–6 and 7" last week, about 30 pp. Hence out of the usual supply of stationery. Shall have to roll down the hills to replenish. If I get down before evening, I shall, thank guidness, miss the fog. The Californians think it's good for me, but I don't see the point in feeling porous.

"My country foist"—incidentally, there's too much prairie goin' across. Even Bill [Williams] would get tired of it. And I'm afraid Carl is fakin' his sentiments.

Your order & check of $11 for the Jeff & Mad has been forwarded to The John Donne Head, P.O. Box 14, Fox St. Sta., New York. They will also forward if they can find 'em The Midland, The Frontier, and Folk's Say—I daresay they have bookstores down below—but the Univ. of Calif. is dedicated to football. —All the issues of The Midland I ever saw was full of "lyrics" of the affections and the affectations. Prof. Raymond Weeks used to bring copies of it to class. He also waited for 12 ladies to pass thru a turnstile in the subway station, before he bowed finally to the air & threw his own nickel in. Unfortunately Taupin arrived too late for Weeks to be his boss.

As far as I remember The Frontier & Folk's Say are of the same bland calibre. But maybe I never saw 'em.

The last I heard of Buntin' some mysterious "they" wuz plannin to send him to Colorado.

The Adams letters I sent you are for keep—even if they take up too much space.

Echanges has written & asked me to be American correspondent. Since they have "revue anglaise et française" on their letterhead I presumed that I could offer to send 'em my "Am. Posey since" in English. (That shd. not interfere with your passing it of[f] on T.S. Eliot.) I can follow with my essay on Reznikoff. ⟨??⟩ All this material obviously "⟨American⟩ correspondence" despite its length. If Mlle. Harper wants 'em in French I suppose she can get a translator. Or am I known to her as the trans. of my E.P.? She probably knows the woiks since she wrote me in English, but mebbe that wuz just continental courtesy. No copy of Échanges arrived yet. Will send Freeman rev. of Taupang when she come out. Also "poesy" which I am anxious to have you see when typed—

Also anything else.

May go down to Monterey befo' I got to goo bye Wisconsun. I don't spose you want me to say hullo to Mistur [Robinson] Jeff[e]rs for you.

Yrs

Z

P.S. The Golden Gate ain't as per adjectival specification but it does for a poor easterner.

Carl: Possibly Carl Sandburg or Carl Rakosi.
Weeks: A professor of Romance languages at Columbia University.
Echanges: A Paris-based little magazine edited by Allanah Harper. Though she did not print "American Poetry 1920–1930," she did take the Pound essay. See her memoir, "A Magazine and Some People in Paris," *Partisan Review,* 9:4 (July-August 1942), pp. 311–320.

22. ALS–5.

Sept 8/30. 1110 Miller Av. Berkeley, Calif.

Dear E:

I. Here y'are—give Boy a mark.

I mean I finished the Review of the Cantos for the Indice last night, and if my host will continue, and finish, typing it to-night you'll have it sooner than I expected. You might compare date of this letter with postmark on envelop for an indication of the efficiency of one inhabitant* of this great state. No need to come to conclusions about the rest. *I meant my host.

You will notice that for an English instructor some of the sentences are improperly long. But that's the modicum of infant fun I got out of writing the thing. I should prefer that the entire review be printed, but if L'Indice objects to my exceeding your limit of 1200 words, you can cut as follows:

Pg 1 entire

Pg 2 down to "When the major criticism of Pound's very beautiful indeed etc." Begin there.

Pg 4 — The sentence beginning "That the numerous dramatis personae" etc. and ending "is not strange." Begin: "It was but natural"

This should make matters simpler for the spaghetti eaters. Also for salon criticism if I send it (Review) to Cambridge, Box A. Let me know which version you prefer. Tho by the time your letter gets here, I suppose I will have sent the thing as I prefer it. I am assured that saying "reminiscent of Basil Zaharof" instead of the original "i.e. Basil Zaharof" will save us a libel suit.

The review was done before your copy with inscription arrived. Hear that's the way reviews are usually done. My host insists that I copied my original essay. —At any rate, thanks, XXX Cantos is now very much my copy—barring t.t.r. (till the revolution), Tovarisch!

Hours Press copy not yet here. Will follow orders in case it arrives.

II As for the revision of The Cantos themselves—"tidying up the mess"—about which I say nothing in my article—you know what you're doin' (ya bet) but my primitive faith in the matter is once you know how to spell the finished first guess is correct. I See what you're doin' changing Ityn, Ityn to 'Tis. Tis. Ytis, but am not sure that the second is more like a bird than the first or that the first was becoming repetitious.

Did you have "But Sordello, and my Sordello?" and the first two lines of VI in de luxe edition?

Too bad, it seems to me, you had to loose the image i.e. effect of people singing a round in

Mar-
ins
vieux
Ce sont les
— son-

for the word Marsouins, even tho' the "line" in H[ound] & H[orn] version was not absolutely apparent. Who axed me?

III Don't think you're degeneratin' into trained seal in prose articles. Have enjoyed their thought as well as the unusual utterance very much. Even more than seeing my own things printed. So has my host whose intelligence I respect and whooze quite contrary about such things—believing I'm taken in by your thought because I think you "know" poetry.

IV You kin see wut I'm doin in Calif by looking to the left of the picture of a house I'm sendin: seein views, also fruit exhibitions, not growin 'em, am too lazy to push a lawn-mower and don't see the point of it anyway. ⟨At least right now 12 P.M. with the fog from Golden Gate around.⟩ Also bein told by my host who reciprocates exposures to human weakness to fill the gaps of my ignorance and to read Veblen—Thorstein Veblin [sic]. Outside of the amusement involved, and the fun of being shown up as ignorant, I'm sure the net result will be a singling out of the works of this very fine intellect, methodologist and what not as a remarkable example of his law of conspicuous waste. But that's because I'm not a mind and my host's wife realizes that I can be as amusing as my poetry. Now that confession's done——

Also decided (host and I) on a prospective wish-fulfillment. Should like i.e. publish his essay "Paper" and my Hen Adams, E.P.—His Cantos, Chas. Rez[nikoff]. & Am[erican]. Po[etry]. 1920–1930 under title Four Essays and Paper. Have already written the foreword:

"The essay Paper by 'Roger Kaigh' is presented as the work of an Arunta, a native of central Australia, who used an Anglo-American name for reasons of his own. The author of the other four essays in this volume has, to the best of his knowledge, the only copy available, and it is printed here because it would have been manifestly impossible to take cognizance of its thought consonant with points of aesthetic criticism in the other essays, unless their author divulged the relation." —You have seen "Paper" and are asked not to divulge its authorship.

V. Would you please send to Mlle Harper of Echanges, 22, Rue de Condé, Paris, the Reznikoff (after you have read it) and your copy of the Am. Poetry 1920–1930 after Indice's thru traducing it and tell her they're the "correspondence" I promised her. Haven't seen Échanges yet, nor money in payment for E.P. Stuck in the mails? Enclose wrapper of XXX Cantos to prove that they passed U.S. Customs.

VI. Hear that Midland & Adams' history have been sent to you. My bookdealer will also try to find Frontier & Folk's Say. Djaver get extras of Pavannes & Instigations?

VII Been readin very little of Jefferson, but shall probably begin in Madison. Which of the profs am I meant to lay for, that is which one have you instigated to a Wiscon Sinn univ. press. Hear Lathrop won't be there this year.

A 6 & 7 not typed yet. Think, if I may humbly say so, that A–7 performs the revolution in the sonnet I hinted at elsewhere. May be. . . .

VIII. 1. Shd. like you to send Draft of XXX Cantos to Taupin, if you haven't already done so.

2. Shd. like to know what Hours Press has decided about publication of "The"—negative decision won't incriminate you in these eyes. ⟨Matter pertinent to Gug[genheim] re-application now bolstered by academic standing.⟩

3. Shd. like to know what happened after an advertised brochure on the Music of Beowulf. Has it appeared?

4. Shd. like to know what "arcane" means as applied to my Amerik Poessy 1920–thoity.

Thanks, again, for returnin' Mockel's letter 'n everythin.

Z

If "new magazine" gets started, you could use some of the material I got together for Varietés?

Review: "Cantos di Ezra Pound," trans. Emanuel Carnevali, *L'Indice* (April 10; April 25; May 10, 1931).
Cambridge: That is, to *Hound & Horn*.
Zaharof: Sir Basil Zaharoff (1849?–1933). European arms dealer and manufacturer. He appears in Canto 18 as "Metevsky."
Hours Press: Pound to Zukofsky, 19 August 1930, "Copy of Cantos XXX started toward you this a.m." This was the Hours Press edition of *A Draft of XXX Cantos*. Gallup A31.
Ityn, Ityn: See Canto 4.
Marsouins: See Canto 28.
H & H version: Cantos 28, 29 and 30 appeared in the April/June 1930 issue of *Hound and Horn*. Gallup C764.
Veblin: Thorstein Veblen, American sociologist.
"Paper": This essay seems not to have survived, nor has the "foreword" Zukofsky mentions.

Lathrop: Henry Burrowes Lathrop, Professor of English at the University of Wisconsin.

Music of Beowulf: A projected work by Pound that never materialized. Gallup E6g.

"arcane": Pound to Zukofsky, 19 August 1930, " 'Indice' says it wants to print yr. much too arcane note on murkn poesy since 1920."

Mockel's letter: Mockel had read and rejected Zukofsky's essay on Pound. His letter does not appear to have survived.

"new magazine": Pound to Zukofsky, 19 August 1930, "There 'is talk' of a monthly in the Englisch langwidg." This was probably Samuel Putnam's *New Review,* which published its first issue in January 1931.

23. ALS–4.

26 Sept 1930 Livorno.

Dear Z: Coming perfessership casts ominously shadow before it. Ditto W.C.W[illiams]. behind?

Read the Rez[nikoff]. up till train time but hadn't finished it. = on hasty - = insp. == You must stop tangling yr. sentences = got to ~~learn to make~~ simplify. write subject predic. obj. = AFTER you have abs. mas-
1 2 3

tered simple (even to platichood) style you can start convolutin' =

my letters done to save time are NOT model for print =

I know its very hard to keep mind on what reader dont know & has to be told.

I don't think either essay any use fer Yourup = I think they both (after emendation) ought to appear in Poetry. & will write same to Harriet [Monroe].

= You have two gordorful mistakes in simple grammar. — (no ⟨more⟩ for any)

Last I heard Carnevali was translating yr. 1st essay on me for Indice. = ergo this one not needed. = But also as so much of it is answering fools whom Italians won't have hea[r]d speak—it is more adapted to U.S. pub.

The Reznikoff. long citations about p. 17 very fine & convincing

=

for the earlier short quotes, your comments rather annoy.= if the reader can't see point without yr. telling him This word illustrates this principle

= ———————— etc. I mean you are too lectury. and R's lack of technique worries me too much.

I will write to Harriet today or tomorrow = and if you like will edit the mss when I get back to Rapallo.

R. not using speech wie im Schnabel gewuchsen. — I don't know if simple effect of using foreign language.

= In the long citations (along p. 17) the rhythm (contrary to yr. op.) does seem to me satisfactory.

———

The essay on me more recondite than the 1st. You know more & really continue on assumption that the reader has read your earlier opus. —— good fer the development of criticism but not for purp[ose]. of intro-d[uction]. to thorny subject.

I think H[ound]. & H[orn]. have intentions for a review. — any how if they don't take it try it with Harriet. == desperate attempt ought once more be made to get hold of that gun pit.

=

The only regular monthly bulletin cd be useful. — anyhow the only place where one can assume enough interest in poesy to print yr. Rez. etc. ——

E

P.S. Have writ to Harriet
Have told her she ought to print the Rez. — & that you ought to do crit. for her regular & that she ought to do a special number devoted to people D[onal]. McKenzie believes in & that you are willing to write about.

Rez[nikoff]: "Charles Reznikoff: Sincerity and Objectification." Zukofsky later revised this essay and printed it as "Sincerity and Objectification: With Special Reference to the Work of Charles Reznikoff," *Poetry* 37:5 (February 1931), pp. 272–285.

Carnevali: Emanuel Carnevali, Italian-American poet and short story writer.

wie im Schnabel: In *ABC of Reading* Pound asserts, "You receive the language as your race has left it, the words have meanings which have 'grown into the race's skin'; the Germans say 'wie ihm den Schnabel gewachsen ist,' as his beak grows." *ABC of Reading* (New York: New Directions, 1960), p. 36.

McKenzie: Donal McKenzie, Marxist literary critic and co-editor of the little magazine *Morada.*

24. TL–5.

24 Oct. [1930] Rapallo

Dear Zuk:

Wonners will nevuHH cease. I have just recd. nooz from Harriet [Monroe] that she is puttin you at the wheel for the Spring cruise.

I dunno whether in L'annonce fait a L.Z. she mentioned the foreflying occasions????

At any rate since it was a letter from donal mckenzie that smoked me up into writin Harriet the letter that awoke in her nobl booZUMM the fire of enthusiasm that led her to let you aboard

I

wd. appreciate it if you wd. invite mckenzie to do one of the prose articles for the number and state his convictions as forcibly as possibl . . . .

after which I see no reason why you shdnt. add a editorial note saying why you disagree.

Poetry has never had enUFF disagreement INSIDE into own wall.

need hardly say that I am ready to be of anny assistance I can. I do NOT think it wd. be well to insert my point of view. I shd. like you to consider mckenzie's point of view and your own.

IF there is anyone whom you want to include and cant get directly, I might be of use in raking them in, but I dont want to nominate any one.

I shdnt. be in any hurry. Take your time and you can produce something that will DATE and will stand against Des Imagistes.

I think I wrote you that I refused to contribute to Aldington's Imagist mortology 1930 ⟨(or 1929 or whenever it appeared) . . . "20 ans apres"⟩

I don't know that I mentioned my statement to R[ichard]. A[ldington]. or praps it was to W.C.W.[illiams] that I shd. have considered tying up with ⟨that lot of survivers⟩ game a species of betrayal of your generation. (or some less rhetorical term, probably a list mentioning you and McA[lmon].)

As H[arriet]. says she has invited your prose comment, it strikes me that you need not limit yourself to unpubd work.

The body of the issue shd. naturally be new stuff, but there is no reason why you shd.nt have a small print senction of 8 or 12 pages with the classics of the intervening period.
(I have in mind Hemingways "They all made peace" and the Neothomist poem (with title correctly spelled).

Can't think of anything else that you wd. be likely to overlook, or of any other writer who wdnt. stand perfectly fair chance of having an unpubd poem as good as anything he has already pubd.

The thing is to get out something as good as Des Imagistes by any bloody means at yr. disposal. (also to learn by my errors).

mckenzie might provide the conviction and enthusiasm (which you somewhat lack) and leave you to provide the good sense

I shd. in general be inclined to neglect anything already on file with "Poetry" waiting to be printed, and INVITE contribution from the active sperrits who wdnt. normally send their stuff to E. Erie St.

I can not GODDDDDAMMMMIT find mckenzie's LIST of just men but am asking him to send it to you.

It mentioned ⟨I think⟩ McAlmon, Johns that edits Paganny, you, norman macleod et j'en oublie, several I did not know but all whom I cd. verify by ref/ to current periodicals seemed good.

(he also mentioned Dunning, not knowing that Cheever was ten years older than I am and already dead (in physical sense).

I cant see that you need be catholic or inclusive;

detach whatever seems to be the DRIVE

or driving force or xpression of same . . . .

an now lemme layoFFF.

That is to say.
I shd. try to get a fairly homogenius number; emphasis on the progress made since 1912; concentrated drive; not attempt to show the extreme diversity; though it cd. be mentioned in yr. crit.

This also wd. make it a murkn number; excludin the so different English; though you cd. be broadminded an mention 'em in a brief article (Basil[Bunting]'s from L'indice; or a condensation; or yr. own.

If you cover yourself with glory an' honour, H.M. might even let Basil try his hand at showin what Briton can do.

or you in yr. now sproutin advisory capacity cd. tell her that Basil (often tres constipé) had done an article that has appeared in a furrin tongue. . . . .

Or still also prejektin into the future; Basil cd. crit. your number after the act, that wd. prob. be the best; you do yr. american damndest and then call in the furrin critic to spew forth his gall and tell what the Britons wd. LIKE to do that you aint done.

//

with mckenzie; I shd. carefully consider anything he nominates. Then let him know what you have chosen and ⟨have him⟩ base his article on his disagreement with you; simply let him say what he wd. have done if he had been editing the number. That will give your decade from two pts. of view temperamentally as opposed as anyone cd. wish (at least I shd. think they wuz. opsd.

venerabilis parens

donal mckenzie's address
Theresienstr. 14/ III Munich Germany

thet wummun she nevuh trusted me lak she trusts you!!!

Des Imagistes: Des Imagistes (New York: Albert and Charles Boni, 1914). Gallup B7.

mortology: Imagist Anthology, 1930: Poems by Richard Aldington, John Cournos, H.D. . . . forewords by Ford Madox Ford and Glenn Hughes (London: Chatto & Windus, 1930).

Neothomist poem: Published in *The Exile,* number 1; erroneously printed as "Nothoemist Poem."

E. Erie St.: The address of *Poetry.*

Johns: Richard Johns, editor of *Pagany.*

macleod: American poet and co-editor of the little magazine *Morada.*

Dunning: Ralph Cheever Dunning, American expatriate poet. Pound had published him in *The Exile,* numbers 3 and 4. He died in Paris in July 1930.

Basil[Bunting]'s: Probably Bunting's "Scrittori inglesi contemporanei," *L'Indice,* 20 May 1930.

25. TLS–5.

[25 October 1930] Rapallo

⟨re/ Potry an Arriet⟩

nex day.
25 Oct

Dear Z

I continue to feel gratified: shall prob put my fingers into the matter too often, still . . . . . you may as well have what I know, at yr. disposal to use or leave.

///

You have at least 30 or 32 pages for verse. I don't think you can show more than a dozen authors, three or four unassailable chunks, and others held down to a single page or poem.

Get what is least attackable or arguable.

Mere surface or trying to be clever cant carry the thing. Cummingsities cd. enliven the shorter manifestations.

BUT the chaps that mean what they say have got to give the weight.

there's got to be enough difference in contributors to indicate a circumference; but NOT to disperse and scatter the energy.

///

It is a better chance to launch Reznikoff than you cd. have expected.

The essay on Rez. is too long to include in such a number, but (poss. with the revisions I suggested last month) feeling yr. way you cd. prob. slide it into a later issue.

///

The other expert advice is: Invite the men you believe in. IF they don't send stuff up to level of their best KEEP AT 'eM. Be takkful. Say you want to show what they can do, havent they something less open to attack. After all the position is xposed, challenges the record etc.

IF the number is convincingly better than the usual numbers of Poetry there is a chance (happens to be damn good chance) of rescuing the magazine from the slough of Zabel, Dillon and co. and making it what it was in 1912/13, the forum in which the Zeitideen WERE presented and discussed.

Much better to conduiser la danse in a well established and subsidized mag. than in a new indigent 6 leaf peryodiuncle likely to last for three numbers.

I don't know anything about mckenzie's verse. He deserves perhaps a page of verse; and as much of the prose section as you can give him. I don't see that you need stint yourself in the prose. Dont be prolix and dont be professorial any more than you can help. ⟨& fer XTZake be ~~lucid~~ direct.⟩

i;e; state anything you like, but dont stop to argue.

IF anyone attacks your STATEMENT it will implicate you into a reply in later issues; which is all to the good.

mckenzie to attack you IN your own number;
BASIL [Bunting] to add the "Foreign critic sees us" in later issue;
dependin on yr. diplomacy with Harriet. and hardly to be mentioned YET; or as you see it.

///

Whom the dvl cd. you get to form an "⟨permanent⟩ advisory committee" ⟨for Poetry.⟩ to replace the present staff of boiled vegetables"??

You, McAlmon, gardnoze, I spose that committee HAS to live in Chicago 2 months of the year.

///

As Reznikoff is your own special, it is very important to get something of his that wont be arguable.

Time enough for your readers to THINK later; your job in this paricular issue is to make them believe.

The prob. differs from mine in Des Imagistes. There, it was to make a very exiguous quantity go as far as possibl

You ⟨on the other foot.⟩ have got to disentangle a far
more multitudinous etc. etc.

plenty of chaps meaning

what they say (with no lit. capac.)

they are your basis. you've got so to choose 'em as to hide their defects.

By getting the ten good lines the barstuds have writ, you compose more or less one hole man out of the lot, or one author.

Keep at 'em till you get stuff that is good enough.
Fight with 'em the day after; that don't matter.

If they don't send in something good; relegate 'em to the historic section in small print. ten or a dozen poems wd. cover that.
Carnevali can prob. do as well as he ever has done.
Cummings and Hem[ingway]. ??? hist. sec. only.

Fer the rest, it is up to you to tell me. I can NOT be expected to know wot the young are doin'

///

I see NO reason ⟨for you or for me⟩ to tell anyone that I have had an indirect participation in the whatshallwe nego=well=ci=moreorless=ation.

The fact that it will be hard for you to satisfy yourself among yr. con'emporaries is all to the good.

The Imagiste movement was made with four or 5 poems of Hilda[Doolittle]'s, three or four of Richard[Aldington']s and one ole Bill Water Closet W[illia]m's. plus y.v.t. or if you like manipulated by y.v.t. whereto were added about the same amt. of stuff that wdn't damage (i.e. one hoped it wdnt. damage the effek).

Prob⟨lem⟩. ain't now the same. I go on burbling merely to indicate that mere extent of the verbal manifestation has nawthin ter dew wiff it.

E

essay on Rez.: See Pound's letter of 26 September 1930.
Zabel: Morton Dauwen Zabel, an assistant editor of *Poetry*.
Dillon: George H. Dillon, an assistant editor of *Poetry*.

26. TLS–5.

[25 October 1930] Rapallo

NOT to be read till you have digested 2 preceding epistles
of yesterday and today

25 Oct.

Dear Z

Yet again; yrs. to hand. this being third epistl I do to thhee indite.

DONT spoil sheep for ha'p orth of tar. You can't get number done RIGHT in time for Feb. issue. take one of the later dates H[arriet Monroe]. has offered.

///

The number ought to be NEW line up. You can mention me and old Bill Walrus [Williams] in the historic section.

if you dont know nawthin about your contemptoraries you'll have to lean on mckenzie who hath faith.

I don't think you need the English. I don't want to queer their pitch, but as the aim is not limited by the immediate objective. i;e; not to STOP with your special number but to regenerate and redemivirginate Poetry; the Eng. wd. natcherly git a show after you have blossomed.

Rakosi' may be dead, I wish I cd. trace him.

His last address was

61 N. Main St. Kenosha, wisconSin.

///

Loomis is too tired and sophisticated. You can get some other one of yr. dozen without lapping over Exile.

I have a pome by Carnevali in desk that I will send on (I spose that's what you mean by Covalesci).

I am glad the Rez[nikoff]. essay is taken elsewhere. It wd. have been out of scale for yr. special number.

I have already given you enough hints in letters writ. last eve. and this a.m.

I WANT a new list of men NOT chosen because they have already got in touch with me.

Let mckenzie nominate and you weed out. ALSO weed out the fellers' stuff when you get it.

Bill [Williams], Hem[ingway], Cummings ought to go in historic ~~section~~ ⟨selection.⟩, or rather I think Hem. and Cummings cd; go there,

unless you can get new poem from Cummings, certainly you can write to him, I have done nowt to cloud the horizon.

I do not think contributions from ANYone over 40 shd. be included; and preferably it shd. be confined to those under 30.

You can in ten lines of yr, prose cover the facts re/ Bunting and J. Gorrdun Macleod. whose Ecliptic is now pubd.

The opportunity is larger than you had grasped on 13th inst.

To save time I spose I'll have to "indicate".

you'll have to go thru Pagany; New Masses, Morada, for talent.
Horace Gregory's book has been pubd. by Covici.

I can not damitall MY recommendation now means too much.
You can make twenty bad guesses and have 30 expectations without doing yourself any harm and without injustice to the men you omit.

Take New Masses, Pagany, Morada and start to debunk and eliminate.

Insist on mckenzie's getting hard solid stuff from his list of hopefuls.

Don't lean on europe. Certainly NOT a translation of an essay on Salmon.

The thing is to cut a line livlier than H[ound] & Horn. with just 8% more sense than N[ew]. Masses.

Get good stuff from people not perhaps good enough ⟨in themselves⟩; but who can get through 8 lines or a page without giving themselves away;

AND

a little really solid.

⟨3 or 4 men can do the needful. Rez. McA[lmon]. & y[ou] & the fringe⟩

ONE notable difference between yr. position in 1930 and mine in 1910 is that you would LIKE to include several older american authors. Bill, Me and I suppose Possum Eliot, with Cummings an already known name.

It is not a factor that makes your ⟨immediate⟩ job any easier but it may on the other hand have made life in general etc . . . .

If you cd. define and dissociate the whatshallwesay impulses depulses etc. of yr. elders (not AT length; but in say a sentence or three paragraphs) Not merely epigramatic whoop.

Anyhow; the young cd. learn something from the three of us and praps from Edward Estlin [Cummings].

The ~~number~~ ⟨issue of Poetry⟩ NOT to be overtopplingly retrospective.

Mr wozisname is NOT content with his uncles.

I am glad you asked about Rakoski. The chap was feelin blue as a sambohillbo in his last letter, I wudnt be sprised if he'd shot himself. If he is still at Kenosha, you cd. establish personal vivavoce.

Always something to be got out scrap that takes place on the premises and not merely over a typewriter.

Obit. H[oward]. Weeks
"" Harry Crosby
"" Dunning (but that was of a distinctly other generation).

I will try to get a copy of Hem's They All Made Peace.

with which remarks: go to it. I dont think poss to have it ready for press Dec. 20.

Harriet's to me says "Feb. March or May." March certainly the earliest poss. and no great harm done if May is later found to be more commodious.

at any rate GET IT RIGHT.

E

You'll have to suspend Jefferson fer the moment and pass a few weeks STUDYIN the writes of yr. contmps.

Loomis: Payson Loomis, American poet. Pound had published him in *The Exile,* number 3.

Covalesci: Zukofsky to Pound, 13 October 1930, "Who is Edmund Covelesci . . ."? Unidentified.

Rez[nikoff]. essay: Zukofsky wrote to Pound on 13 October 1930 that "I can fill in the prose with maybe my 'Reznikoff' which contains general references to the history of the subject. The Am. Poetry 1920–1930 would be better, but, I'm afraid, 'Symposium' has accepted it." Pound seems to have gotten confused about which essay had been accepted by *Symposium.*

Ecliptic: The Ecliptic (London: Faber and Faber, 1930).

Morada: A little magazine based in Albuquerque, New Mexico. Donal McKenzie was one of its editors.

Gregory's Book: Chelsea Rooming House (New York: Covici, Friede, 1930).

Salmon: André Salmon, French poet.

Crosby: Crosby had shot himself in November 1929.

They All Made Peace: Zukofsky quoted it in full in "Program: 'Objectivists' 1931," *Poetry* 37:5 (February 1931), pp. 270–271. Pound thought well enough of this poem to reprint it in his *Active Anthology.*

Jefferson: Zukofsky's projected essay on Thomas Jefferson.

27. TL–6

28 Oct. [1930] [Rapallo]

Z/

I repeat that Arriet's letter t[o] me says you are to have Feb. OR March OR May, as you like. Don't fire till you see the whites of their eyes.

If the thing not in shape to CONVINCE, hold it for later date. I don't see that you CAN be properly ready by 20 Dec. ⟨up to you to produce effect that Poetry has come to life again. as a seereeos orgum.⟩

NEVERTHELESS

I am trying to hasten matters.
I. by asking mckenzie to forward all the best stuff he has collected for Morada, with the bait that you will either call it Morada number (IF Arriet's shd. consent) or ref/ to this material as "Morada group" or "the men mckenzie believes in"

that latter prob. the more tactful, as some of the men he believes in might feel umbrage at bein' "grouped" but none cd. object to havin' a credulous mcK.

Have also suggested he take a chance on writing his CREDO before he has time to hear from you.

If you approve this please cable me. simply Pound, Rapallo yes.
you neednt sign; no other cable will be coming from wisconsin.
mebbe you'll have to add Italy to the address. I will refund.

I REPEAT, the Reznikoff article is too long and wd. overbalance the whole number and chuck it all out of proportion. Harriet might use it in some other number.

A ~~number of~~ ⟨few⟩ brief credos and arts. on state of things since 1920: a longish exposition by L.Z. plus whatever mckenzie' can provide.
AND the verse used MUST be good.

preferably by men under 30; or with Cummings' as the most venerable figure.

The device of historic method, used to drag in stuff like Hem's "All Made Peace" and good stuff already printed (better NOT from volumes) but printed and left scattered since 1920. at any rate the equivalent for that period to my French number of the Lit. Rev. (repubd. in Instigations.)

Ref: to me / Bill [Williams] / an Eliot as the sinister shadows or whatever; O.K. IF you diferentiate between us; with Cummings in mid. distance.

(also any divergent ops/ you may have.
////

Will take up matters of editin: yr. mss. recd. as time permits. Saviotti due this p.m. etc.

///

I dont think Basil [Bunting] was bein' smart in the Villon. Dont quite know what you take to indicate the tendency. Certain procedures of F.V[illon]. himself??

Neither can I see anything that isn't puffikly clear. I objected to his trans. of "La bonne Lorraine", but that's how he wants it.

At any rate bloody well the best thing has been in Poetry fer some time.

since we are committed to intrigue, you might in due course tell Harriet it shd. be "prized".

am for omitting foreigners from your number. That number shd. establish the new American line up.

always better to plan a series of things even if one can only do ONE. If the ONE is intended as start of series it gains a certain potentiality, and gets perhaps completed later.

DONT comment ON Madison ⟨City of⟩ out lound, unless you have already done so. Yr. aged parent was once relegated to Crawfordsville Ind. which MUST be worse, it aint even a state Capital. Bear, observe and BEEEEE silent. Surtout point de zele! In time of stress reread Adams opening chapters on Jeff's time.

Am not strong on the Darrk night of the soul. But still you've got somethin to okkerpy yer mind fer the next few weeks. by which time you'll git a Xmas vac.

ce qu'il aurait pu encaisser /////

Belgion hare need worry one no more than Harpers mag. it reps/ analogous slum in Britain. Eliot ought not to print such drivvle without edt. footnote. The pickled foetus without the bottle.

///

Point re/ Carnevali is that there IS the energy. Sentimentality can be trimmed off by edtr. ⟨to some extent⟩ but the energy has to be provided by the author.

Invalids very hard to deal with. Man lies in bed shaking with encephalitis, stupified by scapolin for several hours daily; then period of comparative controll.

One can't insist on same dicipline one wd. with a man not so afflicted. At the same time he is civilized male reading french, Italian and capable of discussion same. ⟨contrast to barbarians like Hem[ingway]. & McA[lmon].⟩ curious effect of calm voice and intelligence unconnected with shaking body.
Personality intact in middle of it.

All of which must not blunt one's crit. sense. The stuff has to stand by what finally gets onto page.

Merely: it is case where one is justified in doing what one can as edtr.

One is not so justified if the author is merely a [Aldous] Huxley being too goddam lazy to try.

Yes; the stuff needs to be cut. He can't hold a pen. Typing full of errors.

Believe H & H has asked Blackmur to do XXX.

Have never seen "Symposium" have you an old copy.?

///

State of things to be disinfected// scence covered by dilutations of me; Bill [Williams] and Possum Eliot:: also praps of Ed. Estlin/ [Cummings]

plus mess caused by reaction against these dilutes. I mean the Tennysonian sonnet etc. now being done, and NOT so well done as in 1898 or when they were all tryin to do it as well as Miss Edith Thomas//

then the whole nrg and "sensibilité" of the bleatin nashun wuz concentrated on that cambric tea effort.

Since 1912 it has been divided.

Your li'l heave fer the KALON KAI AGATHON has got to make a

clean up, as was done by the Donts and Des Imagistes. (the anthology; or its justifiable parts)

as distinct from the Amygists.

///

proportions of space in number: tentatively ⟨without trespasin on rizin edtr's liberty, we suggest⟩

A. 6 pages (8 | 7) ⟨relatively
B. ditto (4 | 3) ⟨any how 3 main items⟩ speakin.
C. ditto (4 | 6) & thereabouts.⟩

D.E.F. 6 pages for the three of 'em

G.H.I.
J.K.L. 6 or 8 pages fer. the six or eight of 'em/

thats 32 pages of verse.

Prose. 16 or less in short bursts. 16 or more Zuk. on the waste land about bhloszuMMMMMM.

The historic survey with quotes; etc. prob. needs 20 pages; with 12 fer the incidentalia.

⟨over⟩

As to Basil/ I spose his six months visa will make it oblig: fer him to git out of the U.S.A. I want to insert him as Eng. correspondent for H & H or Poetry or everywhere possible: to choke off snot from Beligions Ray Mortimers and bloomsbuggers in generl/ ⟨confidenshul as is most of the rest⟩

French number: "A Study in French Poetry," *The Little Review* 4:10 (February 1918), pp. 3–61. Gallup C327.

Saviotti: Gino Saviotti. Italian art critic, novelist, and translator. Associated with *L'Indice.*

the Villon: "Villon," *Poetry,* 37:1 (October 1930), pp. 27–33.

"La bonne Lorraine": François Villon's "Ballade des dames du temps jadis" contains these lines: "Et Jehanne la bonne Lorraine / Qu'Englois brulerent a Rouan / Ou sont ilz, ou, Vierge souvraine? / Mais ou sont les neiges d'antan?" Bunting's rendition: "In those days rode the good Lorraine / Whom English burned at Rouen, / The day's bones whitening in centuries' dust." "Villon," *Poetry,* 37:1 (October 1930), p. 28.

opening chapters: Of *The History of the United States during the Administrations of Jefferson and Madison.*

Beligions: Montgomery Belgion, British essayist. The "drivvle" was his article, "What Is Criticism?" (*The Criterion,* October 1930).
Blackmur: The *Draft of XXX Cantos* was reviewed instead by Dudley Fitts. "Music Fit for the Odes," *Hound & Horn* 4:2 (January-March 1931).
Symposium: Edited by James Burnham and Philip E. Wheelwright. Extant 1930–1933.
Thomas: Edith Matilda Thomas (1854–1925), American poet.
KALON KAI AGATHON: The "beautiful and good."
Donts: "A Few Don'ts by an Imagiste," *Poetry* 1:6 (March 1913), pp. 200–206. Gallup C74.
Des Imagistes: Des Imagistes: An Anthology (New York: Albert and Charles Boni, 1914). Gallup B7.
Ray Mortimers: Raymond Mortimer, British art historian associated with the Bloomsbury group.

28. ALS–7.

Nov. 5/30 419 Sterling Place Madison, Wis.

[At the head of this letter Zukofsky wrote, "new address," and drew an arrow pointing to the address.]

Dear E: Moved agen as you see—this time to stay the year: one room and bath, entrance private, not leading thru a gudgeous hall in which lighted bald heads pore over newspapers. Much more pleasant for the salubrious Zhiukovskiy to enter his own bath in the morning—unattended by the rest of the naked faculty showing what they haven't got and gazing sidelong at his own John the Baptistry, torse etc remarkable for its lightness. Always suspiciously of course—what is this boy doing here?

As to my proper behaveyour—"surtout point de zele"—Bill [Williams] will tell you I am a very tractable person, but I naturally say yes and no and mean it. C'est à dire brevity to the soul of shit—

However, so far I have made only friends—and as Bill says, "remember the professors have wives and children": Mr. M.L. Hanley, philologist, Mr. Dodge, the head of the Department, even Mr. Wm. Ellery Leonard, whose poetry we have refrained from discussing and who has with something of personal interest regretted the fact that he did not get to know me in time for me to register for his Old Norse course—for the material in it offered much of human values. And I think the students are saying good things about me.

All the more to be regretted since I'll probably be offered an instructorship next year—and if nothing hooks me out in the meantime Gord knows what will become of me. Till now, however, I have managed to lose or quit my jobs.

I do not know whether I wrote you that I am supposed to be studying to be ordained to a doctorship (like hell I am)—but on the face of it—I am, for the faculty, "pursuing graduate studies [″]: Old Provençal and English Research. In the one class there are some five or six others, in the other I am alone. What's funny about Eng. Re. is that Prof. Beatty one of the older members of the department ran the "course" last year, but I chose to be "advised" by one of the younger members, H.H. Clark, an authority on Freneau, and Beatty is jealous of Clark, and gives him advice how to run the "course" and tells him about the necessity for giving an examination—but Clark and Beatty both know nothing of the material of the course—since I outlined it—ergo I must submit a list and outline of my readings and make my own examination—i.e. make believe Clark is making it. It all has to do with the Jefferson—what interests Clark is that J- got his ijees from Rowsow via Blackstone or maybe Blackstone got em from Rowsow and gave 'em to Locke who in turn gave 'em to J- what interests me is how J uses the names of flowers in his garden book—and so we talk. What's still funnier is that you—favver—should have started the course. But I don't tell them that.

Miss Lucy Maria Gay ⟨who gives the Provençal⟩ is a lady of about seventy—and, considering the small number of her students, it was really very sad to hear her mention the other day that Abelard had 20,000 students in the streets of Paris. Gave the old lady who has still a little flare for dwelling on what a roué was Guilhem de Peitieu your Daniel (Instigations) to read. Also your Spirit of Romance which she'll probably find more to her taste—since she's down on the trobar clus and will probably agree ⟨more⟩ with your chapter on the other Proenca.

One might think that with your studies' being 18 years or so in the air, I might get the thing as a heritage. But this goddurned little linguist (me) has to sweat like hell to find things in Levy, Bartsch, Appel etc. Wish I knew some mediaeval latin so as I could recognize a word when I saw it. As for the music, and the reading of it (I wish I could hear you some day!) I suppose it's hopeless— The old lady reads it eight syllables—nothing, up, nothing, up, etc—and can't for the life of me see why you translate "Ab la dolchor de temps novel" and give it the peculiar rock and pause—not that she ever sees that pause after sweet, repeat, meet no more than she does after bosc, chascus or hears the bridies—

But maybe I don't know what I'm talking about. Will have to look up Beck or somebody if I can find it—

Also been trying to read an elegy or so of Propertius each week—that is for the sound of it (a lady translates—this is private and not connected with the univoisity)—and am told I slip up on quantities, and accent, ⟨the words⟩ as as [*sic*] if I were reading English. Granted I know how to pronounce the Latin (which is possible—never having heard anyone pronounce it) how much is the pronounciation altered in the reading of the line to "meet" (or whatever the word should be) the quantity ⟨or the verse line⟩. What has word accent, in other words, to do with musical accent? What's his order of speech or is it all intoned? How much more ⟨intoned⟩ than "Music to hear why hears't thou music sadly," for instance? (i.e. Shakespeare is writing something else besides syllablic & accentual verse)—Or don't you want to be bothered? Point is Allen & Greenough's section on prosody don't tell me nothin' and no English manual including Robert Bridges & Omond etc etc never did.

As for being "srious"—How can I evangilize the H[ound] & H[orn] & write "chatty letters" to Mr. Linkköln Kirstein if whenever I write him a letter Mr. Stroocke answers. Ditto: MSS—the E.P., Am. Poetry, the review of The Cantos, of which Stroock writes "I don't think there is much chance of our publicishing [*sic*] it because it had already been assigned before you sent us yours"— but how could they have assigned it if only 2 copies entered these states?

I'm afraid Mr. K. is sore because the Am. Poetry 1920–1930 disposed of a good many of his?—What's the use of telling 'em Robert Hillyer is bad, if they think "A" isn't any good.

I told 'em long time ago to get in touch with McAlmon, told 'em Bill [Williams] had good stuff lying around, gave 'em what I had (incidentally The Symposium, 100 Washington Sq. ⟨N.Y.C.⟩, ed by Philip E. Wheelwright, Chairman of Philosophy Dep't, New York Univ. is publishing Am. Poetry 1920–1930—probably in January).—"It not availeth"

H & H & Symposium mortal enemies—

And reward cometh from nowhere—now that I am 1000 miles away the H & H ask me to bear with their financial predicament—& then Bill writes me they're going into publishing instanter—Now how do you expect this innocent to handle such people?

I'm doing what I can to get good stuff together for my Feb. issue of Poetry—

I'm trying to outline a French girl's doctor's thesis on Imagism—(Taupin supplied the business) so as I can in six months or so have a dollar instead of half a dollar a day to live on

I'm translating Taupin's Salmon including the quotations—

Correcting themes—a hundred at least

Trying to read 20 volumes of Jefferson, 20 related volumes, Boas' Indian Languages, Frobenius' Paideuma—

My correspondence has become as enormous as yours is (probably)—

"Be srious." Sure, if you'll let me stand on my head

Z

Shd. have told you not to read this letter to begin with

New Freedman (of which I too am a sub/er) pewk pretty much all around including Suzie's flapperish economia

I suppose Mike Gold is alright—but that's his affair—I don't think I've missed anything not seein more of him in N.Y.—saw him once anyway. N. Masses a pretty bad best—I'd just as soon have H & H

Again please send me a copy of Indice—give 'em my address (when you have time) Thanks a lot.

Forget: Showed Miss Gay trans. in Echanges—she agreed with what I had to say about poetry but didn't see how it applied to you. Said I wrote French very well. "Be srious." Calls me Zrfsky.

Will look into the State Capital the next time I pass it & see if the mum⟨m⟩ie of our martyred Abe is there

Eau Claire-Chippewa Falls 7 hrs. from Madison by train.

Hear Black Sun's publishing some new essays of yourn?

Beer sold to every man, woman & chile in these parts

Sonny will eventually go back to N.Y.—the only Jerusalem—Probably for 2 wks Christmuss

Please speed revised Reznikoff if you haven't done so

Leonard: William Ellery Leonard, author of numerous books of verse.

de Peitieu: William IX (1071–1127) of Aquitaine, an important early troubadour. Pound mentions him briefly in *The Spirit of Romance.* (See also the note to *Ab la dolchor* below.)

trobar clus: Troubadour poems that contained hidden meanings.

Levy: Emil Levy (1855–1917), author of the *Provenzalisches Supplement-Wörterbuch.* Pound's visit to Levy is commemorated in Canto 20.

Bartsch: Karl Friedrich Bartsch (1832–88), author of numerous works on Medieval German literature as well as Provençal.

Appel: Carl Ludwig Ernst Appel (1857–1934), author of numerous works on Provençal.

Ab la dolchor: A poem by William IX of Aquitaine. Pound's translation was titled "Avril" and appeared in *Quia Pauper Amavi* (London: The Egoist, Ltd., 1919). Gallup A17.

sweet, repeat, meet: The first stanza of "Avril" is: "When the springtime is sweet / And the birds repeat / Their new song in the leaves, / 'Tis meet / A man go where he will[.]"

Beck: Jean Baptiste Beck (1881–1943), author of numerous works on the troubadours.

Music to hear: The first line of Shakespeare's Sonnet 8.

Allen: Allen and Greenough's New Latin Grammar for Schools and Colleges, by Joseph Henry Allen (1820–1898) and James Bradstreet Greenough (1833–1901).

Bridges: Robert Seymour Bridges (1844–1930), British poet laureate. Author of *Milton's Prosody.*

Omond: Thomas Stewart Omond, author of *English Metrists* (Oxford: Clarendon Press, 1921).

Stroocke: Alan M. Stroock, business manager of *Hound & Horn.*

Hillyer: Roberty Hillyer, American poet.

Wheelwright: Philip E. Wheelwright. American philosopher, critic, and editor. Co-editor of *The Symposium.*

Taupin's Salmon: "Three Poems by André Salmon," *Poetry* 37:5 (February 1931), pp. 289–293.

Boas: Franz Boas (1858–1942), American anthropologist, author of many works on American Indian languages.

Paideuma: Leo Frobenius, *Paideuma: Umrisse einer Kultur- und Seelenlehre* (Munich: Beck, 1921).

Suzie: Suzanne LaFollette, editor of *The New Freeman.*

martyred Abe: Pound to Zukofsky, 22 October 1930, "You might find out if old Abe is still in the state house (he'd be stuffed . . .)." Old Abe was an eagle that had been the mascot of a Wisconsin regiment during the Civil War.

new essays: Imaginary Letters (Paris: The Black Sun Press, 1930). Gallup A32.

29. ALS–12.

Nov 6/30 419 Sterling Place Madison, Wisconsin

Dear E: After last night, yr 3 this morning. This ans. will be haphazard, but will, never the less, follow yr. letters point by point.

1. Will invite McKenzie to do one of prose articles, but what makes you think we'll have anything to disagree about?

2. See your pts. for the Crepitation of the Spheres, but I'm no good at argymint. Damn it, I want to write poetry—even if I ain't being let.

3. Not being soft-minded, however, the poet puts a period in his lapel and says 1 & 2 will depend on what McKenzie sends or writes.

4. Disagreement or at any rate variety shd. be furnished by poets own contrib. I'm not interested in program music.

5. Want to get material ready by Dec. 19, because I want to get the thing off my mind—I can't be an editor, a midwife to boys & girls, a hysterectomer in private and a poet in public all at once. I'm not a universal. ⟨(Naturally, if all material isn't in by Dec. 19—I'll have to wait. But I won't wait if I have enough).⟩

6. Yr. refusal to contribute to 1930 Imagists duly recorded forever and ever. I appreciate it.

7. 8 or 12 pages of the classics? of the intervening period? who for instance? According to my Sassay Am[erican]. Po[etry]. 1920–30—I'd have to reprint one of yr. cantos, Bill [Williams], Marianne [Moore], Eliot, Stevens, Cummings, McAlmon? Small print not desirable to Harriet. How wd. that fix me with copyright of above authors' works etc?

8. Shd like to see Hemingway's They all made peace. Can't say I want Neothomist Poem, particularly, especially after appearance in Exile 1 (not that I'm going back on yer—but why repeat)—maybe Donal [McKenzie] could quote it to express his attitude.

9. Present list of names of possible contributions includes Whittaker Chambers, George Oppen, Jerry Reisman, S. T. Hecht, Henry Nolan (pseudo), Reznikoff, Me, Bill (I've accepted his Alphabet of the Trees—the man isn't dead, he's younger than any of us), McAlmon (if Bill can get him to write me, he's written him I know), probably two or three other unknowns, Rakosi if he's somewhere, Cummings (I'll send him the best contributions to tell him he'll be in good company), Bunting (a poem or so, because, I wrote him, & to introduce him previous to the subsequent English issue you plan. I don't see why—Eng. issue be damned—I shdn't get [Joseph Gordon] MacLeod & J. J. Adams & other

Ingles if I can get 'em—and if they're good. ⟨Maybe Spector, [Charles Henri] Ford—maybe—⟩

10. I am not referring to Poetry's files for anything

11. Johns of Pagany no good as a poet—I'll write him, ⟨tho',⟩—even if my reject will probably cause him to neglect me in turn.

Norman MacLeod better, but generally not a poet. He has a potential matter but is for the most part bad prose.

12. Don't care if Dunning is out of it. Thought you'd like him in. And I sometimes like his work. Obit?

13. My only catholicity will extend to poetry—Seems to me I have no group but people who write or at least try to show signs of doing it—Will cut down to the marrow—For this reason best plan wd be to print 6 or 8 new poets (unknown) and about 6 or 4 old ones (new work only—Bill, McAlmon, Cummings, you—I won't ask Eliot unless you know his later work is improving

14. The only progress made since 1912—is or are several good poems, i.e. the only progress possible—& criteria are in your prose works. Don't know ~~that~~ ⟨my issue⟩ will have anything to do with homogeneity (damn it) but with examples of good writing.

15. Don't mind, as I said, McKenzie saying ⟨in prose⟩ what he likes & why, but he can't print ~~it~~ ⟨poems⟩ unless I like ~~it~~ em

16. Your idea of a dozen authors, 3 or 4 unassailable chunks, & others held down to single page or poem agrees with mine.

17. Cummingsites have Blues, Pagany, etc etc. No need for anybody unless he can stand on his own.

18. Reznikoff may not have anything as good as his contribution to last "Pagany" (which contrib. I got across) or as good as my quotes in Essay. Therefore, essay must be printed in Poetry—(what gave you idea someone else accepted it)—The historical small print matter you suggest is covered in said essay of mine—You said you'd revise it—you got this poor poet into a fix by asking (H.M. to ask) him to edit a maggerzine So please revise the Reznikoff—relegating first paragraphs to notes—leaving the historical section mentioning you & yr. generation (note the section deals with accomplishments etc not with crap), leaving whatever you think is good of my handling of the poetry (Reznik's) & omitting section on prose, but including section on glosses & quotation which gives some more historical matter. If you chew it down to half or less than half its length & circumcise my rhetoric we'll have a good essay—

I want you to do it because you said you wd. And it will give my attitude concretely & present Reznikoff besides. If Donal disagrees I can answer him in brief footnotes which wd. sharpen my style & give more of the air of argymint ⟨than is present in me generally.⟩ Moreover, you must lop the Reznikoff & send it right sune because I'm not going to repeat what I said in Am. Poetry 1920–1930 which will appear in Jan. "Symposium" a month before Feb. issue of Poetry. Also I don't think I've anything else to say except footnotes. Can't be pullin' the pud about these things all the time. You think I'm a Rabbi or something? Or a Cabala? Also your revision will cut out the professor—Sotzup to you!

19. You speak of later issues of "Poetry"—but it's alright: you say, "hardly to be mentioned yet"—

20. Another reason for getting my essay on Rez. is that Harriet has seen it & thinks highly of it—thinks it must get in in abridged form—

21. If I'm asked to edit another issue we can talk then about advisory committee—

22. Don't know McAlmon wd. care to work with me—We've pretty distinct tastes—& I don't know he won't always damn me. & Vice versa. But I shdn't mind trying.

23. Agree with you about my generation—"plenty of chaps meaning what they say (with no lit caapacity"—[)]

24. I'll keep at 'em. Postage costs are busting me—I'll die of hunger before I edit the issue ("passons")

25. No use ~~of~~ ⟨for⟩ a "historic section giving" bad stuff—what's the use of preserving names if they don't represent literary capacity—didn't know you favored literary history—besides can't ⟨see that⟩ certain bad stuff (i.e. of Robinson Jeffers, for instance) represents a current as J[ohn]. G[ould]. Fletcher did in the old days, or yr. friend Amy [Lowell]. —If the people I reject don't have the decency to admit they're bad—they can go pull the chain. I ain't gonna "relegate" no one to "historic or any section" if they're no good. "Blues," "Morada" & other truck history enough.

26. Carnivali doubtful—I've seen nothing that I like since "Day in Summer" & maybe a short thing or so in "Hurried Man" (Contact Press)—stuff in "Pagany" very poor. Don't tell him so—he's evidently sensitive.

27. You have faith, I know my generation as well as anybody? I

think I do I also at one time edited Mr. Wms' Descent of of [*sic*] Winter—which recommends me for the job?

28. Think I'll have as good a "movement" as that of the premiers imagistes—point is Wm. C. W. of today is not what he was in 1913, neither are you if you're willing to contribute—if I'm going to show what's going on today, you'll have to. The older generation is not the older generation if it's alive & up—Can't see why you shd. appear in the H & H alive with 3 Cantos & not show that you are the ⟨younger⟩ generation in "Poetry." What's age to do with verbal manifestation, what's history to do with it,—good gord lets disassociate ijees—I want to show the poetry that's being written today—whether the poets are of masturbating age or the fathers of families don't matter.

29. You shdn't be allowed to lay off—that is to exempt yourself from contributing—if you say what Norman MacLeod wants to say. ⟨i.e. express what he's perhaps trying to express—⟩

30. Of course, you shd. appear merely as one of the contributors not as favver.

31. Again—I think I know as much about my contemporaries as D. McKenzie does—not that we're fightin already—

32. Will write to Rakosi—maybe one of the millionaires here can drive me out to him—if he's still alive and kickin

33. Won't lap over Exile, if you don't want me to—certainly not in case of Heming[way]'s Neothomist Pome.

34. I know Carnevali's work as you have made out by this time. Covalesci was mentioned ter me by Parker Tyler who said you praised him—but Tyler was evidently being American about remembering the name.

35. Again—you must do over my Reznikoff essay—You can strike out what you don't want in a half-hour at the most—

36. Most of the men I choose will not be people who have been in touch with you. Satisfied?

37. If I can't get a new poem from Cummings—what I say of him in the Rez. essay will have to do him—

38. I am not going to reprint any old work.

39. I can add a note to Rez. essay or work one in with Donal [McKenzie]'s criticism that wd. tell about Bunting & MacLeod & other Englishmen. Will not write to them (except Bunting to whom I've already written) unless I haven't enuf to fill 30 or 32 pp.

40. No talent in Pagany, New Masses, Morada—or very little. Ditto Horace Gregory. Have read 'em—believe me

41. Won't lean on Europe, but Taupin's Salmon will serve purpose of a book-review and a bolstering of nominalisme which is probably my attichude if I know what it is—besides René's style and matter is up to date or ahead of date.

42. If with your help, I don't do 100% or 1000% better by letters than New Masses you can call me a bum.

43. Sorry H[arry]. Crosby appeals to me more as photographer than as poet. Up to Donal to find any unpublished stuff that's good—or to say something about Chariot of the Sun—alright there's whoop & occasional fire but what am I to say? Never saw too much in Weeks either, but very little outside of Xile was printed—Have you any?

So
Z

P.S. I don't think I lack enthusiasm when there's something to be enthusiastic about.

PSS. Excuse simplicities of my other letter—especially with reference to Latin verse. I know, of course, where to find out how this ode in Horace etc shd. be read according to this measure—but that doesn't answer my question—I know also that if we knew how Latin verse lost its quantity (or if we know) that we can bridge the gap ⟨btwn Latin & Romance & English⟩—but maybe you can illuminate the business in a sentence—as usual.

Reisman: Jerry Reisman. A friend of Zukofsky.
MacLeod: Author of *The Ecliptic* (London: Faber and Faber, 1930).
Adams: British poet.
Ford: American poet.
contribution: "The English in Virginia," *Pagany* 1:4 (October-December 1930), p. 31.
Fletcher: American poet and translator.
"Day in Summer": "The Day in Summer," a poem in Carnevali's *A Hurried Man* (Paris: Contact Editions, Three Mountains Press, 1925).
stuff in "Pagany": "The Girls in Italy" (poem), 1:3 (July-September 1930) and "Italian Farmer" (poem), 1:4 (October-December 1930).
Covalesci: See the note to letter 26.
Tyler: American poet and editor.
Chariot: Harry Crosby, *Chariot of the Sun* (Paris: The Black Sun Press, 1928).

30. ALS–6

Nov. 9/30. 419 Sterling Place Madison, Wis.

Dear E: Yo' sure are an engineer! Keeping me working all day Sunday—and probably the only warm day of this slaughter-house ice-box of a winter. O well, got a ressurected fly to keep me company. Zum . . .

No need to cable you: Matter not important enough to rumble the deeps of the Atlantic. Wrote Donal [McKenzie] yesterday or day before & invited him to contribute his credo, poetry—his'n & others.

Certainly Not a Morada number—God's gut, have you ever seen the thing? I mean Morada—promised foreign number may improve (my D.R. is in it!) but can't trust them.

As for a group "McKenzie believes in" I don't object—if I agree with what he believes in. We'll see.

But why "McKenzie believes in" or "Zukspewsky presents"—why not a date or a region or a tendency—Poets, 1931, or The Twelve, or U.S.A. 1931, or 606 and after. Or what do you suggest? Or Objectivists, 1931, or The Third Decade, or The States? Objectivists or the equivalent minus philosophical lingo is what it shd. be, that is the poems will be such as are objects. Or Things.

Your distinction between the calm voiced Carnevali and the barbaric Hem[ingway] & McA[lmon] very profound and moving. Why not send me his translations (the best) of Rimbaud, instead of my writing him now to invite him for MSS. An older voice, you can suggest to him whatever changes in the Rimbaud translations you think necessary. And I can write him later to thank him for them, as well as for the translation of my E.P. Translations of Rimbaud interest me especially—& if his ⟨Rimbaud's⟩ technique is not too evident among the "group," I think the temper he represents is very much evident—a kind of recalcitrance which says we're doing this, but we might as well be doing anything else—giving things the cold shoulder and yet taking 'em on. So send the translations.

Sorry I haven't a copy of the Eng. of my essay on you. The following corrections need to be made in the Echanges trans.:

pg. 145 – comma ⟨(no period)⟩ after glaze in quote from H[ugh]. S[elwyn]. M[auberly].

pg. 148 – ne serie de mouvement – not quite accurate for makes mock of motion—tromper?

pg. 150 – quote from Canto on Kung—excesses not sing.

pg. 152 – Arnaud ⟩ Arnaut

pg. 154 – line 8 le verbe I don't remember English but probably verbalisms
pg. 154 – Two references to Keats shd. be Yeats
pg. 154 – End of third paragraph—no capital letter 〉 nature
pg. 154 – Don't remember English for fantoches
pg. 155 – Question mark after quotation from Lustra ed. of Cantos
pg. 159 – 3 Mts. Press—shd be Hours Press—now?
pg. 161 – Passage from Canto XXII printed incorrectly
pg. 161 – la gosse?
pg. 164 – La musique etc. b), c) chant, chants shd be canto, cantos
pg. 165 – chant—shd be canto
pg. 165 – Ityn 〉 Itys?
Passage printed wrong (4th Canto)
pg. 166 – mutatis mutandis—not in Pavannes—in new ed. of Collected Prose?
pg. 167 – English spelling of pony.
pg. 167 – quot. from Canto XXVI—printed wrong
pg. 169 – Last paragraph after la fragilité de fragments
I think I had something about Imagism, Circa 1913 in English—Don't really matter in context.
pg. 170 – Example 3 printed wrong.

You might send above to E.C[arnevali]. if you have time & thank him for me. Do send 300 word hist. of europ thought since 1912 you mention in yrs. of 27 Oct, and anything else including new poesy which you probably don't want to send for fear of putting us to shame.

Fevvins Zake! If you think I'm gonna miss impt contemporaries please send me their names. Chooz to do it! Don't be afraid of overburdening me with work—I'm prone to complaint in any case. I think I know my contemporaries but I'm not SEAS ALL, NOZE ALL.

What's bunf?

I repeat the Reznikoff article the thing for issue if you 〈cut〉 out the aching appendix from it—It's not a question of Harriet using it in some other number—It's not a question of greed for print but of saying what I have to say without repeating, with generalities, credo etc applied to a particular case. Also doubtful whether I'll give 〈R.〉 much space in the poetry section—He's working on things now, but may not have much (4 pp) that is now ready. Two pp. of his poetry and 10 of prose (devoted mostly to my credo & not really to Rez.) will not overbalance the issue. Besides the article will be called Sincerity and Objectif-ation (with special reference—or leave out the special—to the work of Chas. Rez). Parenthesis, as I have it. The historic section in it—referring to you, Bill, Eliot, McAlmon, Cummings, Marianne makes the distinctions between yuse you call for in yours of Oct 28.

The verse will be good—it'll be great etc.

Don't think there'll be need for historic section—unless you send me The Return or something to reprint. If you send new work—it's obviously contemporary. Since no one has probably seen Hem's All Made Peace it'll be new. Bill's Alphabet of Trees no more than 2 pages & not history—tho it'll go down into the anthologies. Define history as a story which it takes time to tell (Roger Kaigh)—but we deal with duration, the instant, NOW etc. Cummings may not send anything—in that case you'll have no grief over the young ones being bullied by their elders.

Re Eliot—aptness of your epithet Possum more striking than ever, after reading his latest (?) Marina. It's a fine thing. If he isn't feigning death again can you stir him into sending me something as good as that. The first good sign from him since Waste Land—tinkering with English influence not in vain & infusion of Classical Latin (as probably taught in English schools?) a veritable blood-transfusion. And it's only a page and a half. If I can get something equivalent to it for Poetry—why blubber about him as history. The poem wd. present exactly what has happened and what is happening.

Basil: Will be the only Englishmun I'll print. Apprenticeship or Debut for his appearance as coming Eng. corresp. If he doesn't send new stuff—I'll have to choose from Redimiculum (of which Harriet doesn't know)—possibly Sad Spring or Against the Tricks of Time or While Shepherds Watched or Chorus of Furies or To Venus. None of these as good as Villon but handling of quantity always pretty expert. Myself—liked his traduction of La Bonne Lorraine—ending possibly too uniwersul. However, the first stanzas of that section remarkable. "Smartness," if any, is dilution of you & Eliot, cf. opening, end of 2, 3 especially last two lines. Will hint to Harriet he should be prized when I see her in Chicago Dec. 19—Do you think my youthful appearance will harm any or will facilitate further her taking me unto her bozum? Better let me know, if you think personal visit ill-advised. Usually ladies (age immaterial) like me—exceedingly.

And you said it again summing up [Aldous] Huxley—

Shall be interested to see what Blackmur has to say about XXX—Used to be most interesting & reliable (or perhaps the only reliable) younger critic—not so good recently, cf. his poor reviews in New Freeman. Mr. Boyd (Boid) has definitely taken over litcherary deputment—result: my Taupin review won't appear after all–tho' they paid for it—i.e. Mrs. Gove did in June when she accepted it. Suzie la Follette struck me as a flying hart or something—at any rate she said nothing to me when I wuz onc't there talking to Mrs. Gove, & I wuzn't introduced. Cy gist.

Will write to Wheelwright to send you number of Symposium. Haven't one here. Looks as respectable as H[ound] & H[orn]. Last number contained article by I.A. Richards, Poetry & Logic by Wheelwright, Jules Laforgue by Bonamy Dobrée, Paris letter by Stanislas Lumet. Sells for 75¢. I suppose you know that H & H wanted to combine with them. Idea of thing is a Symposium—the last issue on Poetry.

Please trust me—you ak as if you ain't seen one of my critical opiniums of last 5 years—of course, I'll disinfect dilutions of you, Bill, T.S.E., Cummings etc. And certainly you don't think I'll turn to the [Malcolm] Cowleys, [Edmund] Wilsons, Boids etc.

The only sonnets to appear in issue will be seven of mine making up seventh movement of "A"—I'll send the thing to you tomorrow—so you can judge whether I've any taste or not.

Worked all morning cutting out line after line of McAlmon's Fortuno Carraccioli (Italian Ex-patriate satires) evidently Em. C[arnevali]. in mind, but you needn't tell anyone. I think I have six or seven pages now, if M. R. McA. approves & don't cuss me publicly, which wd. occupy position in present group. Eliot occupied with Prufrock in your generation. That's not saying McA is Eliot. I'm trying to measure energy by analogy. ⟨If McA. objects to my revisions—he ain't got no sense that's all!⟩

Have also been trepanning others.

Prose section probably limited to 25 pp. There won't be room for historic survey in small print & as I said the rotten stuff needn't be codified & dated.

Thanks for advise as to how not to droop and wilt in Madison. Too bad if I gave the impression I was doing it. But it really isn't bad. Haven't time to look around or even hear the peeannolays. My new room is among roofs, and tops of trees, & brick chimneys of respestuble old houses.

Will go home Xmuss—friends will see to it I get my fare. Have become civilized enough to act on the knowledge that they want me as much ⟨as⟩, if not more than, I want them.

Z

my D.R.: The second part of Zukofsky's "Two Dedications." *All,* pp. 33–34.

bunf: Pound used the word in a letter to Zukofsky of 27 October 1930. "Am also cogitating a note on criticism which you cd. have IF necessary, but it wd. do in some other issue of Poesy just about as well. Depending on whether you found yourself pushed for space, or embarearsed to fill the issue without using bunf." Pound to Zukofsky, 24/25 November 1930, "Bung?? a cartaeous substance commonly sold in rolls or flat packets and used in vicinity of domestic plumbing."

Kaigh: Irving Kaplan.

Redimiculum: Redimiculum Matellarum, Bunting's first collection of verse, published in Milan in 1930.

Bonne Lorraine: See the note to Pound's letter of 28 October 1930.

Mr. Boyd: Ernest Boyd, author of a weekly column, "Readers and Writers," in *The New Freeman.* Irish-born American literary critic whose specialty was contemporary Irish literature. See his *Ireland's Literary Renaissance* (New York: Knopf, 1922).

Mrs. Gove: Marguerite Gove, secretary of *The New Freeman.*

I. A. Richards: The noted literary critic. His most recent work had been *Practical Criticism* (London: K. Paul, Trench, Trubner, 1929).

Fortuno Carraccioli: Poetry 37:5 (February 1931), pp. 247–252.

31. TLS–3.

18 Nov. [1930] Rapallo

Z//

Re p. 3. yrs of whatever.

Look into thine owne eare and reade.

All ballz and a great deal more are talked about prosody. If it dont "read" good whasser use of it. Obviously the ole bokos that have a theory and read it ti tump ti tump ti TUMP
do NOT understand anything.

I don't think a rehash 2000 years late of what some Roman perfessor faked up to prevent his students understanding Sappho better than he did, is likely to help any one much.

If there are rules they work in 51 percent of the cases and 49 are special exceptions. (in an indef. number of kattyGORYs.

On the other hand of course, latin words do have a hackscent on some syllables more'n on others, like in English and amurikun but mostly you have to learn it a word at a time. The fun comes when it pulls against the verse accent,

alle samme jazz etc. depending on whether the guy has nigger blood undsoweiter.

Re/ yr/ 43 articles. O.K. The Reznikoff I was in act of placing or trying to place elsewhere. However I will recall it. Am trying to write Cantos 31 to 35 and am not anxious to disguise myself as my grandson. Howeffer . . . . . will see what can be did.

re. article. 25. My idea of historic section was NOT to record vile names of the incompetent. My model historian is the chink whose name I forget. sic “Then for nine reigns there was no literary production”.

the current down the cloacae don't need no munnyment. You record the sewage flowed or the sewage was clogged. but do not git down with a rake to see whats in it. (risking thus the loss of milady's poils IF you insist on scroughing the metaphor to death but not otherwise)

///

I cant recall any “Co[illegible] reckon Tyler invented him.

///

Fer the rest. Yr/ 43 article perused. An I dont raise no objexshuns. Save that my existence can be “covered” by statement.

In 1913 les jeunes did not respect their papas. In 1930 there are a few middle aged bokos that we can afford to let live.

////

mckenzie has now shrunk downt to : : kalar, fearing, mangan fitts (?) macleod (?) k. boyle (you never can tell) michael mass (a new guy) reznikoff. I reckon I must have passed him yr/ opus. otherwise how'd he know.

I won't bother you with HIS correspondence. NOR need you bother to tabulate reasons fer disagreein with any of my suggestions. What you say in yr/ note is O.K.

(Yes [Ralph Cheever] Dunning died several months ago.)

Dare say McAlmon wd. write a essay BUTTT. . . and thass thaat.

I have writ enough about this venture.

ebnedictions

E

of whatever: Zukofsky's letter of 5 November 1930.
43 articles: The 43 sections of Zukofsky's letter.
Reznikoff: Zukofsky's essay, "Charles Reznikoff: Sincerity and Objectification."
"Then for nine reigns. . . .": Zukofsky borrowed this quotation for use in his "Program: 'Objectivists' 1931," *Poetry* 37:5 (February 1931), p. 269. See also letter 33 (12 December 1930).
kalar: Joseph Kalar, American poet and labor activist.
fearing: Kenneth Fearing, American poet.
mangan: John Joseph Sherry Mangan, American poet.
fitts: Dudley Fitts, American poet.
macleod: Probably Norman Macleod rather than J. Gordon MacLeod.
boyle: Kay Boyle.
mass: Unidentified.

32. TLS-3.

[27 November 1930] Rapallo

27 by Herbie's proc. Nov. 1930

Yeees, Yeas,

allus sober n industrious.

Wot you want me to tell you about it that you can't find out for yourself??

recd. one development or fugue or fuagal etc. produced by Ludwig von Zuk und Sohn, on not always digested meat of his forebears but with a ditional and final contortion or fugal (quasi) termination in form of canzone (miscalled 7 sonnets) but still a conzone a la sestina but with 14 lines to the strophe.

Crit. wd. be

A. eliminate top dressing inherited.

You'll have to work at that, just as hard as I did to get Roberto de Brownening's his vocablary outer my system.

Wd. be B. the purely rational and commentatarian expositions a bit perfessorial in parts.

Wots to be done about that? Possibly PATIENCE.

Not spoiling the sheep for a ha'porth o' tar. But conserving reservativeness and returning to the poem. with ought not to end with a "to be continued"

At least I don't think it ought to go on after your seven wollups. NOT unless you are making it a life work. Which; if I remember rightly; was not yr/ orig. intent.

"A" a work not in but showing progress.

You have not wasted the year or however long it has been.

I strongly suggest that YOU send me a crit. of it before I say anything more about it.

/////

I got round to sending a line to Payson Loomis yesterday. Mebbe in light of yr/ precedent epistolary etc. . . he might fill in a chink, at any rate no harm in seein wot he"zgot.

If you want to quote Brancusi go ahead, "La sculture n'est pas pour les jeunes hommes.".

Calvin Coolidge dh' pvwezident
He vudn't go but dh' family vwent,
Vuddunt giff notding but his name vass lent
For deh yidtischer Charleston pband.

You might sometime look thru my trans. of deSchloezer's Strawinsky. Not gospel but has a few good things in it.

///

On the whole yr/ mss/ has succes d'estime, but if you can refrain from releasing it for a few months I believe you will not regret the forebearance.

I think best procedure is for you to send me a crit. of it. Detach yrself/ as much as poss. and I will correlate my op/ with yr/ statement.

At any rate you are further along than in box of mss/ you sent me (note paper size). ⟨year or so ago⟩

Certain things can be remedied more or less by procedures known to yr/ venbl/ frien' but it wd. even better to remedy them by procedures evolved by L.Z. ipsissimo.

Have you seen J.G. Macleod's Ecliptic? I mention only to show the "need" being felt for longer poems built on a plan.

yrs
E

Herbie's proc.: Probably a reference to President Herbert Hoover's Thanksgiving Day Proclamation. Thanksgiving Day fell on November 27th in 1930.
one development: Movements 1–7 of *"A"*.
Calvin Coolidge: A supplementary verse for Pound's "Yittischer Charleston." Gallup B29.
my trans.: Pound's translation of Boris de Schloezer's *Igor Stravinsky* appeared in *The Dial* for January, February, April, May, June, and July of 1929. Gallup C733, C738, C742, C743, C745 and C749.
Ecliptic: The Ecliptic (London: Faber and Faber, 1930).

33. ALS–12.

Dec. 12/30 419 Sterling Place Madison, Wis.

Dear E: Re- "A"

How shall I begin?

You see-saw my heart ups and downs. When you say "I have not wasted the year etc", it goes ups. But it misses some beats at "A a work not in but showing progress." I should want it to be both—"showing" and "in". i.e. if you dont feel it weighty enough to go on—the notes in my desk—3 or 4 times the quantity of the finished (or as you say to be evaluated with patience) MS dont mean anything. But they'll have to if I'm going to remain (?) a poet. I mean I don't do as Bill [Williams] does—notice something and write the note down and then type it off (or write it out) and—another poem! He's kept young—and it's damn good he has. Considering your statement that the lines of poetry in a generation are few—and I believe it with all my heart—how I wish again and again that I could still be writing short poems—be excited into a song or something as brief and essential ⟨(!)⟩ i.e. I'd rather be the troubadours (or one of them) than Dante, Burns instead of your papa's Ring and the Book or Sordello, one of Shakes' Songs than any long poem "built on a plan." (Wonder if same feeling prompted the opening lines of your Canto XXX—whatever other reasons you have for it in the scheme . . .) But them early natural days don't come no more. This—that—I don't even bother to jot the things down any more after I get home (you see, it's not sterility, I'm afraid of, it's ⟨not⟩ anything I'm afraid of, there's as much juice here I think as in anybody or more, but it's a kind of witsful (?) dissatisfaction ⟨with what one's possibly good for⟩ again expressed by your papa in One Word More) as I was saying this—that—it's there, it'll go into the design—"A"—next summer, or the summer after, or ten years from now when I have two weeks of leisure to do it in. No hurry. It'll go in, but there's no time for the occasional thing—song etc.—it'll maybe return again 20 years from now—when A's done but A'll have to be done first. So one misses essentials?—You'll have to excuse your infant chile, but had to explain the pisscology of the matter before the criticism.

Yes, as far as I'm concerned right now "A" will be ⟨a⟩ life-work. I don't see how else, if it's going to be 2 movements a summer and 17 more to go to complete the "epic" 24! My plan as outlined to the Guggenheim last year ⟨was⟩, of course, only a plan to satisfy them—I mean the time element, "A" ⟨to be⟩ completed within a year etc, the tag sentences describing the contents still O.K. as far as they go. (I don't know whether I've told you that I'm renewing my application this year—it will be fun if they give it to me this year because I'm 2/3 of an ass. at Wis and have five addtl., sterile recommend.)

As for the history of the matter: when I started the thing late 1927 or early 1928, I had not seen the 3 Mts. edtns of your Cantos. Had read only the early ones in Lustra & 4, 5, & 6 in Poems 1918–21; the ones on Sabotage, Metevsky etc only after A 1 & 2 had been completed. "The" was a direct reply to The Waste Land—meant to avoid T.S.E's technique, line etc (tho I see how much more lucid it is than my own) occasional slickness, but intended to tell him why, spiritually speaking, a wimpus was still possible and might even bear fruit of another generation. Didn't like his Wagnerian leit motives, so I ended, or so I think, by doing something more discursive, more a matter of sequential statement–Pope maybe in modern dress, but the positive getting the better of the satire in opening First Movement, parts of two and most of 5 and 6. But on the whole, left merely with the promise of the last lines trans from Yehoash—"shall be."

"A" 's intention was to make that promise good. The design, the unity to be got by binding it all with the theme from the Matthew, etc was my own—at least consciously—a direct development of The ⟨line 309 which first appeared in poem in last Pagany—poem, however, written in 1925.⟩ You remember that I had read Cantos 4, 5 and 6 as separate poems, or poems dealing with the histories of several periods—I still had no inkling of the main intention of The Cantos. Had I seen Cantos XIV, XV, and XVI and the later American ones before I wrote A 1 & 2, the poem would never have been written—certainly not the invectives in the first movement or the instinctively beautiful (!) 2nd (I had seen your Homer in Instigations, but I had not seen your Second Canto). But since it was done, and since the malign disease of being unable to write any more short verse (Two Dedications, 1929 the only exceptions) had already set in, I couldn't see any way out but to continue. I had started ⟨without knowing it,⟩ something in 1928 which you had started in 1908 (?)—the dangers of being young and too poor to get hold of the books that matter. The only things that might possibly save me would be the objective evalutation of my own experience, an indigenous emotion controlling a versification which would (possibly) be my own and a natural ability (or perverseness) for wrenching English so that (again, possibly) it might attain a diction of distinction not you, or Eliot, or Bill [Williams], or anyone before me. Of course, that's no mean program . . .

When "The" came out, the charge ~~by~~ ⟨of⟩ those who are "supposed to know" was Waste Land. I didn't think so—Bill said no, you implied (?) no (?) by printing it in Exile 3, Taupin with a foreign ear has said no.

The charge now will be The Cantos: 'the same personal obscurities, but never Mr. Pound's brilliant diction'—Mr. Kirstein when I sent him 1 – 5. Well, you wanted to know and I've given you the history—What they won't know about the indebtedness and then they won't see the relation is that A–7—the canzone—you're right—is a direct outcome (an acceptance of your challenge) in The Dial for July 1928—The sonnet occurred automatically when some chap got stuck in effort to make a canzone. His genius consisted in the recognition of the fact the [*sic*] he had come to the end of his subject matter"— The intention of A7 is to justify the attack on the sonneteers in A1—which again was conceived before I read the above quotation. As for subject matter people had written sonnet sequences—damn 'em they had—but what moved 'em was concepts, not a subjeck matter like two or three balls juggled in the air at once and the play got from the reflected lights in the colors of them balls—development being; not over a space.

And this is the intention of the whole seven movements so far. The themes all stated in 1 & 2 repeat in different guises in the remaining 5—the juggler, if you will, has moved into a different ring and continues—the same process, the balls spinning different only as things from minute to minute—i.e the mind back of 'em or the orbs seeing 'em have something to do with it. For a "synopsis" of intentions 1 – 5 see p. 26 and 27 of the MS. I sent you.

Now as to development: 8 – 12 will continue with "particulars"— 13 – 24 will be—if I get to them—12 Ballate beginning An—with the intention of seeing whether the longer Canzone such as you write about in Dial July 1928—can't be brought into English—as English. I think A–7 but for a palpitation here & there "sonnet 4," for instance, lines 4 & 5 (and damn it I don't know what to do to make it seem absolutely inevitable, as the 1st "sonnet" or the last ~~2~~ ⟨two⟩ with possible exception of open, O fierce flaming pit, which isn't as effective ⟨as⟩ at end of 1st Movement)—yes, I think, A7 is quite a long breath towards the longer breath I want to take in coming movements 13–24. (But Oooo don't Sonny have to learn a lot—and he no more will [be] staying around in these sunk parts, than he'll do the Jefferson this year if he works with the University. (Cheenius can't be restricted—ergo I'll drop my one minute conference with the "authority" of Am. liter. here & not pay 'em 21.50 a semester & trust it'll cost me my job—as it will—and then write the Jeff. without having to tell him that I read 50 pp. this week and the Kentucky bugger writing it down. —Pardon the vent.)

Continuing with "A". Movement Six—Longer than the others on purpose to see whether I could keep it up under so many words—I wonder if I swaller some—at any rate beginning with the paraphrase of the Dies Irae—"On that morning etc" pg 32–45 it has more impetus than 24–32, more Zookawfsky—etc—The danger of accessories as defined in the poem. Probable lapse pg 16 & 17 saved by "gentle humor" of pg 18? Five I think goes as I have it, so does 1 & 2 (especially 2) & 3 & 4—i.e. pg 13–15 of Four

"Professional parts"—pp 24–32, 16–17?

What worries me: you say—"rcd one development on fugue or fugal ⟨by LZ⟩ etc on not always digested meat of his forbears but with aditional & final contortion or fugal (quasi) termination in form of canzone"—does forbears refer to those in the poem, or to what?

As for eliminating the top dressing—vocabulary etc—when one's as Wordsworthian as I am—i.e. plainness of diction (Rakosi says the worst that can be said of "A" is that in places it escapes banality by ellipses)—it's pretty hard for oneself to find "the top dressing". Your corrections or suggestions for A 1 & 2—a year or two ago—were about as helpful as your recent corrections of Reznikoff—You wanted to omit Staccato in A1—& I think emphasized it—I could if I wanted argue why two prepositions might some times want to go together—even as English. But the fault, if it exists, etc must be more essential. In the case of the Reznikoff—it's probably that the thing shouldn't have been written—And maybe the same's true of "A".

I'm willing to stand by it, however, for the next few "years" or so (maybe less if the Lo'd will open my eyes & I can see better). In the meantime if you can spare the time & it doesn't interfere with your own processes, I'd like to know what particular things can be 'remedied by procedures known to you.' Be hard on the damn thing—slash it—if you think it's a dilution of The Cantos—and no one ought to feel that better than you—and that it's dead to begin with say so—I won't be hurt. I don't think there's Bill [Williams] in it—& I don't think there's anyone else in particular—but I wonner if you can pick it up and say that diction, that ictus, is Z—if you can't say so—and maybe I'll start a new procedure in consequence.

Will not release what there is—unless McA[lmon]. publishes the entire thing in the spring—but "A7" goes into Poetry to save (?) my face. I'll just have to print that on the faith that it is good. If I'm honest with myself—and I think I am—I do feel it shows more sense of form and ability to last (I mean the endurance of the words as you read them) than anything else in the issue with the possible exception of Bill's Botticelian Trees—which is, however, more ornamental & more in tradition of ye old English. And yet I think A7 is not a contortion (what did you mean exactly?) I think it's English allright but can stand up against a furin tongue. Rakosi's Finmarkin more mordant—more bare sensation when not "modernistic."

And this bothers me about "A"—you've got to chant ⟨(declaim?)⟩ the thing even in the "purely rational & commentatarian expositions"—

otherwise it don't go. You gotta become seereeous—ooo!—it's probably a work of "art" allright—but it don't let itself be spoken—witness the Hen[ry]. Ford quotations—the words exactly his own (pp 29–31 MS.) ⟨& yet you got to intone them.⟩ Now when you do that kind of thing—! It's speech, conversation! Hell, maybe what I say in the last paragraph is its ⟨—("A" 's)⟩ only reason deter (d'tre?)—It has to be read as a pattern.

Well, now please correlate with my statement—and don't spare the rod and spoil——

Just r'cd list of addresses from Walt Carmon of New Masses—including names of Martin Russak, Raymond Kresensky. Asked for the durn thing weeks ago—but Mike[Gold]'s in Russia & I guess they didn't open his letter. Will have to go to press without seeing their new work. Occasionally they had something in old numbers of N.M. that was good. Fearing, Langs[ton]. Hughes, Herald, also included—don't matter. ⟨Hugh⟩ Kane, Joseph Kalar? Probably not much from bits I've seen.

Anyway, I'll have to launch the issue with what I've got. Mike shd. be pleased with my redemption of Comrade [Harry] Roskolenkier—& you shd. see what I had to do to wade thru the stuff & then come out after putting it together (???) with—dignity. I mean certain lines in one poem naturally belong in another—signed L.Z. —But what will happen if I stop running my correspondence courses? If I redeem another "poet" after Sat. Nov. 13, I'll shoot myself.

Will send Program: "Objectivists 1931" sometime tomorrer—plagiarized your phonetics—Kukchuh, & the line about the Chinky Man—"For 9 reigns there was no etc" but the rest is so sedate they won't know who the orig. owner wuz. Serves you right, anyway—I don't like writin edtrl—and—— Don't quite get Brancusi—La Sculture n'est pas pour les jeunes hommes—what's jeune got to do with it—if Abram could have a chile at 110 & at 16 what's the difference. La Sculture etc–is that why "A" shouldn't have been written?

Has ⟨your⟩ transl. of Strawinsky by DeSchloezer been published in Book Form—can't lug 12 Dials with me wherever I go—tho I lugged the July 1928 to Berkeley & back to here——

I forgot to say I mean "A" to end at end of every movement, but if I go on—that's a different matter!

N.B.— "A" better'n "The"?! Answer—

⟨Saw only xtract of Macleod's Ecliptic—2 pp. in Criterion Someone ought to buy my books for me—Liked the versification—fall of ⟨rhymes and⟩ quantities as prose—(?) but wasn't sure of virility The whole—very good? What do you say?⟩

your papa: Robert Browning.
Sabotage: Canto 19. "Sabotage? Yes he took it up to Manhattan. . . ."
Metevsky: Canto 18. "Metevsky" was Pound's pseudonym for Sir Basil Zaharoff.
Yehoash: Pseudonym of the Yiddish poet Solomon Bloomgarden. Zukofsky quotes some of his poetry in "Poem Beginning 'The' " and "A"–4.
Matthew: Johann Sebastian Bach's *St. Matthew Passion. "A"* begins with an account of a performance of the *St. Matthew Passion* at Carnegie Hall.
line 309: "Our God immortal such Life as is our God." The poem in *Pagany* is "For a Thing by Bach." *Pagany* 1:4 (October-December 1930), p. 23.
Homer: "Early Translations of Homer." Reprinted in *Literary Essays of Ezra Pound.*
Two Dedications: All, pp. 41–44.
The Dial: "Donna Mi Prega by Guido Cavalcanti with Traduction and Commentary by Ezra Pound: Followed by Notes and a Consideration of the Sonnet," *The Dial* 85:1 (July 1928), pp. 1–20. Gallup C717.
Botticellian: "The Botticellian Trees," *Poetry* 37:5 (February 1931), pp. 266–267.
Finmarkin: "Fluteplayers from Finmarkin," *Poetry* 37:5 (February 1931), pp. 238–239.
Ford quotations: "A"–6, pp. 25–26.
Carmon: Managing editor of *The New Masses.*
Russak: A silk weaver from Paterson, New Jersey, whose accounts of life in the Paterson mills were printed in *The New Masses.*
Kresensky: Raymond Kresensky, American poet and short story writer.
Herald: Leon Srabian Herald, American poet.
Kane: Unidentified.
Roskolenkier: The "Objectivists" number of *Poetry* features his "Supper in an Alms-house." He later changed his name to Roskolenko.
your phonetics: In "Program: 'Objectivists' 1931," Zukofsky writes, "The small magazines are to be praised for standing on their own against the business of the publishing racket, the 'pseudo-kulchuh' of certain national liberal weeklies published in New York, and the guidance of the American university." *Poetry* 37:5 (February 1931), p. 271.
nine reigns: In "Program: 'Objectivists' 1931," Zukofsky also writes, "Implied stricture of names generally cherished as famous, but not mentioned in this editor's *American Poetry 1920–1930* or included among the contributors to this issue, is prompted by the historical method of the Chinese sage who wrote, 'Then for nine reigns there was no literary production.' " *Poetry* 37:5 (February 1931), p. 269.
DeSchloezer: See the note on Pound's translation in his letter of 27 November 1930.

34. TLS–4.

25 Dec. [1930] Rapallo

Z/

Re/ yrs/ re/ "A"

I concurrrrr. I see no reason fer yr/ being discouraged. No pale regrets. And printing "7" in yr/ issue has my O.K.

The whole thing is an advance. The Whistlerian dictum that a picture ought to be finished at every stroke of the brush, comes from Japan and has to be taken cum grano. (Danger of a thing that stops at end of every chapter and yet DONT stop.

Tha fact that a danger exists, merely means that it has to be WATCHED, not that one has to sit pretty and avoid risk.

////

For the rest. I don't know that my crit. (restrictive) amounts to more than saying that:

As I am readin Jeff. and J. Adams correspondence my style becomes momentarily more aulic etc. IF one reads at all the vocabulary of the last thing read floats on surface of mind and slips off into what one writes.

The elimination of this alien substance is fairly easy AFTER a period of several months. Attempt to eliminate at once not always successful.

The minute one is conscious of a bit of Browningese or Shx-ese or whatever one can by very simple change eliminate it; OR give it force of quotes.

You can't <u>un</u>consciously multitudinously incarnadine the sea.

Consciously you can play the whole bally rainbow, from Joycianly "inviolet" etc. . . . . .

When one has just done a job, and for varying periods thereafter the surface vocab. sticks to it.

The process of eliminating this cd. ⟨& shd.⟩ be personal. Much better the elim. process shd. be yrs/ than mine.

hence ⟨my⟩ reluctance to particularize.

La sculture n'est pas pour les jeunes hommes. Simply there is so much that can come ONLY with time. So much that only fits the particular and unforeseen case. Skill that is not reducable to precept.

Mr Antheil just having hell's own sorrow at this discovery.

The geenus at 20 knows what the dud will NOT know at 80. But the geenus at 80 will know quite a lot that he didn't at 17 or 27 or 37.

Ref/ note on Boschere on Elskamp, in Instigations

NO the Schloezer is NOT reprinted in handy vollum. And NONE of my prose wisdom is available in handy vollums. And it is gawd'zone outrage, and one of the minor functions of you brilliant y.m. (including the eliptic p[arker]. tyler) is to create a false demand for folio edtn. or any damn edtn. of my indiscretions (in the wider sense) voluminous and ill-sorted data.

///

"A" is more important than "The"

at least I suppose it is. But "The" is done.

Your problem coming after T.S.E[liot]. me an' Bill [Williams] is very dif. from what ours was coming after Yeats and Bliss Carman. Praps best for you not to worry about it at all, and cease considering it as a problem.

Simple lyric, at 17 when the artist is unborn and dont know.

Simple lyric later when knowledge has reentered instinct.

Which don't mean that the pote can go to sleep in ditch and refrain from intermediate processes.

If "A". is a life work of course it don't end at 7.

⟨Fer⟩ The middle period an its difficulties // ref/ my study of H. James.

And who is going to come through.

In the U.S.A. you and McAlmon. Rakosi already given up??

In England Bunting and Gordon Macleod, isolated; no connection with each other. Haben kein Zweck as it were. Look at G.M. Hopkins, he happened, not IN any current. Insulated and isolated. ⟨England. dif. state of things.⟩

The rest go into anthologies. of the dacade. The better the anthological level (caused by the outstanding but in way reacting) the better the top lights.

pardon sententious dullness of this

Guess it reduces itself to: Fergit A1 to 6; for the next seven months. Do next sections. Don't look at 1 to 6 NOW. If and when Mac[Almon] is ready to print the whole, look over it for fortuitous associations of words vaguely resembling those ⟨of other writers⟩ now known to you but unknown to you when you did 'em.

yrs/
E

"7": "A"–7.
Boschere: "De Bosschere's Study of Elskamp," in *Instigations of Ezra Pound* (New York: Boni and Liveright, 1920). In this essay Pound notes his own "inability to make anything of Max Elskamp's poetry[,]" but does not directly address the matter of artistic maturity that comes only with time.
Carman: Canadian poet and essayist (1861–1929).
H. James: "Henry James," first published in *The Little Review* (1918). Gallup C316, C381 and C382. Reprinted in *Literary Essays of Ezra Pound.*

35. TLS–4.

[29 and 30 January 1931] Rapallo

29 Jan.

I seebythe papersSEZ Mr DooOley thet Mr Phuthnumb's review is afther bein printed,

and by thet thet it may git

here in the looseness of the fullness of the unincumbhered elasticity of Einstinian (thak godnot GertSteinian) relativity.

as fer this Chimpanzeeum, DOES it PAY its dom conthributhers and IF SO does the eminent blacksmith or wheelturner want me to conthribute ⟨?⟩
and tell him why the hell people misunderstand Mr MARX??

and in the course of same to "answer" Mr. Fernandez whom I can't be bothered to read (at me own risk, of course).

Saviotti says he is printin yr/ me in Nos. 4 and 5, I spose that means Feb. 20 and March 10, but dont know how much time sense he has.

The presence of yr/ 1920 to 30 in the Imposium may accelerate sombastud to traduce THAT. The Genova traducers seem to dally and dolly and not git on wiff th woik.

Does Mr Wellwright insist on ALL his contributors except YOU carrying on in the verbose and indef. manner and always drifting out of concrete statement of an idea into the question of Hegel nd the infinite?

or is it merely that the buggahs can't write and try to hide the fact under a cloud of witnesses' arzsses.

I began Tuesday a note De DUOBUS IMPOSITORIBUS (meaning Marx and Thos. Aquinas tho I think rather better of Marx than of Tommy. . . .

IF Wheelwright wanted the article I shd. remove the DUOBUS so as to include some of his contributors.

This number better than the others, less taint of Bloomsbury snail-smear.

Have read yr/ delousing article with comfort.

///

IF both Poetry and H[ound] & H[orn] have given Cantos to Fitts to review it is a goddam bore. . . . only interest wd. be in seeing to what xtent it penetrates <u>different</u> mentalities . . . . .

How well do you know Wheelright? . . . . dont in any case

say I said so . . . but ask if he has anyone to review it . . . if so, I dare say another rev. copy cd. be xtracted.

E

30 Jan.

NEXT MORNIN

The followin useful ideas occur to yr/ aged friend.

It is god damn well time for some agitation re/ publication of my collected prose. Did you see the Aquila announcement of the vol.?? ENNYHOW I have a contract, BUT the goddam firm is bust (hanging up, as you know, the Cavalcanti) AND also the prose.

As you know, my first poems were pubd. abroad. A fukin disgryce to the onanystic States. It wd. have been a equal buggerin disgryce IF my prose had been pubd in Europe. The first seerious "colleced prose." It ought to be done by my bastud comphathriots.

Agitation shd. not start in YOUR name as you are known sustainer. It cd. start to better advantage in Symposium than elsewhere as I have as yet no connection with that review.

////

2. Random House ought to be attacked. There is some son of a bitch in that shanty that needs a red hot poker Edward the seconded into his anus. The bastard has boycotted me for a number of years (despite suggestions even from Yeats that they ought to print me). It can't be mere avarice because my edts. de muxe of Cantos have made a good profit. It is just purely and simply that the bastard is a son of a syphylytic bitch and ought to be flogged. ⟨fer obstructing the traffic⟩

The general attack can be that of trying to make a de luxe book trust and stifle even the faint flicker of independednt selection that before functioned in the separate printers. Hell blood and damnation on the sniper and all his fambly the kursse of Mowses ⟨unnecessary⟩ on his phostherity, ⟨as the heredity is enough⟩

These general matters cd. be made subj. of letter to Wheelright with the partic enquiry re/ the Duobus Impositoribus at the end. You can state the facts NOT saying I suggested the communique to HIM, also re/ the article, all you know officially is that I am writing it. And that H & H dont git on with the job quite fast enough to suit me. (or praps not mention H & H at all)

E

Mr. DooOley: A character who commented in dialect on current events and the social scene in a series of books (1898–1919) by Finley Peter Dunne.
review: The New Review.
Chimpanzeeum: The Symposium.
wheelturner: Philip Wheelwright, co-editor of *The Symposium.*
Fernandez: Pound refers to "Thought and Revolution" by Ramon Fernandez, *The Symposium* 2:1 (January 1931).
yr/ me: "Cantos di Ezra Pound," *L'Indice* (April 10, April 25 and May 10, 1931).
1920 to 1930: "American Poetry 1920–1930," *The Symposium* 2:1 (January 1931).
Genova: L'Indice was published in Genoa.
De Duobus: This article was never printed, nor does a copy survive in the Ezra Pound Archive at the Beinecke Library.
collected prose: See Gallup E6h.
son of a bitch: Unidentified.

36. ALS–7.

Feb 5/31 419 Sterling Pl. Madison Wis

Dear E: Good news about Basil [Bunting]'s British number: Harriet [Monroe] evidently thought I was a nice boy suggesting it and accepted Basil's proposition after I told him to write her. He ought to criticize my number—and perhaps invite one American to contribute—preferably one who did not appear in my Feb. issue.

Your French issue is an idea. For one thing it wd. save many of the boys the trouble of doing resoich themselves. Secondly, it should help to clean up the mess of recent translated anthologies from the French—Jos. T. Shipley etc; also useless critical opinion by Peeaire Loving and other high authority. —I suppose Harriet—if she agreed to a French number, and she has some pretensions to French herself, lawd, did she almost want to butcher my traductions of Taupin & Salmon—wd. even give you 100 dollars. That is I got 53 bucks for my job, and I haven't a family to support—ono.

Not that you need help—but if you want it there's Taupin at 80 Riverside Drive, New York who knows a thing or two and keeps up with the latest periodicals and has been looking for something to do. If you wish, I could do a "free" translation of what you select. I'm sending the galley of the rest of the Salmon for you to look over (there may be some errors, I'm too tired to proofread thoroly), and if you approve—the translation cd. appear in small print in back of the issue.

Don't know how much I'll do on the Jefferson, this spring. I've quit working "with" the department on this project—i.e. I told them I had too many things to do & that I cdn't promise to fulfill residential and exam requirements as a grad. student and I didn't pay 'em 22.50 Univ. Fee to keep up a bunch of fools. All done, of course, with great tact and approved by Mr. Dodge, chairman of the dep't. So I may work on the Jeff. As I told you—did I outline what I wanted to do?—the project is at least a three years job, and then it may mean little or nothing. A popular book on the freedom of the press & Jeff would be a stunt for a journalist, but I'm not a journalist. Incidentally, there isn't so much (almost nothing) on the free press in Jeff's writing. I don't know what there is in the Jeff. papers in Lib. of Congress—20 or 30 or more volumes never printed. I'll see—I'll have to do something to keep alive here—and I can't write pohtry just now. Can't do anything very much but feel that I've sent myself up into a jail to stay. Not next year I hope. You see, fare to Chicago is $10 and when one gets there—what?

Translating your frenchmen wd. please me most. Translating Taupin & Salmon gave me the only genuine pleasure in months. So try & get the scheme across.

Martha Champion (vide. Feb. issue Poetry) who knows Greek & I have been amusing ourselves during hours of parole "translating" the Iliad. Here are two extracks:

"And you bet Kid Paris stops playing around right then, and up on his legs quits that damn Sherry-Netherland (leaving Helen in room 69), his gun flashing to kill, (and have his legs sox appeal!). And like one well-fed stud bustin' his harness runs like mad thru Central Park wanting to get drunk in the lake, hits on a couple of swell truck horses, sure he's got "it"— boy that's just the way Paris whinnied."

also:

"Bad egg Alec, lady-killer, rotter, too bad you were ever born to screw—I'd feel swell to ⟨see⟩ you in hell."—

Do you think there's any use for a Homer in slang? Anyway, keep the idea under hat—the pornographers might get hold of it and make money on it—i.e. it = the wrong slang translation.

You say you wd. have a word on Rooshan poezia in your French number. Do you read Rooshan?

Now as for the bizness of the super book-club: of course, I'm willing to work, and as one of the commissars you can assign me to some sensible duty. I don't think I'd be good at organizing 300 or 400 or 500 people who will buy at 50¢ or 1 buck etc—i.e. I'm not a salesman—however, maybe your subsequent letters (I am answering your "incomplete statement" of Jan 22) will convince me different.

However—why not begin with your suggestion in Morada 5 and organize a writer's syndicat ⟨(membership rules up to you)⟩ You can get 100 writers to contribute $5—or you can get 50 writers to contribute $5 and 10 to contribute $10 and use that to pay for your first or first two volumes. You can, or should be able to, get free advertising (or credit) from Hound & Horn, Symposium, Blues, Pagany, Morada, Front, The New Review, Criterion, etc. That should give you the 300 or 400 or 500 subscribers you want. There are also the subscription lists (?) of these magazines to circularize.

Breathes there a pote with putt so dead he wd. spend more than 10¢ for breakfast even if [he] had the $5 I suggest he "give away" to his syndicat?

Anyway here's comment on your list:

Dahlberg (Edward?)—met him once and he seemed rather pig-headed personally—but if he has the time & you know he's honest—I didn't like him

Tyler—been working for Henry Harrison, Publishe recently
Ford— ?
} boys will be boys?

Wheelwright of Symp—has money—and probably plenty of it—nice chap—sense—probably reliable.

Kirstein—haven't seen him personally—doesn't seem much of a business man from what Stroock says—and never reliable as a correspondent—at least not with me.

Price—haven't heard from him since I last wrote you about him—of course, no occasion. You might write & try: he was interested in publishing.

Rakoski—write 301 Gable St, Houston, Texas. He calls himself Callman Rawley down there and wants no one to know of "Rakosi["]; teaches school & studying to be a doctor. Maybe I shdn't give you this information—but if you can handle the case tactfully, & I daresay you can—he might be able to do something.

MacLeish—don't know him personally.

R. Johns—evidently still going on with Pagany—don't know how he does—very quiet when I saw him in N.Y. this Xmas—said he wd. do at least a second year of Pagany. Shd. be useful in way I suggested above.

N. Macleod—"young" & flighty according to McAlmon. Never saw him. Working on New Masses now.

Zabel—Harriet doesn't think he's a true believer. And I think he wd. work if he had the right party to work with.

Reznikoff—why not write him yourself—if you have a definite project in mind. 225 McClellan St. Bronx New York. He's been in business and is a lawyer but does not practice the profession. Older than most of us—36 and absolutely honest and dependable—if you can get him started.

Joseph Freeman—don't know him personally—have heard nice things about him—I shd. think tho as a member of The Communist Party etc he wdn't be free

H. Gregory—don't know.

Mangan—wrote me several nice letters—but probably a little erratic—at least Tyler thought so which is funny. Seems sensible from his critical woik but a little off and why not?

You might write Kenneth Rexroth, 403 West Channel Road, Santa Monica, California (Santa Monica Canyon).

I think I can get [Jesse] Loewenthal, Hecht, Roskolenkier & a few others to work if you need them.

Don't see how you, Bill [Williams], Eliot & Marianne [Moore] can work together—but I suppose that depends on you & your directive genius. By the way, where is Marianne. No one in N.Y. seems to know. Bill didn't.

Z

British number: Pound to Zukofsky, 22 January 1931, "Basil writes me that our sportin' frien' Miss Monroe has axd him to do a Bri'ish number." This British number was *Poetry* 38:5 (February 1932).

French issue: Pound to Zukofsky, 22 January 1931, "Spurred however to still higher flights of fawncy I wonder if Harriet wd. stand fer a french number edited by your elderly friend." Pound did not edit a French number of *Poetry*.

Shipley: Probably a reference to Joseph Twadell Shipley's *Modern French Poetry* (New York: Greenberg, 1926).

Loving: Pierre Loving. American dramatist and translator. Author of *Gardener of Evil: A Portrait of Baudelaire and his Times* (New York: Brewer and Warren, 1931).

my traductions: Zukofsky's translation of René Taupin's "Three Poems by André Salmon." The translation appeared in *Poetry* in two parts (February 1931 and March 1931).

Champion: A student at the University of Wisconsin. Her "Poem" appeared in the "Objectivists" issue of *Poetry*.

Sherry-Netherland: An elegant New York hotel on Fifth Avenue. Zukofsky mentions it in "A"–1.

book-club: Proposed by Pound in his letter of 22 January 1931.

Morada 5: "Mike and Other Phenomena," *Morada* 5 ([Dec.?] 1930), pp. 43–47. Gallup C974.

your list: In Pound's letter of 22 January 1931.

Dahlberg: Pound to Zukofsky, 22 January 1931, "I have just answered a letter from a chap called Dahlberg who seems to have time on his hands." Edward Dahlberg had published *Bottom Dogs* in 1929.

Ford: Charles Henri Ford.

Freeman: American political writer and poet. He was one of the founders and editors of *The New Masses*.

Rexroth: He contributed to the "Objectivists" number of *Poetry*.

Loewenthal: Jesse Loewenthal. He contributed to the "Objectivists" number of *Poetry;* a friend of Zukofsky.

37. TLS–2.

12 Feb. [1931] Rapallo

Dear Zuk:

Feb[ruary *Poetry*]. just here. Only thing I have time to crit. I mean to see as needin amendment is in the Taupin. The rest is good job.

In the Taupin the DATES of Salmon's books shd. be put. Pub. will mix him up with Albert Samain; and think he was the fountain of light.

You shd. distinguish clearly between Imagism and Amygism and then weed out "imagistic" from metaphorical on p. 291.

Re/ the dates. Taupin in "L'inf; symb." makes the error of sposin one NEVER thinks of anything for oneself.

The INFLUENCE is over emphasized (I know he had to etc.) however . . . .

AS in my French No. Lit. Rev. I give the frawgs plenty of credit.

and AS the frogs are too damn conceited to recognize and to provincial ever to KNOW when someone else did it first . . . . no use your contributing to error.

Be just; but generosity can be over done. If WE growing out of Rimbaud; Corbiere; LaForgue etc . . sprouted, discovered, grew BEFORE the young frawgs; there is no use obscuring the fact.

Even Barzun's pourquoi doubler 1 image is inherent in the three tertets. Though I can't swear who said it first;

however ⟨& whichever⟩ all the virtues ascribed to Salmon and THEN some were I think done in our lingua materna before Salmon (Andre) cut his teeth.

any how, you can look into it.

////

Have writ Harriet [Monroe] to do eleven numbers MORE as good.

I can see three? Bunting's; a proletaire, my french number.

Your left overs. plus augment of critical section by me; Bill [Williams], and the elect. including yr/ next sassay.

If they git good enuff I' cd. give a couple of cantos. etc.

(not that they want 'em)

⟨Hugo touch bunk.⟩ ⟨Keep at Harriet⟩ E

the Taupin: René Taupin, "Three Poems by André Salmon," trans. Louis Zukofsky, *Poetry* 37:5 (February 1931), pp. 289–293.

Samain: French poet and essayist.

"imagistic": "The best argument against the use of the imagistic word has been furnished by the linguists themselves. The most direct contact is obligatory, more striking than any metaphor tainted with impure interpretation." (Taupin, "Three Poems by André Salmon," p. 291.)

"L'inf; symb.": Taupin's *L'Influence du symbolisme français sur la poésie Américaine (1910–1920)*.

French No.: The February 1918 issue of *The Little Review*.

Barzun: Probably Henri-Martin Barzun, French poet. I have been unable to locate the "image" Pound refers to.

Hugo touch: "André Salmon has been able to rediscover one of the secrets of epic poetry, which is neither recitative nor narrative. He may be pursuing Victor Hugo's secret. That he owes much to Victor Hugo is hardly to be doubted. Hugo intermingled poetry and morality; his fact was not entirely pure, depending always on decorative qualities for its framework. Still, he knew the poetic value of the event, and he is the only French epic poet." (Taupin, "Three Poems by André Salmon, p. 292.)

38. ALS–6.

Apr. 25/31 — 419 Sterling Place Madison Wis

Dear E: Ye-ess—deposit Moe's letter in your archives—and when I've "proved them to be wrong" show it to them. At any rate, won't do me any good to have it around—and maybe I've already proved 'em to be wrong. The fruits of consolation!

I think I wrote you that the sec'y of the Gugg. dropped in to see me here in Siberia—and I tactfully (?) corrected him on a few errors about you. Seemed pleased—as far as my poetic simplicitee cd. make out—and became personal enough to confide that Glenn Hughes wdn't do anything of value. Maybe the Kommytea is to blame.

My friend [Tibor] Serly is sailing the seaz on May 7 and hopes he will find you in Paris. After a while, I suppose he'll go to Budapest till September. How long do you expect to stay—in Paris? The lunatic Stokowski who was going to play his viola concerto and his orchestration of Mozart's Simfoni for a Musical Clock—at any rate, goin' to give Serly a trial hearing of these things—didn't after all. Serly talks the Eng. langwidge in the most peculiar way—but you will find it a crime to stop him if you meet him: the gentleman I recommended to you last year.

I'll see M. Moore & Miss [Helene] Magaret when I get back to N.Y. late June if eyether of 'em is around.

Basil [Bunting] being controlled by 'Arriet [Monroe] is something of a hair-raising event— However, he shd. go to it anyway & remove some of the monthly manure by the way. My best to him & Mrs. Bunting—when you go to the house on the hill.

Of course, I don't want you to pay my boat fare. Wdn't, even if you got the Nobel Prize—but God knows in the case of a rampage like that—even my beautifully generous nature might be overturned. Thanks for thinking about it anyway. —When is the Cavalcanti coming out–or blast everybody—isn't it?

Your last on Moscowism etc very beautiful. I suppose one cd build more than a shack on it. I suppose every young man of my age wants to go to Rhoosia to escape the spiritual undertaker. But I don't know anything about farming or chemistry or— and I don't think the C.E.P. wd. see the brode proletarian basis of "A"–6. The American representatives at the Charkov Conference were, of course, nothing— that is, omitting the several cartoonists. Naturally, to them, even to the blank Magill, I'm the sediment of the bourgeoise—tho I don't think they've ever read me— I shall, however, have the satisfaction of setting several proletarians on their writing asses—Roskolenkier—etc if they profit by my lessons. But I'm afraid they need continual tutoring. —I suppose I cd. drop in on [Norman] Macleod & the rest of the New Asses—when I'm in N.Y. but they'll probably fire me out because my name has occasionally been associated with E.P. & W.C.W[illiams]. and that lump Kewmangs (comme dit my German-translator-friend-Chambers). Incidentally, Whitt. Chambers' stories in New Masses have, and wd. have, style—if they didn't time and time again, Lenin preserve his pore gentile martyrdom, just patently fire off one's communistic (so-called) vas deferens, "patented." ⟨He⟩ Can't see, I suppose re his Chink story, that your Bowmen of Shu said it a long time ago. —Anyway, if you come across his contributions to Mar. & Apr. New Masses you might tell me what you think—if you care enough. Whitt—I should say—wd. be a better man to have at the Plenum of the Int[ernational]. Bur[eau]. of Rev[olutionary]. Lit[erature] than Micky Gold. O well—

No,—it's not the comfort of Rapallo, I want, but a vacation of six weeks wdn't hurt me. At any rate, not after the Katorge of Madison. The dep't here has seen fit to reappoint me at the salary of a $1000—but I've ⟨about⟩ decided not to stay—or have I told you. Might have got an instructorship if the Univ. Regents were so low as to accept eleemosynary grants, but they just can't think of it, and the State Legislature has cut down on the Univ. Budget and so a great man like me must go without a raise. Doubt if even a raise wd. lure me—will send in my resignation in August. —Prospects: spending the summer in N.Y. on $75. Next—??!

No—no use communizing Am. boneheads—or even teaching 'em literature. They* like me well enough—and one is even smart enough to read 25 pp. of Ulysses with me a day—but I think it's my poisonality—and that I've decided needs the annual renovation.

Z

*Everytime they hear yr. surname mentioned they sigh for verreh blisse—because they're sure they won't fall asleep.

O yes—try & persuade [Samuel] Putnam to come across with an "Objectivists" Anthology ed. by me—and a volume of my woiks—I need prestige.

H[omer]. L. Pound wrote in praise of mine in Apr. Criterion—for which all I am grateful and happy.

When you get back to Rapallo say what books you want me to send and I'll send them.

The enclosure has the distinction of having been typed by Taupin. The punctuation after "leaf", line 1 is a hyphen. This opus has also the distinction of being flatly contradictory to the aesthetic theory I so distinguishedly set forth in Feb. Pohtry. The reference is to Spinoza—Bk IV—Desire which arises from reason can have no excess.

Enuf.

Moe's letter: A letter from Henry Allen Moe, Secretary of the Guggenheim Foundation, notifying Zukofsky that he had not received a fellowship.

sec'y: Henry Allen Moe.

Hughes: American poet, dramatist and critic. Author of *Imagism and the Imagists* (Stanford, California: Stanford University Press, 1931). He had received a Guggenheim fellowship.

Stokowski: Leopold Stokowski, conductor of the Philadelphia Orchestra from 1914 to 1936.

Magaret: Helene Magaret, American poet. In a letter of 3 April 1931, Pound had advised Zukofsky to "look up" Moore and Magaret when he returned to New York.

boat fare: Pound to Zukofsky, 3 April 1931, "I shd. be glad to see you but can't pay yr/ boat fare."

Moscowism: Pound to Zukofsky, 3 April 1931, "We cant exactly have Moscowism / and heaven knows what better or worse we shall get. Are you young enough to enter New Masses and get invited over to Rhossia?"

C.E.P.: I have been unable to find any organization with these initials. It may be Zukofsky's acronym for "Communist Economic Plan."

Charkov Conference: The conference of the International Union of Proletarian Writers, held in Charkov, U.S.S.R., in November 1930. Mike Gold was one of the American delegates.

Magill: Abraham Bernard Magill, editor of *The Daily Worker.*

Kewmangs: E. E. Cummings.

Chink story: "You Have Seen the Heads," *The New Masses,* April 1931.

Bowmen: Pound's poem, "Song of the Bowmen of Shu."

Am. boneheads: Pound to Zukofsky, 3 April 1931, "In anny kase communizing american bone heads wont work."

Apr. Criterion: "The Cantos of Ezra Pound (one section of a long essay)." *The Criterion* 10:40 (April 1931).

get back: Pound to Zukofsky, 3 April 1931, "dont send me ANY books till I get back from Paris."

enclosure "Prop. LXI," *All,* p. 47.

39. ALS–3.

Sept 3/31 50 Morton St N.Y.

[For this letter Zukofsky used stationery from the New Weston Hotel, 34 East 50th Street, New York. He seems not to have known that Pound's great-aunt (Frances Amelia Weston) had opened the hotel in 1906. She was forced to sell it at a loss in 1909. See James J. Wilhelm, *The American Roots of Ezra Pound* (New York: Garland, 1985), especially pp. 156–159. Pound to Zukofsky, 8 September 1931, "IZ it a coincidence, or do you know what the Noo Weston is the drain wot swallered all the fambly forchune & left me bareassed on the pavement[.]"]

Dear E: At lah'st the clippin'! [Samuel] Putnam's story appeared in The N.Y. Sun of Fri. Aug. 21. Maybe he'll get you a copy—or maybe he'll send one to me I'll forward.

Mr. Kirstein will probably use the enclosed poem. Doesn't know—probably—I stole it from Waller, but thinks my Helen Kane-Jefferson poem takes off from Mauberly! Oyoi—and then he wants me to read half the poems of half a nation & advise him & will probably take my advice?!

You might show "her soil's birth" to Basil [Bunting]. I think he will admire—shall I say—its chastity?

Hear indirectly from Serly that you're a "good scout." Now what manners are these? Also that you will write no more in English—If that's true I resign the whole shebang—I just can't afford being the clearest Anglo-Saxon mind in print (i.e. current).

Aw—dun't leaf the ole' mudder—

Z

Putnam's story: "A Paris Letter," *The New York Sun,* 21 August 1931, p. 11. Putnam reports on Pound's visit to Paris to meet with representatives of the B.B.C. and discuss the broadcast of *The Testament of François Villon.*

the enclosed poem: "Her Soil's Birth," *All,* p. 49.

Waller: Edmund Waller (1606–1687), English poet. Zukofsky "stole" from his "Go, Lovely Rose," in fashioning "Her Soil's Birth."

Kane-Jefferson poem: "Madison, Wis., remembering the bloom of Monticello (1931)," *All,* pp. 45–46. Helen Kane (1904–1966) was a popular American singer. Zukofsky to Pound, 2 April 1931, "Re my uncanonical use of Jefferson in verses sent some time ago–seeing Greta Garbo won't help. But hearin' Helen Kane wd. if she consented to recite them as she recites her own matter."

40. ALS–2. Enclosure.

Oct 12/31 New Address:—214 Columbia Hts Brooklyn N.Y.

Dear E: I cannot know how to too much offer my thanks—

Yr. Chaston Blues-uues—now being typed by Mussyou Reenie Toe pan and will be before the booblik if [Samuel] Put[nam]'s reliable.

The whole business goes to Putnam on Oct 19 with this dedication—if it pleases you—

To
Ezra Pound

Of course, if I came up for judgment to my 'art of 'Arts I might possibly use the enclosed dedication (on separate sheet)—written down in a few moments of acute thought, understanding, humility, and considered paideuma.

If you think it (the enclosed dedication) is better than the one above—

you can in a few moments of Ta Hio type it, forward it to Putnam, and tell him to use it instead of the one above. If you don't want any dedication—write Putnam & tell him I gave you permission to retract it. Always thanks.

The new quarters the size of a bathtub overlook N.Y. harbor from Bklyn—a few streets away from Basil [Bunting]'s old 'otel. Why didn't I ever hear from him re- the ["Objectivists"] Anthology. Too late now—but give him my best—the Trotzskiite.

Yrs
Z

O yeah—see how I put you into the Sun?

Zuky the Manhattan Mauler
(Wot Ted Serly the blustering
Magyar of a mudgear calls me)

[Enclosure]

"And that was the revolution . . .
as soon as they named it."

To
Ezra Pound
who despite the fact
that his epic discourse
always his own choice of matter
causes him in his Cantos
to write syntactically almost no two lines
the consecutiveness of which
never includes less than two phrases
"And doom goes with her in walking,
Let her go back to the ships
back among Grecian voices."
himself masterly engaging
an inference of musical self-criticism
in his Fifth Canto
(readers can afford to look for the lines)
is still for the poets of our time
the
most important.

Chaston Blues-uues: "Yittischer Charleston," *An "Objectivists" Anthology,* ed. Louis Zukofsky ([Le Beausset, Var, France & New York] To Publishers, 1932), pp. 44–45.

Ta Hio: Probably Zukofsky's code for "great learning." Certainly a reference to Pound's Confucian translation, *Ta Hio: The Great Learning* (Seattle, Washington: University of Washington Bookstore, 1928). Gallup A28.

the Sun: In his review of *The Poems* of Wilfred Owen, Zukofsky said, "Owens's poems as a rendering of the very form and pressure of the time in any case never approach several of Hardy's war lyrics, Ezra Pound's 'These fought in any case,' 'There died a myriad,' or the body of Canto XVI." *The New York Sun,* 10 October 1931, p. 13.

Manhattan Mauler: Jack Dempsey, heavyweight boxing champion of the world from 1919 to 1926, was known as "The Manassa Mauler."

"And that was. . . .: A quotation from Canto 16. The enclosed dedication was used in *An "Objectivists" Anthology,* except that the word "never" in line 9 was deleted.

41. TLS–5.

28 Oct. [1931] Rapallo

Deerly beloved son:

Second performance of my Villon 100% better than first/ the god damn frogs ought to do it next.

Re Oppen. Benedictus, benedictus inter hominibus. IF he wants to do the collects of E.P. he had better have the How to Read also and at once.

Young H[armsworth]. says it is in press/ IF Opppen is going to do the series, he shd. write AT ONCE to

Desmond Harmsworth
13 Hyde Park Gardens
London W.

and ask what his terms are on H.T.Read. brochure. I believe 1 shilling in Eng. but cd. be 40 or 50 in U.S.

Yes I approve the idea of 50 cent installments. I ALSO think they can be combined with ultimate FOLIO. Folio double col. made of 4 pages of the brochure.

merely means taking electro[type]s as you go alon.

I honestly think it wd. sell (bizniziz) better than yr/ Adams. There is no partic. justice in these matters. The nearer one approaches senility the more buyers exist. vultures approaching carrion.

I think Bill W[illiams]. ought to be printed. But (friendship thy name!)

[A page appears to be missing from the letter at this point.]

I believe a young biz house). Announcing my collected. but only pledged to bring out 50 cents worth at once. . . .

. . .

Has the nobl. Oppen ANY capital or ANY sources of inkum?

Not that I greatly care a dame, like the Rabbis. But as Clara Leonora udes to say "Plesset are dey dot eggspect nothink fer dey shalls get it."

Rexroth SAID he wanted anything I d. give him; but have heard nothing SINCE then / or seen or had any sign that he is pib.ng anything either by me or by other.

//

Better to have H.T.R. with same firm (firmer, firmest) that hopes to do the hole job.

100 against possible royalties. O.K. with Ez. Has O.P.N.
GOT the hundred bucks???
if so what is he???
Amy [Lowell] said to "Bryher": (by letter I think) "We are in wooll whereas YOU are in ships."

On a 50 cent book; I think 100 bucks against 10% royalty wd. be equitous.

I had 20% from Macmillan on Noh. and Liv[eright]. gives 15. but the cheap bk. ought to arrive.

At any rate I shd. like there to B a pubr/ with a decent edtr///
wreats and posies.

By the veh; did you ever look up H. Rella.
now at 107 West 3d.
suitable member I think for the Taupin/Zuk/Oppen circl.

E

28 Oct.

Continuing

Z//

You don't say whether Oppen has ANY capital. If he hasn't? In any case he prob. hasn't ENOUGH.

I am perfectly willing to be used as a lever. Had lunch with Otto the Kahn in Paris and used evangelism but not with immediate intention. Otto SAID he wd. speak to a couple of young ploots. (I spose he aint nevvuh seed 'em since.) but still.

If Oppen (and he damn well mustn't say I told him) choses to try Otto or anyone else; on grounds that he intends to pub/ my collected prose and damn well OUGHT to receive facilities; extensions of credit etc. for the nobl/ purpose I see no objexshun. Joyce tried to work up some interest in the subject in London. Oppen cd. also apply to to the Gt. Jhames Jheezus Aloysius for moral (not fiscal support).

The prose is considered capable of paying (in the long run). Whoever seriously does the prose with decent assurances and on decent basis of FINISHING the job; wd. as a plum get the first cheap edtn. of the Cantos.
I.E. 2.50 (two bucks et demi or something like that).

Oppen can take position that IF he satisfies me as to prose (his; Oppen's security to finish it) he wd. get the Cantos; which (judging from sales of Personae (Liveright's edtn.) I suppose ⟨is or⟩ are a sure payer.

It is also or ought to be obvious that I can NOT give the Cantos to a ramshackle house likely to cascade at any moment/
gottttamit ve gotter liff // though damnd if I see how we do.

You (i.e. oppen cant APPEAL) he wd. have to putt it as pizznizz proposition, conservative estimate/ etc.

Mister KKKhann ⟨M or N.⟩ dere orter be a decent publishinkg housse in Jew York, I tink I can magke it pvay. if I can't ennyveh dere orter be.
~~or some line of that sort~~

E

Villon: Performed over the B.B.C. on 26 and 27 October 1931. Gallup E3h.

Oppen: Zukofsky to Pound, 15 October 1931, "Geo. Oppen is planning a publishing firm–To, Publishers, and I'm the edtr."

Harmsworth: Desmond Harmsworth published *How to Read* in December 1931.

Adams: "Henry Adams: A Criticism in Autobiography," *Hound & Horn* (Spring, Summer, Fall 1930).

Clara Leonora: One of Pound's classmates at the University of Pennsylvania. She is described in Canto 28.

Rexroth: Kenneth Rexroth was attempting to start a small publishing house, RMR Publications.

Bryher: Winifred Ellerman, daughter of British shipping magnate Sir John Ellerman. Novelist and companion of H.D.

Noh: 'Noh' or Accomplishment (London: Macmillan, 1916). Gallup A13.

Rella: Ettore Rella, American poet.

Kahn: Otto Kahn, American financier and patron of the arts.

Personae: Personae (New York: Boni & Liveright, 1926). Gallup A27.

42. TLS–3.

22 Nov. [1931] Rapallo

Dear Lodovico

Ivory?? The impot'nt old gentleman seems to have been annyoed about sumfink. Or praps thats the way emotion takes 'em in Baston.

Seems at any rate to show overwhelming intellectual capacity in meeting an argument.

Yaaasss I rekon the inelleckshul ammosphere in them paats is something of which no one resident fer two decades in Europe can form ANY idea whatso-bloody-ever.

DeVigny, thaat's apt, now. ⟨(i.e. Il prend une bonteille et il la choisi très forte)⟩

You are a bit indefinite about Oppen. Have you any idea whether either he or Rexroth has sent in a bid to D. Harmsworth re/ importing "How to Read".

I have corrected the proofs, and thing wuz to have been pubd. last week.

(along with, I suppose, a lot er plop).

Waal, I rekon Serly is right, an its time fer you to come to Yourup. Gard noze HOW. I can't employ you at an eating wage. Z'a mystery how I bloody live ennyhow. Mebby its on imagination.

Intellectual life costs about ten dollars a week in europe. Basil [Bunting] must do it on less, but he is a bit torpid and can't be said to be plumb in the centre etc. etc.

Damnd if I see any more action here than any where else. I answered two questionnaires in one week re/ mod/ lit/ in Ita. and in U.S.

"Si noi non lo facciamo, non si farà.
and
Let us pray.

I dunno if the Indice got yr/ sub. more important to know whether you GIT the Indice. apart from that there back number which cant be got. at least I dont thinkit is.

::::

I wuz on pt/ of ritin you two days ago, that I am about ready to look thru yr/ revised ⟨revised to Dec 1931⟩ version of "A." and also to make the crit. that I pussnly dont believe "A" is geared for a life work. I think if you cut it off about the length of "Homage to S[extus]. P[ropertius].", you wd. hold something.

Not because I objekk to peepul writing epicts;

//

Me, I am ritin another opry. more musical.

///

I bloody wonder if there is any way you cd. get at Otto [Kahn] or any of the large local lights.
IS Antheil still in America? I dunno how anyone breaks through. There is no opening for a y[oung].m[an]. of talent. one has to cork screw. Antheil is or was in with the high. Undoubtedly a question of "knowing people". Not that it ever does any good.

//

Wuz it (Villon) a success. My mother in law's cook, now cutting out clippings about the Bard of Pontoise. Manchester Guardian had two lines to say it wuz one best shows B.B.C. had putt on. Forchunately it wuz mostly in foreign language. Orchestra inaudible, but the few bars of mandolin sounding like a regiment of cavalry. On the whole a success. And 50 quid, even though the sterling down, were useful though not to wipe out all indebtedness.

///

Damn it all, how badly do you want to get to europe, if at all. And what is the extreme limit of degradation to which you wd. submit, in the way of menial servitude etc. . . . ??

How your job with Taup pan out??

etc. . . .

E

Ivory: Yvor Winters had written to Williams, "Your pet bull-pup, Zukofsky, is getting on my nerves; one of these days I am going to kick his teeth out past his tail." Zukofsky reported this to Pound in a letter of 11 November 1931. Winters' negative review of Taupin's *L'Influence du symbolisme,* "The Symbolist Influence," *Hound & Horn* (July-September 1931), prompted Zukofsky to write a reply. This in turn elicited a response from Winters. The editors of *Hound & Horn* proposed to print the exchange (and set it in type) but never did. The proof pages that were sent to Zukofsky are now in the Zukofsky Collection at the Humanities Research Center, the University of Texas at Austin.

De Vigny: Zukofsky noted in his letter of 11 November 1931 that Taupin was annoyed at having to teach the works of Alfred de Vigny.

another opry: Cavalcanti. Gallup E3a.

job: Zukofsky to Pound, 30 June 1931, "Since times are hard & fast Taupin and I are taking on the propulsion of a new racket. I will write on Apollinaire & the period & other loci when I know something about 'em. He will appear with me as the author—or the entire author in French (without me) & then I'll 'translate' my work or book into the original English. For which I'll get

$50 a month (and, probably, Taupin's other liabilities). Not a word of this to anyone. I don't know why he asked me to tell you this, but we both think it's amusing. Literature is best when anonymous. Any other principles of yrs. we can live by, Mr. Pound? If Columbia Univ. finds out we'll both lose our jobs–René with the univ. & I with René. Taupin can work this racket because Columbia Univ. has given him a leave of absence beg. Feb. 1932 & full pay."

43. ALS–16.

12/7/31 214 Columbia Hts Bklyn

Dear E —yes:

Just some intercallary notes, before the real business letter is sent off to you. Haven't heard from Oppen re- your complete works (it'll have to be that eventually!), but I spose I shd. any day now. And you've probably heard from him—already. Anyway, let's remember two things:

1. The first volume of your prose can contain (& shd) 125 pp. Which is How to Read—+plus what you decide. —The point is not ⟨so much⟩ to show Oppen's French printer what the canny Scot can do—the pg. out of the Harmsworth catalog ⟨tho I'll let Oppen see it & ask him to show it⟩—but to get you printed in six to 10 volumes, so as I can take you off the shelves, like any French author, when I want to.

2. No use worryin' about a commercial edtn. of Cantos now. Of course, if you can get reg'lar publisher—Boni etc—to do it within a year—the next year—alright. If not you shd. keep To firmly in mind, if in the background. The point is Oppen if I know him—wd. be delighted to give you every bit of profit on an edition of Cantos, and that shd. amount to—if you're at all a commercial fit—something

At any rate, I'm itchin' all over to get a view of what'll come out of all this.

Rexroth—if the business end of him still bothers you—said some months ago that he had got a "very friendly letter" from you and that only an extended vacation in the Calif. rockies was preventin' him from answerin you. Also it seems he has been quarrelsome with his patrons. I hope his scheme does go thru—since he was wantin' to get out my essays & poems.

Anyway, again: if you prefer To, Publishers, we are very highly & personally flattered.

About Geo. Oppen printing my Adams—I'll be durn'd if any friend of mine is goin' to lose money on my works. Geo. can have the poems or what after he's published you, Bill [Williams], Reznikoff, etc—but the editor will remain behind the scenes.

Possibility that Dodd, Mead or Dragon Press (Angel Flores, Ithaca, New York) or Rexroth may do the Adams—at least, all of 'em have written requests.

It wd. seem $ even if Harmsworth publishes How to Read that Oppen could use it to open a volume (Vol I of yr. prose) of yours—if the vol. contains other work prefigurin' a collected edtn.?

Am enclosing the Winters correspondence. Please return it. I wish you could get it published. Maybe if you sent it to Contempo ⟨—(a r-r-rotten sheet!!!))⟩—or New Review? Do you think we need ask Winters' permission. I asked him, but he hasn't answered—& he did as you see write all the truck he did for the H[ound]&H[orn]. My relations with the last definitely broken.

My embellished traduction of Taupin's chapter on Eliot to appear in Jan. Symposium. Look between the lines for our personal jokes. The translation was done—oral, dictation,—several successive Wed. nights at Frenchie's ap't. on Riverside Drive, to the great delight followed by fits of despair followed by ho-ho's of delight of the Frenchman. No dictionaries around.

The Apollinaire is proceeding. Wish it were done. On the whole, T[aupin] has been reliable with his $50 per month—tho goddarn our economic syphilization he hates like hell, profligate tho' he is, to write out a check—and I never ask, —but when he realizes that I may have coyly dispensed with two meals on a certain day & limited myself to a 15¢ breakfast, his heart melts. It's funny—and I don't expect nuthin. Except that I fear the month of Feb. when I'll have to do the writing. And he's a strict boss, tho' very worshipful of my talents.

Incidentally, if you know of anyone who has some rare items of Apollinaire (I know [Samuel] Putnam has—& he said he'd send him, but he hasn't—maybe you can prompt him while you spur him on to print the "Objectivists" Anthol) cd you have 'em lent to me till—the latest—April 1st?

Great difficulty of the work is that it must sound as if it came out of one consorted mind—Taupin's—that is, his next on inspiration & mine must show the same woof of thought. Ergo, I've been outlining bibliography, ideaology [*sic*], etc for his own volume. (Incidentally, Frobenius is puzzling us both & we wonder if he isn't just too smoothly theoretically truthful). I don't know what Frobenius has to do with Apollinaire—but he probably has a lot to do with it.

Not a word, of course, about this to anyone—unless Basil [Bunting] can keep a secret & be amused by it.

Net result: writing as an individual handiwork pretty distasteful. Growing ideas of Mr. L.Z. on the 50th floor of the Empire State, disseminating literature to the 49 floors below. M. Taupin his right hand man.

Symbiosis and art!!!

Lodovico thanks you, my friend. I didn't mean to make ⟨you⟩ sad—or wring your heart—except ring it?

This ¶ of yours, however, interests me: "Damn it all, how badly do you want to get to Europe, if at all. And what is the extreme limit of degradation to which you wd. submit, in the way of menial servitude etc. . . .??"

Correlating all the above paragraphs with–you can see I am not very happy. It is foolish of course to expect to be every minute of one's waking life—which I want to be—but with continual opportunity for being unoccupied and the constant necessity for bolstering one's closest friends, [. . . .] etc, even to the creation of the very air in which they live—Kaigh in Calif, & Serly in Phil. are possibly the only exceptions, & they're (thanks etc balls, stars for that) a bit inuman—'murka has in the last 2 yrs. become an unlivable place. Not that I expect to run aroun in Europe—or kick the gong around, or be anything but my sweet, sober self, but a change of air wd. do me good. And then I cd. always run back, if I felt like it.

Point is: I wdn't mind "menial servitude"—if it wd. involve only me. Say, half a day of it. No, of course no, you can't employ me. But what did you have in mind? For the rest, I don't want to say nothin' but the

Taupin salary shd. expire soon—& there'll be a limit to which I can permit myself as sot so to draw on Geo. Oppen. But say nuthin.

Yes, Antheil, I hear is still in America—but question of my getting in touch with the high not worth discussing. The high wd. have to show signs of seekin me out—& why shd. I expect that?

Which brings me back to "A" goddamit. You had my plaint a year ago regarding that there poem—& I've had ⟨yr⟩ criticism about length etc, which in your last, as it probably shd. be, is still unchanged—and I've had almost a year and a half for revision, & all I cd. do but correct a few typing errors in the script of the 7 movements sent to you, has been:

Pg 17 — line 5 grave of night changed to grave at night

Pg 31 — "For six years you was out of a job"—Omit the rest of that line

Pg 32 — Add a comma after Rimbaud omit a comma at the end of the line above it: To find a thing, all things

That's about all. Which wd. indicate two things

1. Either I've grown pigheaded—failing of critical faculties
2. I'm right as to the essential (or let that word fly) value of the poem.

1. danger of course, of being critically myopic enough to have emotionally—even if it is cranium emotion—evolved a theory to fit my desire of what I want the poem to be. On the whole, the critics I value have been impressed, but, if I can gage hearts, not absolutely. i.e. Taupin has even gone so^far in order to give my affirmations regarding the work the let down to say—jestingly of course but I suspect him an[y]way—that it reminds him of Conrad Aiken. In soberer moments he has less cataclysmically mentioned things, ~~about~~ ⟨such as⟩ 'fearing that "A" is in the wrong direction,' 'alright if you want to give over poetry to structure emulating music, but thinks that shdn't be done'—'difficulty of reading the thing in one sitting—as opposed to the ease with which one hears a piece of music at length etc.' Bill[Williams]'s original enthusiasm, subsequent lack of it, subsequent qualifications of that, not to be depended on: on the whole, he seems ready to praise the work when he sees it in a magazine and uncomfortable before it otherwise.

2. The value of the work.

I— It seems to me to make straight reading—following out of your don'ts

almost to the letter (the only exception being the And to the Sun I bow translation out of Yehoash & a few other spots at the very end ⟨of the 4th movement⟩—not the quote from Veit Bach which is gracious & humorous—which I can't seem to get around.)
II— Despite Taupin's objection as to length, I've reread it time & time again out loud to myself all this last year—and it has not lagged—the 20 or 25 minutes devoted to this process has never failed to—inspite of the original intention otherwise—interest not only my mind, but to stir my Rockerfellers along with it (vide my translation of Frobenius: Er hatte ein Glied, aber kein Skrotum—He had a Cornelius, but no Rockerfellers). And I've experienced moments when I've wanted to hear only one movement of a Bach or Mozart Concerto. That is 1 & 2, 3 & 4, 5, 6 and 7, or 1, 2, 6, 7 can be read separately in 12 or 15 minutes—& I think for the pleasure of sequential structure—3 & 4 as a variation, 5 as a development & prelude.
III—Serly's recent playing of the piano version of the ⟨Mozart⟩ Fantasia which he has orchestrated, has again convinced me that intuitively I have done something in poetry very much akin to good music. (Intuitively—i.e. as far as notes are concerned I can see or hear when they go up or down, & linger or proceed.) Serly has also reassured my skepticism by having in secret bothered to set down the 7th movement as musical notation (mind you, not a melody, or a tune to it) but just notes or rather beats & time intervals) & found in it perfect logical development, sequence, progression. It's more than I have hoped for, but I have hoped for that, & have always depended on that truth to keep me one interval on this side ⟨of⟩ attainment.
IV—You've called "A"—Serly tells me—a glorified "The". That doesn't say much for the diction, but it does say if I understand it, that the impetus behind it is on a higher emotional level than The. Invention: Serly tells me that you have limited that for our age to Joyce, Rexroth, & The Cantos. About as good a choice as any, & better, of course. Tho a lot is omitted—it all depends as to what one means by invention: i.e. I sometimes feel Bill [Williams] & Marianne [Moore] have done a good deal unprompted by anyone—& without embellishing anyone. I think structurally no one has done anything like 1–7 of "A". That is, I feel, the climaxes in each movement and as they proceed over the 7 movements are right.

The value of "A" 's diction, linear technique—no where approaching Cantos. On the other hand, up to now, I think there is a different grasp of sequence, of placing & developing movement out of movement—if even in a more traditional sense—which is, granting the interest of the detail, invention. The building up by section on section, block on block, of the Sixth movement—gratifyingly from a critical standpoint the longest—has not been done otherwheres. If anything like the 7th movement exists in English I do not know it. Maybe it does exist in several Italian Canzoni, and in Daniel—but then it does not telescope out of anything like the Sixth movement.

Speaking of invention: if you will compare Mr. Eliot's recent Triumphal March with "A"–5 you will find that I handled his essential subject ⟨in a⟩ way far superior manner back in 1929.

Pore' me . . . you don't believe "A" is geared for a life work. I wish you did, dammit I wish you deed . . . but I know the difficulty will eventually be not searching for material to eke out the matter into 17 remaining movements (There will be no more than 24—doesn't that make everybody happy?!) but to twist the neck of the material in the movements immediately to follow (the next 1–5 years) movements 8–12, so that all the ⟨preceding⟩ detail gets a new head. And, mentally & in odd notes that's what I've been doing the last year and a half. That is, to so handle the setting of the piece—the Jheezus material—so that eventually by development nothing of it remains etc. At any rate, when I feel good sometimes—creation seems more certain, almost assured. The last twelve movements 13–24—the twelve Ballate beginning "An" shd come easy & with mirror like grace with maturity & a clear and richer head.

Incidentally, I take it that Rexroth's contribution the moving, isolation of words above each other, instead of alongside—as in a Gregorian chant[—]is also partly in the 7th movement, with a certain fluidity added to the static: i.e. R. is more primitive.

The difference between Cantos & "A" aside from diction ⟨& quality of line⟩ in the matter of musical approximation—The difference between polyphony (many voices of angels, if you will permit it) and one human voice thematically split in two—but so far the fugal principle is more obvious in the last. We both partake of the cinematic principle, you to a greater & more progressive degree, tho' it wd. be pretty hard to distinguish in either case where montage leaves off & narration begins & vice versa.

Reverting to business of diction: incorporation of slang etc in "A" done in accordance with the canons of a work of art, i.e. when Cummings has printed fuck in a Calligram there is still no relief. I used to think I had a great deal to learn from him—I see now that I haven't, that even "The" is much better etc—

And now your criticism: "I think if you cut off about the length of "Homage to S.P.", you wd hold something." That wd. cut it down to about half of what it is now— I wish I could see what to cut, there's nothing I wd. enjoy more. Yr. original suggestions for movements 1 & 2 really very slight. That is, you wanted to get rid of staccato, & occasionally went in for more of it. For the rest, there were 2 or 3 sins in the matter of "don'ts," i.e. a circumlocution now & then—English, after all, being a continual training for me. I wish, if you cd. spare wasting (or not wasting, as you wish) the time, that you'd do the cutting you think necessary on the script I sent you & forward it to me. —I know that takes a lot of time, & if eventually it wdn't mean anything to the general good, as you see it, I don't naturally want you to do it. But I do want to know what you mean by I "wd. hold something." It wd. be the length of Homage to S.P., but wd. it in its own way give as much pleasure? Good man, be honest with me, this isn't life, but poetry! And I haven't died of remorse till now, I guess I cd. linger on.

I feel foolish sending you odd leericks—leeriques??—now and then, & receiving your deferred silent opinions in answer. I get you—but funny, I can't help feeling specifically what you once said generally that there's something to 'em. And more than what I see done anywhere around. I hope I'm not greedy.

The Apollinaire is the first in the Il y a collection. I tried to do him one better, trepanning the 90ies, the melodrama etc.

I should appreciate it if you guess where Song 8 has been cribbed from.

"Another opry, more musical" sounds as it should—fine.

Best always,

Z

⟨Indice—being r'cd but not regularly.⟩

canny Scot: Pound to Zukofsky, 23 November 1931, "How to Read a very good model for Oppen to show his French printer. (Better work than he will get in france, and very good for the french printer's morale to see the canny scots labours.)" The Harmsworth edition of *How to Read* was printed by Morrison & Gibb, Ltd., Edinburgh.

Flores: Flores' Dragon Press would publish William Carlos Williams's *The Knife of the Times* in March 1932 as its second book.

traduction: "The Classicism of T. S. Eliot," *The Symposium* 3:1 (January 1932).

Cornelius: Probably Cornelius Vanderbilt (1794–1877), American multimillionaire.

Daniel: Arnaut Daniel, 12th-century Provencal poet.

Triumphal March: Published by Faber and Faber in October 1931.
printed fuck: Probably a reference to poem XXX of *ViVa,* which contains the line " 'I will not kiss your fucking flag.' " *ViVa* was published by Liveright in October 1931.
The Apollinaire: Zukofsky's translation does not appear to have survived. The first poem in *Il y a* (Paris: Albert Messein, 1925) is "La Cueillette."
song 8: Probably the eighth poem of "29 Poems." *All,* p. 29.

44. ALS–10.

Dec 10/31 214 Columbia Hights [*sic*] Brooklyn N.Y.

Dear E—. Gees! wut a wad I have to write you. Lemme see, lemme see . . . maybe I better begin by merely quotin' Oppen: (you can form yr. own opinions—with our permission—if I don't offer any—the unquotes are my comment, the quotes, my young boss—How many bosses have you Mr. Z? Two To!!—Y're just our regisseur, Mr. E.)

"A swell guy Pound. And this thing's really swell. All this idiotic consideration of taste!—the thing is, one was so detached that brushing his teeth (if he did so) would be an act of pure intellect"—Refers to How to Read—if I can guess.

"I'll write Pound. He wants the thing business-like? I might send him a new year's card; we'll be getting one from our dentist and the dept. stores. or:

Dear old Pal:

Well, well, well; I wish you could see me now. Butlers cars and all the fixings. Nothing like the good old days, eh what? Things has broken right for me finally, and I'm hittin up the old high spots. Lemme hear from you

Sincerely
G. August Oppen
Treas. Rudemintary Insurance Co.

"Wrote Pound—assuring him of our financial stability. I told him we don't mind considering the hundred dollars a guarantee on a ten-percent royalty, but we'll pay twenty percent on copies sold over the number (about 3000) necessary to pay 100 dollars on a ten percent royalty. That comes to the same thing as my original suggestion to you, except that it gives us our clear (almost) profit on the copies sold from 1600 (which is necessary to break even) to 3000. Which profit we'll probably have use for if we ever get it."

—You can't say Mr. Z. is not honest, but you can say he's a naif copying all this out for you!

"Got a letter from Pound—expressing satisfaction, insisting on the folio, and exhorting me to write at once and direct to Harmsworth to get "sheets" of "How to Read." He says it wd. save us money. I don't understand whether or not Harmsworth has abandoned his purpose to print the How to Read, but I wrote him, asking, & asking what the price of sheets wd. be if has, exactly—I hope—as if I knew what they are. Electrotypes? Better tell me; I may not be able to find out here. The word translated litterally into French seems to mean nothing unusual."

You better tell him—if H[armsworth] doesn't. I can't till I buy J.A. Holden's Bookman's Glossary—which won't be for some time—it costs 2.50—MR. Z.

"Pound says you've agreed (I have—MR. Z) to the folios—which naturally (is O.K.—MR. Z). Tho I'm sorry that they'll have two columns to the page."

—Yes, that is sort of funny. Got any suggestions—or do insist on resembling an early American (Gothick??) text?? Better write Oppen about it—& let me know what you say to him. Fair is fair!! The following has nothing to do with you—it's about our stationary (the business'). "Must the envelopes be American size. I'm afraid they're not going to be. What is wrong with European dimensions!! (They don't fit my archives—Mr. Z) "Pound's envelopes"? I say, there's nothing wrong with 'em—not a thing—I retract (Mr. Z.).

—

—

"This'll do for the Announcements of Pound, won't it:
To—etc
Announces The
Prolegomena
(Collected Prose)
of
Ezra Pound
which will be published as a series of brochures, each volume to sell for fifty cents the copy. The series will consist of the following volumes: How to Read, etc, etc, to be released in the order named

The How to Read is available for March delivery (date will be verified—Mr. Z.)

Kindly send me__copies at fifty cents the copy of How to Read vol 1 etc——"

"Pound writes again. He says, speaking of the advisability of starting with H[ow].T[o].R[ead]. that 'it is an introduction to the whole method of my crit. and everything that has heretofore looked like dilletantism and tasting here and there; shifts into place and has its proportion.'

Can you do better than that for announcement. If not, I'll ask Pound if we can use his statement—over his signature or not, as first you and then he wants. Wacha think?"

I think I can't do better, that Mr. E. shd. let Mr. August Op. use the statement ⟨over⟩ Mr. E's signature. Please, MR. E., write MR. Op—MR. Z "Pound—to me—asks not for electrotypes for the folios but just to have 500 copies printed from the brochure type, four brochure pages to the folio pages. Which is good–electrotyping wd be too expensive. —What it will cost with better paper I don't know. Covers will have to wait. We'll need better paper." —Considering the growth of a young pub. house, Mr. E, the fact that the complete collected Folio shd. be no more than 2 vols., the matter takes care of itself. You will need several brochure volumes (3 or 4) before you can fill a folio. Haste in this case will not make paste. Believe in us, in our future, in our everything, but do not press us about the glorious volumes before the lesser lights are published. You have our promise that there will be a Folio ed—if yr. collected appears (first half of 'em ⟨at least⟩) at all—i.e. there shdn't be a folio over our dead bodies.—MR. Z.— But don't worry, we'll live.

"Writing Pound to agree—likewise: he seemed to think it might be necessary—to the Folios, I says, says I:

"He better write entirely to you or entirely to me to avoid contradiction or duplication of letters. (You better write to him—and let me know whether you're satisfied, when you can—MR. Z)

"It isn't necessary that we should both agree to any proposal (no, that's ⟨what⟩ wrong with parliaments, congresses—MR. E.Z., but we (august & I) usually agree—MR.Z.)

"That we will pay the advance royalties—this goes because it has to—on each book as it is r'cd from the printer i.e., the first book will be paid for the first of March; the second the first of May, etc (Have you ever known such conscience? I esk yu? If you objek—I know who can use the money—MR. Z. And so do you?!)

"Maybe you better tell him that we won't commit ourselves to printing one installment every two months—we might want to interrupt the series with something else. I don't know if he understands that.

"In fact, we'll almost surely want to interrupt it.

"That's the way I am

Buddy"

I think you understand, MR. E. i.e. we will print at least 2 (two) volumes by you—or rather of yr. prose—I think I can get George to agree—but can't assure you of more—tho there may be more—a year. Two volumes by E.P. a year; possibly, but not probably, more than two.

When the time comes the Folio will not be counted as a volume—but as our gift to you, in addition to the 2 brochures.

Now—answering yrs.

our list runs: 1. Bill Walrus [Williams].
2. E.P. Section I.
3. If Oppen agrees—Tozzi/Buntn.

only objection: we may have to pay Tozzi—is he alive?—& we cdn't afford to pay both Bunting & Tozzi—But you write Oppen & see what he says. No, I don't think we propose to be purely amurikun. In fact, we expect you to be on look out for foreign material and make suggestions all the time.

4. Possibly L.Z.
5. Reznikoff. (probably)
6. E.P. (2nd section).

Bob McA[lmon]—cd be taken care of the second year. We don't want the same homocide squad allee time. By that time he shd. be rejected by everyone else & ⟨have⟩ polished off his Politics of Existence which has fine things in it—what I've seen—but needs to be cut (& I mean cut). Not just circumcised.

If you wish to cede yr. 2nd place to Bunting & take 3rd—it wd. be alright—but Geo. counts on you, second, as a business asset. Up to you & Oppen.

I will write to Geo. ask him to agree to definite list—which he'll send you—& you, please begin hornblowing, logrolling etc as per yr. wish!

Yr. suggestion as to calling the thing a periodical to evade tariff— The customs wd. see that the thing is the work of one author—I phoned 'em just before, explaining & they said they cdn't consider it a magazine. It is barely possible that we'll attach a date to the publications, anyway, & trust that the customs will go cock-eyed, strabismic etc when the time comes for the things to pass thru their hands.

A tax of 15%—damn them, they said 25% if the authors are American! — will be a big blow to Geo's possible outlay of $250 a month—& remember we don't expect profits on our first item—only that it shd pay for the printing, Bill's $100 & mine. i.e. Enough to invest again in the 2nd item—you or Basil. So think of us with fervent heart.

———

———

Please remember when we get started on yr. volume—that it will be faster for you to write Oppen re- all detail of printing, format etc — you can inform me later or save time—he'll let me know——

———

———

Yr. Cavalcanti: I shd. like to review it—tho' I don't know who'll accept it. H[ound] & H[orn] is out. Leaves "Poetry" "Symposium" "Contempo" "Contact" (but I don't think they'll print reviews) & whatever avant-garde, you don't care to be mentioned in, left at the time. I don't know whether Symposium has a mediaeval specialist. Must you have one, that is the point. If you don't—then I'm your man. In case you agree, the proper procedure I suppose wd. be to send Symposium a copy—but then Wheelwright wd. probably want to keep that & not allow me to review the book after all. Or ditto his partner Burnham. The godly procedure wd. be to send me the volume, & I can write 'em a note to the effeck that I wd. like to review it, or better you can say as much to 'em if you think fit. By the way, what happened to that MS. on Marx & Aquinas they were to print? Yes, by all means, please MR. E. send this specialist your Cavalcanti.

Thank you, thank you

Mr. Z.

Tozzi: In his letter of 27 November 1931, Pound had suggested that Bunting translate Federigo Tozzi's *Tre croci.* Pound referred to it as the "only modern wop bk. as good as Dubliners and Portrait of Artist." Pound may have been unaware that an English translation already existed: *Three Crosses* (New York: Moffat, Yard, 1921).

Politics of Existence: A novel McAlmon had been working on since 1928. Part of it had been published in *This Quarter* 1:4 (Spring 1929).
Cavalcanti: Guido Cavalcanti: Rime (Genoa: Marsano, 1932). Gallup B27.
Marx & Aquinas: Pound to Oppen, 23 December 1931, "The Marx Aquinas wasnt unified enough for 'em. They asked me to revise. Their crit. was justifiable, But I have more important things to attend to."

45. ALS–5.

Dec 14/31 214 Columbia Hts Brooklyn N.Y.

Dear E: Well, if the admirable Oppen confirms the idea of printing off sheets for ultimate folio, you may rest assured etc

#

Nuclei of just men in U.S.A[.]? Yes, I guess you have directed me most gratuitously.

#

Frenchie [Taupin] is just a common blackguard to have maligned my bizness potentialities with Basil [Bunting]—or in confidence to him. Did I say potentialities? Mor'n that: Actualities!! i.e. who used to do the rare book sales for my brother way back in 1925? Lil' loo-wee- the prudent bibliographer. i.e. if you know anything about the booktrade—anything which concerns our end of it—you can only sell or one can only sell just the number of copies there's a market for. For the rest, my past history should allay your fears re- my incapacity: i.e. a sale of $500 worth of limited editions in 5 minutes—of course, they were wanted—; the resignation of 6 beautiful ladies to my sales talks, and the even completer yielding of an Italian Catholic Arctic Geographer, aged 50 and married. Not to mention my triumphs over sundry idiots and multitudinous cranks.

#

The bookseller referred ⟨to⟩ in my recent—who might handle the XXX Cantos wuz my brother—or is—he owned several bookshops i.e. successively & wd. be quite prosperous if he weren't too imaginative: i.e. he planned Renaissance arches instead of considering his overhead, & the fact that as his greatest aid I was perhaps getting too much, earning a bar of chocolate each day. Anyway, he's never got over his failure—brought on by lunatic integrity: another reason why I will eventually leave the U.S.A. unless I can get some money for him to lose in another bookshop.

No, I guess he can't handle the Cantos. And it wd. be too much of a job for me to keep record of his books—if he took 'em on tick.

Nancy [Cunard] writes 50 copies at a lesser rate than 25%, but doesn't say whether 33 1/3 or 40 or 50.

It wd. seem to me the safest plan for you wd. be to ask Nancy to let you have the number of copies remaining. Then, for To to take on agency for that item, the Cavalcanti & the Stravinsky—or whatever other items by you (we can't fool around with everybody i.e. I can't, the burden of the work wd. fall completely on me) & indicate on its list Orders taken for etc. I needn't have you send more than 10 copies of Cantos & perhaps not that many—because my place is not insured & I don't wish to be responsible for goods over value of $50—& then pay you as they are sold & you can write me what commission to deduct for myself. Naturally, I will also have to deduct for shipment (distribution) costs of each volume—includes parcel post charges, insurance etc.

If this is satisfactory, please, to save time, write Oppen & Nancy—& I'll also drop 'em each a note by the way, saying they may hear from you. i.e. tell Oppen to add the 3 titles mentioned above, or whatever, to the bottom of his announcement list.

#

Marianne [Moore] is in exile or self-inflicted solitary confinement: She wrote me a very fine letter recently, but won't come out or allow me to do so. I doubt if I can presume again upon that cincture even by corresponding. How, anyway, could she be helpful?

#

Who is Jean Foster?

#

Hear from Rexroth again? Remember, I don't want him to feel I've done him out of "sponsoring" you—I value the work of the man & the man himself very much. So you'll have to be better'n Polonius! Especially since there's a little Hamlet in R's gestures & movements.

#

Yr. efforts towards London & continental distribution of To's Publications wd. I needn't say be of extreme value. Do what you can & we'll be beholden.

Jerce [Joyce] 'opkins, again? That's funny!! Napa—a kind of weed growing in Napa, Calif. I don't know why Persephone's husband, romanized, shdn't be on the west coast now. I don't know that Napa has a university, but it might as well have.

The literal meaning of this famous epigram was the bare statement in a letter of Roger Kaigh to Mr. L.Z.—D. (Dorothy his spouse, who was dispensing pensions to old folk) is in Napa trailing the sterilized. I added the title & lower-cased napa—which word you can find in Webster's international. I looked it up after I myself ⟨had⟩ begun to doubt the meaning of the poem.

The allegorical meaning is that L.Z. in Wisconsin was Pluto in hell following a lot of emasculated peripatetics (tho' it is even doubtful these walked or were ever unemasculated).

The anagogical meaning is that even evil (Dis) implies redemption.

Any other 14 "ambiguous" readings permitted—vide Empson, 7 types of English ambiguity—provided of course you keep each meaning distinct. As you see it's a great poem. Most certainly—is your reading justified, i.e. napa inverted— ⟨in⟩ weeds or in "a pan"—what difference? Or imagine a bottle with a label on it; the label has printed matter all around & down the bottle. As you turn the bottle the poem forms out of the circumference measured around one plane of the cylindrical surface. Advertising & montage, Mr. E.,—Eisenstein has nothing on us. Incidentally, what on earth prompted him to do Romance Sentimentale? i.e. it might well be used in a university course given over to the cinema, but for him etc—.

And as Chaya Tryne moaned when encountered—oi, I'm goink to de operra . . .

Ever

Z

Yr. scheme of fooling the customs of no use—the books printed as magazines wd. be taxed 15% or 25%—as all magazines are, 6 months after publication.

Nuclei: Pound to Zukofsky, 29 November 1931, "I spose I must have given you most of the names and addresses of nuclei of possible just men and cooperators in the U.S.???"

maligned: Pound to Zukofsky, 29 November 1931, "Taupin has filled Basil with firm belief in yr. utter incapacity to transact ANY business operation."

brother: Morris Zukofsky. Louis Zukofsky dedicated "A"–21 (1967) "to the memory of John Gassner and my brother Morris Ephraim[.]"

Stravinsky: An edition of Boris de Schloezer's *Stravinsky,* translated by Pound, that was never published. Gallup E6i.

Foster: Pound to Zukofsky, 29 November 1931, "When you git goin/ both Marianne and Jean Foster . . . might be helpful." Jeanne R. Foster, American poet and editor, was no longer living in New York. Pound had evidently been too long out of touch with her to realize this.

Polonius: The name with which Pound signed his letter of 29 November 1931.
Napa: In his letter of 29 November 1931, Pound had inquired about the meaning of this word. It is used in the poem "University: Old Time," *Poetry* 37:5 (February 1931), p. 251. Though the poem was Zukofsky's, he used the pseudonym "Joyce Hopkins."
Empson: William Empson's *Seven Types of Ambiguity* had been published in 1930.
your reading: Pound to Zukofsky, 29 November 1931, "is 'napa' intelligible in ANY dialect, or simply thieves argotic inversion 'a pan.' "
Eisenstein: Sergei Eisenstein, Russian film director.
Romance Sentimentale: Though Eisenstein was credited as co-director on this film, it was really the work of his friend and colleague, Grigori Alexandrov.
Chaya Tryne: Unidentified.

46. TL–3.

22 Dec. [1931] Rapallo

Z/

Have had a hard day settin' on the printin' press in genova.
But note as I read/:

what the HELL do you mean to convey by the sentence "Serly tells me you have limited that (invention) for our age to Joyce, Rexroth and the Cantos" ⟨??⟩

????

whatever HAS S[erly]. half/swallowed. And why Rexroth? what of Rexroth.

I can't remember ⟨having made⟩ any such summary, or ANY summary

I can't see why I shd. have omitted Bill[Williams]/ Marianne [Moore]/ the Professor (to be) etc// in fact

I don't rekognize

the remark AT ALL.

too tired to go into it now.

WAAAAL. Every generation has to do something its granpap can't quite make out.

I thought I said A.7 was technical O.K. Experiment/ ~~etc.~~ ⟨innovation⟩

what I am doubtin is thechnique of the half (that is one dept. of technique) bein) enough to sustain Throughout limitless prolungation.

IF you are discussin A. at its present size/ that is ONE prop.

if you are diskussin it as the start of a pome of ⟨"some⟩ length/

that is a NUTHER.

And (if you think you are right, go ahead, and dont listen to me or any of yr/ other damned ancestors.

I have not seen Triumphal March (where does it lead TO, Cambridge Mass?)

P. 15. seems to justify my having STOPPED trying to criticze, and tellin' you the thing was out of my critical baliwick, and that my solutions of my jobs. wd. be no use to you in a different one.

Mebbe better if you forgot the Donts, and every godd damn abstract criterion that ANYone has uttered, and concentrate on yr/ own aesthetic.

There is no REASON why I shd. be able to be any more use to you ⟨as critic⟩ 1930 to 1950 than yeats to me 1910 to 1930.

E un altra cosa; questa

/// at any rate if you are working out a new musical structure, you've got to concentrate on it 5 or 10 or 20 years.

Its a whale of a job. I don't see why it shdnt. lead out. to etc. . . . .

⟨Wot you posterlate⟩ ~~it~~ is an abstracter kind of poesy than my generation went in for. Woller TOOT.

If the alternative is [Archibald] McLeishing for KRRists sake go on and do fugues and double cannons and letter puzzles and sequences of pure consonants with no god damn trace of god damn lichercgoor in 'em AT ALL.

Too tired to write Imagin/ Convstn. betn. Confucius and Bar/Spinoza on metric.

more anon

cross ref/ on locomotion of musicality / Antheil in my "Antheil"

⟨good
night⟩

printin' press: Pound was overseeing the printing of his *Guido Cavalcanti Rime,* which was finally published in late January 1932.

Serly tells. . . .": See Zukofsky's letter of 7 December 1931.

the Professor: T. S. Eliot. Pound had learned five days earlier that Eliot had been named Charles Eliot Norton Professor of Poetry at Harvard for the academic year 1932–1933.

P. 15.: Page 15 of the typscript of "A" 1–7. It contains the "Shimaunu-Sān" sections of "A"–4.

the Donts: "A Few Don'ts by an Imagiste," *Poetry* 1:6 (March 1913), pp. 200–206.

locomotion of musicality: Pound, quoting Antheil, wrote, ". . . in musical history names of great men, eventually discerned only through the necessity which they have apart from others to create a new locomotion for their musicality." *Ezra Pound and Music,* ed. R. Murray Schafer (New York: New Directions, 1977; London: Faber & Faber, 1978), p. 263.

47. TL–2.

27 Dec. [1931] Rapallo

IN THAT CASE

The poem "Dis in napa etc." suffers from one of the known varieties of licherary disease

namely a Xcessive complicity or trascombobilation, and is a inferior poem to one enjoying or containing and inlucind the Confucian virtues.

Caligrams: anagogicies etc. .

//

N.B. more or less relevant/ certain orthographies purrmitted with typewriter not permissible with illegible or semilegible script.

That is to say:

you cd. have expressed the same subject matter in a more simple and lucid manner without losing one jot of the meaning.

Eg/ the so often useless article "the" wd. have indicated that napa was a noun general;

Dis the napa or pampas.

etc.

faddy n[ouvelle];r[evue];f[rançais];lack of capital letter if indicating the town.

etc.

senility and sterilization not synonyms. muddld thought at that pt.

Jeanne Foster had some sort of rapport with something or other address apt/ 702 300 W. 49th

wd. favour wider distribution of my woiks.

Iris Barry 344 East 51 st. vide Oct. Bookman will give wot pubcty/ poss to "TO" pubctns.
also might relieve Manhattanism. Have sent her yr/ name cognomen etc. but you might accelerate.

You can discuss campaign with both of 'em. I see no reason why Iris shdn't become president of the Euninted States.

Might tell her Fordie's memoirs are out. She prob. knows it. but it will save me writin a letter.

Nothing noo from Rex[ro]th/ I will answer his letters/ but I can't set on a chiny egg. Too b/y much else on the cawpit.

Barry: British poet, novelist and historian of the cinema. Pound had been acquainted with her since 1916. Her reminiscences of Pound and his associates in London, circa 1916–1919, "The Ezra Pound Period," had recently appeared in *The Bookman,* 74:2 (October 1931), pp. 159–171.

Fordie's memoirs: Reminiscences 1894–1914: Return to Yesterday, by Ford Madox Ford (London: Gollancz, 1931).

48. TL–3. With Prolegomena enclosure.

[May 1932] Rapallo

AWL rite/

Sell um fer wot you can get/ if anything. and remit what's left. when you have eaten/ if ever.

Had s'more proofs (slightly erratic) in Firenze two hours before I went on fer me song and dance, deelighting that audience as they say by my "caustic wit" (as they apparently don't wish to quote any specimens)

Why don't that old ASS Bill grumpus von Vilhelmstrasse [Williams] send me his bleating lamb of a maggerzeen. . . . . . izz ee fraid of my caustic??

Sam Puttenheim [Putnam] is drunk half the time/ over works the other two thirds / worries I shd/ think about his health (which is the worst known to man) the remaining fifth/ His last issue New Rev[iew]. inexcusable on any other base/ass.

Sorry!///he'za sympathetic kuss/ Have said faretheewell to his orgum.

ANYHOW / my corrections of Prolegomena (vol. 1. containing alas sections 1 and 2) has went to Muster Oppen this a/m/

Wd. be good thing to start 3d. issue before printer finishes this job. I mean the issues will have to overlap if O/ is going to bring out six a year.

Yaas/ Profile is that there anth/ done in 1931. copies shd. have reached you. Please plant a review of it / not fer my sake only/ Scheiwiller good guy/ ought to be NNNNcouraged.

Also the fact that I have a crikikul METHOD ought to be rubbed into the blighted pubk/ and that yawp (started by Aldington; about Eliot beink the more seerious schorlar or crik or whatever, ought to be spiked.

fer the sake of everybodys future income.

Did I say that the eyetalyan pypers : vurry respekful to pore ole Masefield, yet did distinguish between the 'most representative Eng/ poet after Kipling" and one whose produk belonged to la letteratura mondiale.

If that dissociation of ideas cd. be rubbed into the american wound with a bit of cayenne pepper . . . .

Masefield "poeta maggiore dell'odierna Inghilterra, dottore onorario di lettere nella universita di Oxford nonché poeta laureato di Inghilterra.

Pound autore prolifico . . etc. .
opere che sono fra le piu eminenti della letteratura
mondiale. . . .

You as pubr/ and adv/ agent can do what you like with it. I have no idea who wrote it. Has praps no crit. val. but indicates diminishing resistence in some quarters.

How the chap found it out I don't know. But the sooner it can be kicked into the consciousness of Sawk Corners The american fartiversary system/ the female clubs/ the female editors/ the lousy bastards settin at the seat of the printin press/ the sooner WE EAT. meanin by "WE"; us, all the just. and a few over.

I've sent G[eorge]/O[ppen]/ some British press notice of How to Read. Herewith a copy of suggested announcement of Prolegomena as a series/ you can improve it if you see fit/ am sendin' carbon to G/O.

⟨all of which has produced enc. blurb which am sendig to Opp.⟩

PAGE IN LARGE BLACK TYPE.

> This second section of PROLEGOMENA is of a very different nature from the first. It should, to my mind appear only in the large folio volume of reference, intended for ⟨such⟩ students of literature as might from time to time wish to look up my personal reports on various sections of that subject. It is given here in pamphlet form because of the ⟨publisher's⟩ desire to make that material available without the delay of waiting for the projected folio.
>
> Any reviewer or critic wishing to do me a favour will confine his attention to "How to Read" and refrain from discussing the following section until the rest of the Prolegomena have appeared.

> Certain irregularities in typography are due to misunderstanding of mss/ indications intended for the folio publication. They are left to avoid delay and similar disparities will I hope be absent from ~~further installments~~ later sections.

In the somewhat delicate position of announcing the series of speeches by ⟨celebrated⟩ foreign authors for the Fiera del Libro, the Italian press referred to Masefield as the greatest poet of present day England, after Kipling, honorary doctor at Oxford, poet Laureate and so on. It referred to Mr Pound's works ⟨as⟩ "of the most eminent in world literature "piu eminente della letteratura mondiale", and this can be taken as perhaps tardy reward for a critic who for more than twenty years has laboured to establish just these distinctions between local and temporary criteria and criteria already adumbrated in his earliest prose volume; criteria which will weigh "Theocritus and Mr Yeats" in the same balance. ⟨internat—valid over long reach of time.⟩ In announcing the publication of

P R O L E G O M E N A

we are not for the moment concerned with Mr Pound's poetry but with emphasizing his work as critic and in demolishing whatever fable's exist in derogation thereto. Most people admit that he has introduced more important living writers than any other critic, we wish to emphasize not only his critical intution but the fact that he has established a critical system, a method. His work on Cavalcanti and Daniel shows this method working a[t] close range and should dispose once and for all those adversaries who have considered his criticism superficial and hasty merely because he has from the outset, insisted in considering world literature as a whole.

No one denies the effect of his example and manifestos on the reform ⟨or at any rate on change in the manner⟩ of American poetry, we emphasize not only this historic aspect of certain simple ideas, but the full program which implies a radical reform in education, and in the whole teaching of literatue. The author is doubtless most concerned with his own work, is in second degree concerned with the actual practice of writing but he has also given something that is of use to any and every reader, any and every student of literature and somehting which the teachers of literature will, in his own words, "either have to attend to or get out lock stock and barrel."

TO PUBLISHERS
announce for forthcoming publication the following installments of
PROLEGOMENA

(list as furnished)

and the following volumes

xxxxxxx by YYYYY
qqqq by ZZZ etc.

Sell um: Copies of *Guido Cavalcanti: Rime* and *A Draft of XXX Cantos* (Hours Press).
Firenze: Pound had read at the Fiera del Libro in Florence that month.
maggerzeen: Contact, second series.
last issue: The fifth (and final) number of the *New Review* contained Kay Boyle's "In Defense of Homosexuality." It was probably this that Pound most objected to.
Profile: Profile: An Anthology Collected in MCMXXXI (Milan: Giovanni Scheiwiller, 1932). Zukofsky was represented by "Poem Beginning 'The' " and "A" 3–5. Gallup B28.
Masefield: John Masefield, British Poet Laureate.
Sawk Corners: Sinclair Lewis was born in the small town of Sauk Centre, Minnesota. He had won the Nobel Prize in Literature in 1931.

49. ALS–4. Enclosure

July 7/32 P.O. Box 3, Station F, New York City

Dear E: Thanks for the distribution tips. Have written, or will write, when the time comes, i.e. when To's circulars bearing yr. blurb arrive in quantity. Have you seen it? Will also then write to yr. agent V. Rice.

Thanks for the copies of Profile. (Bill [Williams] seems to sense an idea behind it, or so he said. Wot he do 'baht "Contact," vie he no send coppee, I dunno, he send me nodink too). "Review of Profile will have to be writ by the included poets." Eez dat so? Woo— whooza dictator arahn heah? L.Z. The enclosed review written with me and a whip over To's offishul reviewer, the young, brilliant J[erry].R[eisman]., me Instigatin! (after Instigations) has been mailed to 'Arriet [Monroe]. I forget what in it I accidentally soothegested. Anyway, it's time I stopped as a seegnature to write critikuhly abaht ya, vut?? Fer verius reasuns, as I will make (un)clear below.

Glad you have seen To's work on Prolog. I. & it is good & that you have stood the shock of a chq/. —Have not ⟨yet⟩ the buk on dis side of the waters. Vil send refew copies to Hatfield etc as you request.

I can't ask Munson to admire me without reserf Yet—who asks him to admire me with reserve? If Basil [Bunting] had an article in The Bear Garden, please ask him to send it: you see, I'm so near The Sun it's blinding & if the Bear shd. sometime run out—Boo!!! Fer instance—I happened on that day etc—Rascoe is a DOPE: underline. Why you troubled to answer him at all, I can't see, or rather I won't, I suppose. Why I shd (I, fer instance) waste my time, when The Sun can print my essay on you—it still never having seen the world beyond my mental vagina in these U.S.A.—i.e. instead of lots of Bear Gardens?? Or why I shd, when I sent them a better review of W.C.W.'s Novelette than the one they printed (the review by J.R.) & they reply they accept no unsolicited reviews, & wd. probably do the same if I were pigheadedly insistent enough to send them the enclosure etc etc. (But I do think The Sun was amiable printing a review on Bill, printing you, etc). Certainly I have need of a "quiet corner" etc "anyone" wd. if he had to spend his time as I have for the last how many years, or more specifically since I have forgotten the last how many years, the last 27 days between a post office box and the Bronx, but if no one ever reprints The, I ain't goin' to hang outside the cages of Bear Gardens because the abstract mind & amber cigarette holder of Gorham B. [Munson] sees o sees so much the need of promoting controversy to air one's views. Even on second thought, I just don't like being the bear towed around. Do they, fer instance, pay? And if they do, why don't Munson ask, if his reserve approves of, me. Or why don't Grey—a gentleman as far as I could see in my two visits—if he wuz so satisfied with the review I did for him. Have there been no books out since? Nussir! Eef dhey vill be meek & 'omble like Canby enclosed, I vill write for 'em. Besides, let the sons of Abimelek eat & the righteous starve—who wants to eat in this heat—so they can write poetry, ask Reb Baruch, For, the resultant line is down (as says comrade soendso in San Francisco, dhey can try dis, dhey can dry that, but the resultant line is down.)

Yes, the reviews in Fifth Floor were indeed a surprise—even if they do from time to time pick up dead matter & recommend it to the taste. But how far wd. they get into The Sun? Besides, it's not enuf, the material they deal with, one shd. wipe the floor with it in a word & behold: Shit.

Really I'm "satisfied" and don't care. When, & if the time comes as in the preface to An "Obj." Anthol.—alright—& then if they don't read it after them the deluge.

I don't suppose, fer instance, you ever placed the ⟨H[ound] & H[orn]⟩ proofsheets of my Y.A. Winters' correspondence I long since sent you—if you still have 'em & can remember you might return 'em so I can keep the relic a longer while. Anyway, Hays' review in Fifth Floor takes care of some of the trouble.

Speaking of fer instance, I had much rather see yr. treatise on economics which Basil survived

Well, give my best to Serly when you see him, I hope he is calmer than I am now.

As ever

Z

Congratulations on Farrar & Reinhart's imbibing of knock-out drops, otherwise they wdn't have seen——the 9 copies of Hours Press Cantos still here; one more Cavalcanti sold, however, & you will get the $4 when I have check account again (or are you pressed?)—in that case I'll send a money order if you will permit me?

distribution tips: In a letter of 16 June 1932, Pound had named several people who might be willing to help spread the word about To Publications.

V. Rice: Virginia Rice, a literary agent who represented Pound in New York.

"Review of. . . .: Pound to Zukofsky, in a letter of 16 June 1932.

enclosed review: Enclosure lacking.

J[erry].R[eisman].: No reviews attributed to him appeared in *Poetry.*

Prolog. I: Prologomena I (Le Beausset (Var), France: To Publishers, [1932]). Gallup A33b.

Hatfield: W. Wilbur Hatfield, editor of *The English Journal.*

Munson: Pound to Zukofsky, 26 June 1932, "Munson would like you in the Bear Garden. . . ." The Bear Garden was a column in *The New York Sun* consisting of letters to the literary editor.

an article: "From Basil Bunting," *The New York Sun,* 28 May 1932, p. 16. Bunting commented on Sherry Mangan's review of Samuel Putnam's *The European Caravan* (New York: Brewer, Warren & Putnam, 1931).

Rascoe: Burton Rascoe, American literary critic. He had a weekly literary column in the *Sun,* "A Bookman's Daybook." There had recently been an exchange between Pound and Rascoe. It began when Rascoe asserted that he had been an early supporter of Hemingway ("A Bookman's Daybook,"

16 April 1932). Pound charged that Rascoe lied ("Pound to Rascoe," *The New York Sun,* 11 June 1932). Rascoe repeated his claim in "Rascoe's Riposte," *The New York Sun,* 11 June 1932.

one they printed: "Incoherent Zigzags," by Clayton Hoagland, *The New York Sun,* 14 May 1932, p. 8. Hoagland found in *A Novelette and Other Prose* "nothing beautiful, nothing that compels one to like it."

the enclosure: Probably Pound's promotion of Prologomena enclosed in his letter of May 1932.

Grey: J. C. Grey, literary editor of *The New York Sun.*

Canby enclosed: Henry Seidel Canby's letter informing Zukofsky that his review of Wyndham Lewis's *The Doom of Youth* for *The Saturday Review of Literature* would soon be published.

Reb Baruch: Possibly Baruch Spinoza or Zukofsky himself.

Fifth Floor: Fifth Floor Window 1:4 (May 1932) contains two noteworthy essays "I. A. Richards' Theory of Poetry," by H. B. Parkes, and "Classicist and Regionalist" (Yvor Winters and Allen Tate), by H. R. Hays. Parkes comments, "His critical theory, if applied correctly (as Richards himself does not apply it–his practice is better than his theory), can only have the most harmful effect on appreciation." Hays says of Winters, "Formerly an excellent imagist poet, in the last years he has been making the gesture of a return to traditional meters with disastrous results." Going on to Tate, Hays writes, "Now this is precisely the kind of blurring of language . . . which began in the eighteenth century and rotted the substance of poetry during the nineteenth until the revolt of the imagists temporarily checked its ravages. The scattered critical writings of Ezra Pound (not yet properly appreciated) are calculated to exterminate it."

proofsheets: See Pound's letter of 22 November 1931.

treatise: Pound to Zukofsky, 16 June 1932, "In iritation at idiots I started a treatise on economics last week. Basil has survived 30 pages (all I had done at the time)." This may have been the beginning of his *ABC of Economics.*

Farrar & Reinhart's: Farrar & Rinehart published the first American edition of *A Draft of XXX Cantos* 15 March 1933. Gallup A31.

50. ALS–3.

Aug 8/32 P.O. Box 3, Station F New York City

Dear E: Latest news from O[ppen]—"Can't continue To." Which means my salary goes as well when the year is up—& will probably be reduced to $50 (if George can spare that much) a month, while it lasts. "The year is up"—may be this Sept. 1932—I'm not sure when my year started, since Buddy and I made no formal legal arrangements.

Hell, all around . . . Sorry about George. Business of my being out on The Street again enuf to drive anyone to an asylum.

And as to your contract re- Proleg[omena]. I'm willing to cooperate, sell, continue working for To at $50 or whatever, if Buddy can make any arrangements to suit you. I can say no more.

Nacherly, I suppose O. will let you use H[ow]T[o]R[ead] etc with other pubs. as you think fit. Tsup to him.

Enclose list of Errata of "Obj[ectivists Anthology]"—in case you will do the review for Contempo. No laurels yet—& if not for Buddy's kindness, I wdn't have my contributors fee of $3.00 at that.

I meant re- Y. Winters in my last that when the most influential H[ound] & H[orn] sets up his vileness as a criterion in this land every quarter yr.—there ain't no chance for decent publishing. I recommend you read the last H & H, for you to see what shit he considers good.—I think you had better send the returned Spanish enclosed to him with a U.S. paraphrase.

Re- the auctour of the two reviews sent you—J[erry]. R[eisman]. He does exist—& will more & more from now on & in times to come if Papa Zhukovskiyii has the patience to keep on prodding a young lazy lout into distinction.—As ever

Z—

list of Errata: Enclosure lacking.

Y. Winters: In a letter of 12 July 1932, Zukofsky lamented, "No use my giving either my poems or criticism to anyone in the U.S.A.," and went on to cite the publication of Yvor Winters' review in the July issue of *Hound and Horn* as evidence that good poetry and criticism would never receive a hearing. See Winters' "Poets and Others," *Hound & Horn* 5:4 (July–September 1932), pp. 675–686. The poets Winters found "good" were: Allen Tate, Wilfred Owen, Alan Porter, Kathleen Tankersley Young, Grant Hyde Code, Howard Baker and J. V. Cunningham.

Spanish enclosed: Enclosure lacking.

51. TLS–2. The first page of this letter is on *Il Mare* letterhead.

16 Aug. [1932] [Rapallo]

pussnl addres az
uzhul
v. Marsala 12

⟨Dear Z⟩

I have said a FEW words to Contempo. Until I finish me new opera, and do 10 italian lectures and a few cantos, I can ⟨not⟩ be the rising american generation (unpaid)

Thanks for copy of Resiman. I spose he can quote my FEW words re/ Objectivists and add some in Leipert.

Will use inf/ with postal auth/ to get the Sup[plemento]. Let[terario] to you. If youv'e any local wops they better contribute or translate their betters.
Serly will report in pussn.
You don't owe me 3. bucks re/ anth. An' Op[pen]/ is sposed to be broke.
Dare say Basil [Bunting] cd. use a few papers of fags. WHEN. . . . but he certainly isn't pressing claim.
We think the heraldry beats Gill's gelding. Sorry the hartist cdnt. rise to doin you a hoss. but thet animal dont interest her.
Have had three days vac/ but otherwise been on job. since midle of last Oct. //
Serly apparently got ticket to yourup and back for 112 dollars.
Have you anything to live on for, say three months, IF you by chance get here??????????

I am sending the enc. on chance. It is in no circs. to be used for anything save transportation (tourist class) to and from Europe
It is ALL I can do and there is NO means of supporting you here; thou' you can live damn well on 50 dollars a month and exist on considerably less. If you can raise 200 bucks you cd. do a three months, mostly here but with a look at Paris.

If not please tear up cheq and return the pieces.

You may if you like "regard it as a loan" to be repaid when AND NOT BEFORE your inkum excedes mine by similar sum.

⟨[minimum 7 years: but no hurry.]⟩

ANYhow it wd. save me writin letters for a few weeks.

yrs E.P.

(an dont mention IT to anyone save Serly.)

EP

opera: Cavalcanti.
Leipert: James George Leippert edited *The Lion & Crown,* a Columbia University literary magazine. The first issue appeared in the fall of 1932 with an accompanying note: "The editors of The Lion & Crown wish to thank Mr. Louis Zukofsky for his interest, and to dedicate to him whatever of the publication is theirs to dedicate." Pound apparently thought that *The Lion & Crown* would regularly publish Zukofsky and his literary friends.
Sup[*plemento*]. *Let*[*terario*]*:* Pound's series in *Il Mare.* Gallup C780.
heraldry: Possibly a drawing by Dorothy Shakespear Pound.
Gill's: Probably Eric Gill, the British artist.
a hoss: Zukofsky often used equine imagery in his poetry.
the enc.: Pound's check for $112, payable to Zukofsky.

52. TLS–2.

[8 November 1932] Rapallo

8 Nov.
and to hell wiff
Hoover.

Wunnerz, me deah ZEdKovski will nuvver nuvver cease/
Where the HELL did you got 43 dollars in the present skate of America passes me minds komprehenshun.

If the Universita Commerciale ain't gone on strike I MAY have yr/boat fare in June.
[Ford Madox] Ford also tryin to sell some stuff for his only begotten offspring.

I shan't do anything re/ the Cav[alcanti]/ until Farrer brings out the Cantos.

I am amused at the fury of Tate sans Tète. Our anthologies do seem to annoy, which is the best possible sign. Nothing the 1920 group produced ever irritated, it merely wearied.

What's Parson Possum doin' at Hawvud?
How wide is the spread of the spreadin' comment?
all for Jheezus?
pale crucifixions asphixiated on the wanderin' cosmos?? or wottell??
Let us renounce.

If only some kind chap wd. take him out lobster fishin or on a Cod schooner.
And if only someone wd. kill off the Criterion crab lice. . . . . . however. . . .

any inkin of wot he is tellin the young?

Something ought to be done WITH that
"jewels bric a brac flowers" on
the last page of Arriet[Monroe]'s advertisin'.

aint life jus' wonderful!!!!!! an Herbie's variant on the "good five cent cigar".

E

8 Nov.: Election Day in the United States.

Universita Commerciale: The Università Commerciale Luigi Bocconi in Milan, where Pound lectured on economics in March 1933. See Gallup A34, note.

Tate: See "Laundry Bills," *Poetry* 41:2 (October 1932), pp. 107–112. Tate reviews *How to Read* and *Profile*. Of the latter he remarks, "It moves one to ask, what kind of arrogance misled Pound into thinking that he is entitled to throw together some odds and ends of good verse and trash and call the lot an anthology?"

Parson Possum: T.S. Eliot, Charles Eliot Norton Professor of Poetry at Harvard for the 1932–1933 academic year.

Herbie's variant: See "What the President Reads," by Christopher Morley, *The*

Saturday Review of Literature 9:10 (24 September 1932). Morley quotes Herbert Hoover as saying, "Perhaps what this country needs is a great poem. Something to lift people out of fear and selfishness. Exery once in a while someone catches words out of the air and gives a nation an inspiration. You remember Kipling's 'Recessional,' and that poem of Markham's suggested by Millet's painting, 'The Man with the Hoe.' We need something to raise our eyes beyond the immediate horizon."

53. TLS–1.

6 Dec. [1932] Rapallo

Delectus mihi filius ⟨1⟩

Have just done a few brief notes on René's "4 Essais" / dont know where to print it.

⟨══════════⟩ ⟨2⟩

Appolinaire just come and have read six pages.

I don't know if it is YOU or René/ BUT in anny kase you MUST now at once start on study of technique of FLOW.

As I may have said⟨:⟩ I started after Tacitus and did learn a bit about concentration/ BUT AFTER that you have ⟨one has⟩ to go out for the NEXT step/ which is clarity/

o⟨n⟩e word must also slide into next and to next and to next (not cradling and hypnotizing; but conducing . . . . .

light secondary writers sometimes achieve it/ but it is not therefore despicable.

NEITHER is this desirable order of words the FIRST order that occurs effortlessly to the brainy writer.

(full liberty to quote this note is hereby granted.)

yrs E.P.

notes: Not recorded by Gallup.

"4 Essais": René Taupin, *4 essais indifférents pour une esthétique de l'inspiration* (Paris: Les Presses Universitaires de France, 1932).

Apollinaire: In response to Pound's advice, Zukofsky wrote in the upper right corner of the page, "See Thanks to the Dictionary for reply." Composed in 1932, "Thanks to the Dictionary" was published as one of the stories in *It Was* ([Kyoto, Japan]: Origin Press, 1961).

54. ALS–7.

12/15/32 39 Sidney Place Brooklyn, N.Y.

Our Favver Who Art on Earth, Thank Gorde!
In re
"(full liberty to quote this note is hereby granted.)
the NEXT step / which is clarity
one word must also slide into next and to next
and to next (not cradling and hypnotizing; but conducing . . . . ."
clarity, in my handy dictionary, has two lines
after it, so: ||. Which means archaic. Exactly:
"gradually advance to the end with a becoming prolixity. . . ."
(The Writing of Guillaume Apollinaire, p 110 of yr. MS., in English by L.Z. & R[ené].T[aupin]., in French by R.T. & L.Z., the greatest critical work in any language since De Vulgari Eloquentia, and written in no less than three tongues, Appollinairise, New Yorkese, pidgin-yddisch, i.e. französich-french)

No, it's not René, as you will see when you see his adaptation entirely in French (remarkable what a difference), but it's L.Z. alright painstakingly obstructing the technique of FLOW.

I hope—still hope, however, that you will give your 'bit for concentration' and that you have by now read the six pages after the first six, and will maybe read the first chapter, and the second, and the third!

In any case, your criticism has made clear once and for all my fear of gliding—the possibility of being left with air forever and continued cradling.

If you have done a few brief notes on René's "4 Essais" and don't know where to print it, judging from appearances, the only likely vehicles would be "Criterion" or "Symposium"? I don't myself see the use of asking Possum [Eliot] to let me review René's book in "Criterion"—not till he answers my previous letters. Besides, yr. review wd. have more influence, even act as a springboard for the Apollinaire, when you have seen fit to go thru the volume?

Please let me know what you will do about this. It doesn't matter if I do a review later. Really too busy to do reviews to-day, without being urged by some mag. that wd. pay and wd. really show signs of wanting to command one, as the noble phrase goes.

As for trans. 4 Essais, again I'm not anxious. I'm not anxious. I'm not fast about these things, and it wd. take me hours to translate a phrase like "des formes" or "ces formes" (the opening page of 4 Essais) to satisfy my conscience and to feel that I'm doing more than justice by René. Besides, translating a work of that length makes one lonesome; if the frog were here to type my dictation I could possibly do it. But he is lost in Haverford all week, and when he comes to N.Y. week-ends he is righteously sunk in a speak-easy.—I understand you would like to see me make some money on it. But who's ready to dispense it?

I think I have said—no more criticism for Zuky unless he gets paid for it—preferably in advance. The Apollinaire paid well, but R[ené] could have used that money—paid very well, considering what I turned in was a post mortem of my Hen Adams, the first Joyce in French (vide chap II) and three chapters altogether doing their best to approximate in weirdest langvidge Debussy's Quartet in G Minor. You're right: no one will read it (except maybe in French). But poisonally, I see no use of any other way of writing criticism, except yr. own or a variation of it i.e. along the lines of clarity which is conscious of concentration.

——

——

I have, however, started at once, at yr. advice on a study of technique of Flow—vide the (prose) enclosure which has been added to Thanks to the Dictionary. I'm afraid tho' very few of the other pages "flow". (If this does . . .). These pages give no idea at all of what the work in progress is like . . .

——

——

I enclose also ~~3~~ ⟨4⟩ poems, the long one probably flows, but I'll let you decide

——

——

I'm sorry that to date your answer to my scheme for a writer's union is only "As fer sassieties vurry complicated." When I see the mess around me, I think that scheme would be the only salvation. Costs to begin would be only nominal: about two dollars or less for mimeographing one side of a sheet of prospectus and simple declaration. Mebbe Serly and I will start one—but we'll wait some time, perhaps till your pressure of work lets up for a spell.

——

——

continued Dec 19/32

All of which—the above ⟨five pages⟩—seemed pretty stupid to me and not worth sending till the frog (René) dropped in by surprise this morning & gave me a new lease of assurance. So I'm sending it. Also some very gross ART, which will probably be enclosed with this letter if René sends 'em back in time (otherwise next year—if)—i.e. before I despair of my very unusual talents in this distinct realm of—I leaf it to yuh. The drawings to the verses from Guido [Cavalcanti] & the Swedenborg quotation were done during a re-reading of yours on Epstein, meaning, Anti-Belching etc; the Monsieur Robinçon occurred gratuitously at the same time—I don't remember exactly why I recalled Bill [Williams]'s brother's joke, during the reading, and your, I understand from Bill, Coda to the Jape of which my drawing is ⟨so⟩ edifying an interpretation. The imaginary portrait of yourself was done at another and baser moment. . .

Would you mind sending these drawings and poems to George Oppen
c/o Thos. Cook & Sons
2 Place de la Madeleine
Paris
and save me the time and trouble? You might just say I wanted him ⟨& lady⟩ to see them & then ask him to return 'em to you—if you like 'em that much & wan't [*sic*] to keep 'em—(!)—or ask him to return 'em to me promptly, registered, no less. Two lines, eh—& they might cheer George? Thanks. And I promise not to bother you again.

R'cd a copy of The Secret International the other day for which I imagine you're responsible ⟨for⟩—at least for the free sending—Much thanks again.

——

——

The newspaper clippings: the one relating to the debt payment—if the resolution of our Senate is acted on, I see where I don't go to France.

The [Samuel] Putnam—what kindness have you shown to the fk. now? Someone ought to write a letter to the Bear Garden, telling him or them that if Mr. Putty returned $11 (eleven) dollars or so he made off with on his last & recent departure from the U.S.A. that at least one member of yr. pore fambly could pay his January rent, or half-pay it. Too timid to point me index at me own bare arse in the newspapers yet.

As ever and evurr

Z

De Vulgari Eloquentia: An essay by Dante on language and metrics.
asking Possum: Pound to Zukofsky, 28 November 1932, "Make Possum let you review it in Criterion."
(prose) enclosure: Enclosure lacking.
4 poems: Enclosures lacking. Pound's reply of 8 January 1933, however, indicates that one of them was poem 22 of *29 Songs,* "To my wash-stand." *All,* pp. 59–60.
your answer: From a Pound letter that has not survived.
ART: Enclosure lacking.
Epstein: "Epstein, Belgion, and Meaning," *The Criterion* 9:36 (April 1930), pp. 470–475. Gallup C766.
International: The Secret International (London: Union of Democratic Control, 1932). The intentions of this 48-page booklet are declared in its preface: "This pamphlet is an attempt to collect the available information and to state as clearly as possible the present case for the public control of the whole armament industry. . . . The conclusion seems to prove beyond all doubt that the abolition of the private manufacture of arms is a necessary element in any genuine work for international peace." In the course of its indictment of armament manufacturers, the booklet makes much of Sir Basil Zaharoff's connection with Vickers, Ltd.

55. TLS–1. On *Il Mare* letterhead.

8. Jan. [1933] [Rapallo]

Dear Z/

There are some things a writer like E.P. ought NOT to be bothered about.

//

Le personnel manque// fer yr/ proposed organization. You ought to read C.H.Douglas.

//

Apolinnaire not interesting <u>enough</u> to STAND or carry all that discussion.

/
Washbasin poem, the best of the lot.
//
You organized Oppen. That was O.K., but destiny etc. . . . no use tryin to org/ me, Basil [Bunting] and Tibor [Serly]. we have already reached the utmost point.

If you can affect the OUTER world, and scattered units that ARENT being useful, O.K. thasss jake.

yrs E

Crit/ invalid when it tries to focus MORE attention on a subject than the subject merits// vide T.S.E[liot]. on that ⟨bloody or rather bloodless⟩ ashbin J. Dryden.

proposed organization: Writers Extant. This was a writers' syndicate proposed by Zukofsky. He believed they could finance their own publication. The group was to include himself (as director), Tibor Serly, René Taupin, Charles Reznikoff, and William Carlos Williams. The name of the syndicate was soon changed to The Objectivist Press.

Washbasin: Poem 22 of *29 Songs:* "To my wash-stand." *All,* pp. 59–60.

J. Dryden: A reference to Eliot's essay, "John Dryden" (1922), which concludes, "In the next revolution of taste it is possible that poets may turn to the study of Dryden. He remains one of those who have set standards for English verse which it is desperate to ignore."

56. TLS–1. The portion of the letter from "I have . . ." to ". . . send me" is a carbon copy. Pound evidently sent this message to several correspondents.

23 Feb. [1933] Rapallo

Dear Z

I have this a/m/ recd/ from a London pubr/ what I take to be a serious proposition re/ a sort of anthology, or vol. containing poems by a group of poets; say from 7 to a dozen. with a small advance, which along with the royalties, I shd. divide between the authors. according to justice or their immediate needs. Cant be bothered to distribute in sums of less than 5 bucks, unless particular author shd. insist on immediate accounting of the 7th. dividend, etc. Complaints to be addressed to this address. Prefarably matter not published in BOOKS, though anything that hasn't been pubd. in England could be used if necessary, or if much better than material that had been in a book.

Please send me

I take it this is a chance to print all of THE and all of A. that is ready/

also send suggestions/ re other of yrs/ the chewing gum poem, and items of interest.
//
also has Rakoski anything new/ or have you any snug gestions.

Oppen meritus causa?? couple of short poems??
lemme know if there are?

Basil [Bunting] seems to think Reznikoff is some good??? any piece d'evidence?

Can you help ole Bill Walruss [Williams] to sort hiz self out.

Anything not pubd/ in England is available. avoiding what is in Profile.

E

London pubr: Faber and Faber. *Active Anthology* was published in October 1933. Gallup B32.

gum poem: Probably "A"-6, which refers to a famous brand of chewing gum: "Outwriggling the wriggly Wrigley boys" ("A"-6, p. 21). Zukofsky was represented in *Active Anthology* by "Poem Beginning 'The' " and "A" 5-7. Others represented included Williams, Bunting, and Oppen. Rakosi and Reznikoff did not appear.

57. TLS–2.

[April 1933] Rapallo

Dear Zuk

The Bill W[illia]ms/ is damn good. Shall prob. omit Footnote/ Ball Game / and Portrait of Lady (the latter simply because the subject is less interestin' than a lot of Bill's other work.) I want another 15 Pages of him.

Your best stuuf is "The" and parts of A.

The Reznikoff will appear to the Brit. reader a mere immitation of me, and they will howl that I am merely printin my followers.
It is I think just as good as parts of Lustra (1915, 1916) neither better nor worse. Very cleanly done but no advance in methodology. ⟨(in most of it.)⟩

Possibly by pickin' out the Hebe element we can get something that will arouse interest. Remember an anth. like this has got to AROUSE interest without AT ANY POINT terminating ANY of the interest it arouses.

Its the sample of next weeks film, not the giving away of the end of the story.

The title of the Anth. is "The Active Element". If I omit H.D. how am I to put in most of the Reznikoff you have sent.

my thesis bein that the ART of writing is (is still now continuously developing.

So far Rakosi weak. Rexroth and the rest unsatisfactory.

Young Oppen has sent in stuff/ think three of 'em good enough to include.

Can jewish gentlemen meet sodomitical gentlemen in New York without the irritations of interactive prejudice, or do ONLY jewish sodolitical gentlemen meet sodimitical gentlemen of other reeligious persuasions???

If unable to make a general an objective statement of local custums, you are at lib. to send personal, if an[y], view.

Alien to this queery

Can you and [Sherry] Mangan get Leippert through his critical ⟨special⟩ number?

I have sent him ⟨Leippert⟩ my pencil script for reprod. I take it he is doin booklets by Bill, Marianne [Moore], You and Basil, to the intended muchool profit of all of you.

⟨Basil goin to Spain⟩

E

Bill Wms/: Williams poems submitted by Zukofsky for *Active Anthology.*
Footnote: "A Foot-Note," *Poetry* 43:1 (October 1933), p. 8.
Ball Game "At the Ball Game," in *The Collected Earlier Poems* (New York: New Directions, 1951), pp. 284–285.
Portrait: "Portrait of a Lady," in *The Collected Earlier Poems* (New York: New Directions, 1951), p. 40.
Reznikoff: Unidentified. Probably selections from the poems included in *Jerusalem the Golden* (New York: The Objectivist Press, 1934).
Oppen: The Oppen poems in *Active Anthology* were: "The evening, water in a glass," "No interval of manner," "Closed car–closed in glass–," "Who comes is occupied," and "Brain." All but the last were included in Oppen's *Collected Poems* (New York: New Directions, 1975), pp. 4, 6, 7, and 12.
Leippert: See Pound's letter of 16 August 1932. Pound was under the impression that Leippert had committed himself to publishing the work of Zukofsky and his associates, but such was not the case.
Spain: A brief glimpse of Bunting in Spain is provided by his "The Village Fiesta," *Paideuma* 10:3 (Winter 1981), pp. 619–621.

58. ALS–15.

Apr. 15/33 39 Sidney Pl Brooklyn, N.Y.

Dear E: Wanted (beggin' yr. pardon in advance) a man who can read 8 simple corrections of a MS., when they're sent to him, without my having to write 'em out again, & without his having to spend three fees for postage to say he has and he hasn't and finally he has, but he hasn't, printed copy of same MS.

Wanted, in addtn, same man in Rapallo (at least on rare occasions—postage rates in this country being extra-exorbitant).

Anyhowl, enclosed is "The" for the printer. If you really have the copy of Exile containing "The"—I wish you would return the enclosed typescript which has cost moneys & which I may need in the distant future for some distant publisher.

If you have Exile containing "The" make the following corrections & send it to the printer, for which cruel task, my heartiest, if boldest, thanks.

[corrections omitted]

Sorry but my copy of Exile, if it is, is in storage.

Since you wrote Bill [Williams] to send 25 pages more himself, before you wrote me that you want another 15 pages of him, I suppose he has send 25 pages more.

Glad you liked what he sent. But it's all in "Obj[ectivists]." Anth[ology]. (which Eng. hasn't read?) & very little of it not in Spring & All (1923). Don't know that there wd. be any objection to that in England.

Have sent him a card reminding him to send more stuff if he hasn't. If he hasn't when you get this, you're welcome to whatever else of him is in "Obj." Anth. which was not included in the first batch he sent.

Wd. be elated to see things other than The & A, of me, in yr. Anth. But it's yr. Anth. & yr. opiniyum. May write out another poem for you at the end of this letter.

Agree with you as to the Reznikoff. However, up to you to make a choice of what's in it that will arouse interest–and there's at least 5 pages of that.

I am sorry no one seems to like Rexroth. I think you're underrating Organon which I sent you—anyway, I think everybody is failing to see

Rexroth's merits. When he's very good, his work has more energy than almost anybody's in these U.S.A & sometimes I'm inclined to leave out the almost

---

Glad you've accepted Oppen

Yr. question as to Jewish gentlemen & sodomitical too vague to make me feel sure of my answer. However, will attempt it: (This is not a personal view, since you can consider me out of the picture for which I have only a "to-hell-with-it")

1. Jewish gentlemen meet sodomitical gentlemen in N.Y. without the irritations of interactive prejudice when the sodomitical gentlemen fall for Jewish gentlemen who are sodomitical, which happens I believe only in literary cases.

2. If sodomitical gentlemen are financiers, their sodomy confined to the female (vide Dali) the above proposition as to ⟨lack of⟩ interactive prejudice is not true. ⟨i.e. L.Z. <u>cannot</u> teach in Columbia Univ. and L.Z. takes it for granted.⟩

3. Granted I know what you mean by sodolitical gentlemen (members of sodalities perhaps ???), <u>some</u> Jewish "sodolitical" gentlemen meet sodomitical gentlemen (of class described under 2, there wd. be no point for them to meet class described under 1,) for their common connivance; i.e. Jewish rabbis meet Catholic priests to save their mutual skins against "religious atrocities" (aside: also, Gov. Lehman meets Al Smith). Also, members of Jewish brotherhoods as bad as members of brotherhoods of other persuasions.

Lieppert can go squirt up a rope. He hasn't answered my letters, so I know nothing of his spec. critical number, & won't bother about it till I hear from him. If Mangan bothers, that's his & yr. affair.

Heard something about Leippert's script no. thru Reznikoff—but that's all. As far as I know L—— is not doin booklet by me for "our" mutual profit. He's never said anything to me about it. If he's doin' Bill, Marianne [Moore] & Basil [Bunting], <u>well</u> & good.

Will get you Roosevelt's books or book as soon as I can get to the bookstores i.e. after yr. check is cashed. Don't know what on earth you want to spend money for it for!

Peepul in Urope must think of F.R. as The Saviour.

Don't see that his reforestration project will make it possible for so many thousands of young Americans to support their families, to buy 2.5 (or less) beer, to pay for whoring, (let alone for an occasional book or mag) all on thirty dollars a month. Besides please note that the whole business is now run by the War Dep't.

As for 30 hr. week, bein' confined to industries trading in interstate commerce, I wonder what its effectiveness can be for the milliyons of office workers etc. Also you may be sure the seasonal industries will try to get out of it & get out of it—I mean the bosses of dressmakers, cloak operators etc ⟨Gettin' the 30 hr. week in America will be like gettin "3.2" 'BEER'—i.e. payin for having something you had before, but paying for it now because the gov't says it's not as bad.⟩

May I ask a question re- yr. criticism of du Von in current Symposium—does the Italian Fascist allow absolutely for the clarity and vigour of "any and every" thought and opinion? What does he suppress, if he does?

Can one say that Mussolini in his conference with Ramsay [MacDonald] really intended to prevent war? (That's another question) Also, I wish I knew what you mean by: "the Russ. Rev. is the end of the Marxist cycle." (symposium)

I am not here writing as a member of the U.S. Communist Party—I am sure that as far as they're concerned papa & childt & Unk Bill Walrus [Williams] are in same galley.

The N.Y. rabbi adores The Choimun peepul, because he's a bastard, like every Jew who made the current pogrom in Choimunny a matter of Judaism.

Wd. as I said appreciate a copy of yr. book on economics—I don't see why it wd. be better if written last week instead of last summer—the time element hasn't counted for much—recently—

I understand the report of the Hoover Econ. Conference wd. be very enlightening to you—at least between the lines & as to what they unintentionally said. ⟨Haven't read it.⟩ "Other" news re econ/progress will follow if I see any.

Has Basil gone to Spain for good? & does that mean the next war?

Yrs

Z

Pome for yr. Anth. follows.

typescript: Enclosure lacking.

Organon: A poem. See Rexroth's *The Collected Shorter Poems* (New York: New Directions, 1966), pp. 113–117.

Dali: Salvador Dali, Surrealist painter.

Lehman: Herbert Henry Lehman, governor of New York 1933–1942.

Al Smith: Alfred Emanuel Smith, governor of New York 1925–1929.

Roosevelt's books: Pound to Zukofsky, 5 April 1933, "Please git me Franki Roosenvelt's book or booklets on economics."

criticism: Pound's review of C. H. Douglas's *The New and Old Economics, The Secret International,* and *Mercanti di Cannoni. Symposium* 4:2 (April 1933), pp. 252–256. Gallup C933.

du Von: Jay du Von. Pound mentions him in the review: "M. du Von can't abstain from expressing uncorrelated ignorance about fascism." Pound refers to du Von's comments, "L'Affair Aragon," in *Contempo* 3:5 (1 February 1933), pp. 1–2.

Ramsay: Ramsay MacDonald, British Prime Minister. MacDonald went to Rome in late March 1933, and conferred with Mussolini on prospects for disarmament.

N.Y. Rabbi: Pound to Zukofsky, 5 April 1933, "Why does the N.Y. Rabbi profess to adore and respect the Choimun people." On 27 March 1933, a mass meeting was held in New York to protest the recent persecution of Jews in Germany. At the meeting, Rabbi Samuel Wise said, "This protest of tonight is not against the German people, whom we honor and revere and cherish. How could we, of the household of Israel, fail to cherish and honor the German people, and of the great peoples of the earth, a people that has made monumental, indeed eternal, contributions to human well-being in the domains of religion, literature and the arts."

Conference: Probably the conference on economic problems held in London in January 1933.

59. ALS–3.

June 15/33 39 Sidney Pl Brooklyn N.Y.

Dear E: Such insistence! It's unhear-r-r-d— ov!

However, I've been convinced. Going on the Majestic on June 30 & shd be in Cherbourg July 6th & in Paris the same day or the next.

Will answer all your unanswered letters, postcards etc then, or if you're away, at Rapallo where I expect to be about the 1st of August and after & into the first week in September.

If you haven't sent your $112 by now, please keep it till I come over.

Short of passage money etc now, & there may be some trouble with passport (tho' the N.Y. officials say Washington will probably grant it in 3 or 4 days)—but I think I shd be all straightened out by June 30.

Will bring yr. copy of Mercanti di Cannoni with me

The Oppens send their best regards.

Yrs

Z

Am spending next week (the next to last before sailing) with the Oppens, up state where I have never been, my diplomatic functions being over, young George August [Oppen] having been introduced to the landmarks, sights etc nearby: Reznikoff, Bill [Williams] etc etc

insistence: In a letter of 8 June 1933, Pound had announced that he and Tibor Serly had decided that Zukofsky should tour Europe that summer.

Mercanti di Cannoni: I have not been able to locate a copy of this book. Its scope, however, can be determined from Pound's review of it in *The Symposium:* "At this point we must thank a correspondent of the *Stampa di Torino* who signs with three stars. The U[nion]. [of] D[emocratic]. C[ontrol]. regards munitions sales as a cause, almost as a primal cause and refuses to look any further. The *Stampa* correspondent, whose essays have just been reprinted by Corbaccio (Milan, *Mercanti di Cannoni*), definitely knows and indicates that it pays the founders better to make guns than to make locomotives. His data are in the very words used by members of the Comté des Forges in their company board meetings." *The Symposium* 4:2 (April 1933), p. 254. Gallup C933.

60. ALS–6. On stationery of the Hôtel du Périgord, Paris.

July 12 [1933]

Dear E: Room 36 very nice, thanks. Tho' it reminds ⟨me⟩ of the room I had in Madison, as does the layout & architecture of Paris remind me of the aforementioned.

Will write to as many of the people you send addresses of (and will see as many as want to see me—but I hope Exclusively for my health)—Tho I can't see what earthly good it will do anybody for me to see Brancusi & Leger.

I presume one has to be in a trance to be allowed to see the Surrealistes. However, I'll try, without getting into a trance.

Taupin did not see Supervielle & is not in Paris now & will probably not be in Paris till about Sept 1. So that's that.

No use I suppose telling you before I see you that I did not come to write about the French (already dealt with in L.Z. on G[uillaume]. A[pollinaire].), but to see you & discuss what can be done for 'Murka. The important job is there (however, if the French join ⟨us⟩ as such-&-such identifying a generation, a state of mind, an accomplishment, & I think the U.S.A. can speak of that at least thru the "names" of a few people, all the better).

Also, I am going back either Aug 31 or the first or second week in Sept, depending on how persuasive & dictatorial you ken be. I mean I had rather spend the time with you in Rapallo (if it doesn't interfere with your work) than in Paris. Absolutely necessary for me to know now how long you want me to stay in Rapallo & when you want me to come: for two reasons 1.) if anything will be done for the U.S.A. you & I will maybe help towards getting it done in Rapallo—I don't think "Contact" in Paris will do it—in any case not the contact you suggest. 2) I have very little money, less than 400 francs at this time & the hotel bill here will amount to 330.

(I don't want to press yuse—but I'll need yr. $112 in about a week in available funds—i.e. a check won't do any good, but some draft made out via Thos. Cook's to be collected in Paris & preferably in Francs i.e. the lire shd. be yr. basis of exchange not the dollar—or you can send half in francs or half in lire if you want to).

As I suggested before I left the U.S.A. this is no year for vacations. Paris is now (except for lodging) about twice as expensive as N.Y.

I don't mean to discourage you as far as L.Z. is concarned, but we might as well get the worst over with.

I dunno wot else—

Who is Mrs Hirsch. Why shd. I call on her? Any relation to Baron Hirsch?

As for your "young lady" . . . (three dots)—I'll see her, as you wish, & if she wants to come to the U.S.A. (if she qualifies) we can discuss "a salon" as far ahead as you want to or as she wants to. I mean, in this case at least it's not a question of continuing a certain tradition. But if she's a nice young lady I'd enjoy speaking to her, nacherally. Whether she & I wd. make a salon, however, I can't promise father.

As ever

Z

Madison: Madison, Wisconsin.

Leger: Fernand Léger, French painter. In a letter of 10 July 1933, Pound urged Zukofsky to meet Léger, Constantin Brancusi, Jules Supervielle, Natalie Barney, Guy Hickok, Hilaire Hiler, Caresse Crosby, Pierre de Massot, Jean Cocteau, Louis Aragon, André Breton, Salvador Dali, Max Ernst, and Mrs. Gilbert Hirsch.

Supervielle: Jules Supervielle. French poet, novelist, and dramatist.

Mrs. Hirsch: Charlotte Teller Hirsch, a novelist and free-lance writer who had first made Pound's acquaintance in London before World War I.

Baron Hirsch: Baron Maurice de Hirsch (1831–1896), German financier, capitalist, and philanthropist. He donated millions of dollars to Jewish groups and causes around the world.

"young lady": Pound to Zukofsky, 10 July 1933, "There is also a young lady . . . I dunno how much patience you have . . . or how serious yr/ intentions re/ a possible life in Europe or how far ahead you are capable of looking. . . .

have you the patience to construct vicariously a salon. . . ." Pound did not reveal her identity.

60. ALS–2. On stationery of Hotel Cannon D'oro, Siena.

[July 1933]

Purr suing further == an inspection of Paris does not necessitate adultation == but an examination is needed for more reasons than I can go into.

also for leverage, you shd do series. Also you shd. NOT find yrself at Bill W[illia]ms age az waz, with miscalculations re/ france. == register what they lack. (that's OK.

== If Taup[in] didn't see Supervielle you'd better. // Understand that the only way I got thru alive was playing London imbecility against U.S. imbecility. Your general education requires you to look at certain diverse objects. whether you refuse to see 'em or not is yr/ personal affair. Better "presume" not at all—it damages the faculty of observation. == at any rate try to find out what you & de Massot do not see alike // of course a persistent & cultivated refusal of experience is bound to leave (ultimately) traces on a guy's style.

I had xpected you in Rap[allo]. from 10 Aug till end of Sept. == hoping the first part of Aug. or more cd. occur in Venice — but material reezuns. == you can't see all Paris in 10 days. == even in the mess of the Louvre. There are a few toiles //

If it still takes me a month to see Paris, I don't see how you can do it in much less

The insufficiency of Paris — is one reason for etc. but until that is clearly stated & proved in detail a refusal to state it is sabotage or at least cunctatorial.

etc. E

61. TC.

14 Oct. [1933] Rapallo

Ac[tive]/Ant[hology]/ was due out on 12th.

Dear Z/ it wd/ be more timely sfar as I am concerned if the show cd/ show a little consciousness of the PRESENT. . .

not so much the "gold watch an' chain, las' chanct before the ship goes down".

IS there any chance of you or Bill W[illiams]. wakin up to where we are in 1933??

Very trying moment/ and advantage of my being connected with purely old style capitalist era, ingrowing individualist eeestehtic urge //// to ‹very doubtful› say nothing of Marx's paddle wheel steamer. . . . which is to C.H.D[ouglas] as hand plow to tractor. . . . yaas yaas Mr Wallace Stevens IS back in Bill's epotch, the retiring daisy esthete. . . but what about Doug/ as MEANS whereby the proletaire can get his??

the show: Pound probably refers to Zukofsky's plans for Writers Extant. Zukofsky had probably written to Pound in late September or very early October, but the letter has not survived. Pound's reply seems to indicate that Zukofsky had informed him that one of the first publications of Writers Extant would be a volume of poems by William Carlos Williams, with a preface by Wallace Stevens.

62. ALS–3.

Oct 29/33 151 Remsen St Brooklyn, N.Y.

Dear E: In re- your card no use arguin' abaht Douglas.

"Where we are in 1933"—see for instance even the enclosure & in The N.Y. Times at that. "Where we are": you're there & I'm here.

Very important, however, that I get a direct answer to my last covering the announcement of The Objectivists Press' program ⟨a very simple statement—we're publishing book we think ought to be read—⟩. i.e. do you or don't you like the company—the titular company which wd. include only you, Bill [Williams] & me. Wallace etc are out, & I don't see why you shd. object to ⟨Wallace Stevens⟩ doing a preface for Bill's book. Didn't know you were an orthodox opponent of opportunism. —Must have a yes or no at once: printing costs are going up & we may still be able to do Bill's book for $400 if we hurry up.

If you can convince the firm that a book on economic theory as you see it is worth doing—that wd. be the step for you. Even then—& even if it meets with the firm's respects—& even if we can rake up the money to do it—I don't see "Doug as means whereby the proletaire can get his" immediately. Maybe your book or some one else's cd. explain it! ⟨And I've read " a couple of books" . .⟩

So it's come to: "I'm the purely old style capitalist era." Well, if you mean, that my vote (if I'm to have one) after the revolution wd. be against yr. decapitation, and that I believe with Duns in the possibility of matter to think ⟨(I mean as against will & such vagueness)⟩, & that in Marx's economy, of all economies, alone there is substance for doing the new canzone, & that in spite of these convictions, after the cultured growth is scrapped I may still want to say something like:

"went over the sea till days end"
"the ocean flowing backward"

And out of respect to a dissociation of ideas One acknowledges it saluting with two fingers (and out of respect, tho respect is all one has known before)

With a salute, with two fingers:
which
Touch, turn aside from, the forehead.
Better that one
Acknowledges at least the personal,
An approximation which compels more than the dissassociation

The impersonal clarity after the voice known has spoken. —then you're probably right. Too bad I didn't show you all my notes on yr. ABC—I'm probably the only one who took the trouble—but I prefer to leave some of these things to the development of yr. intelligence, if not ⟨to⟩ your intuition.

Yrs

Z

enclosure: Enclosure lacking.

my last: In a letter of 23 October 1933, Zukofsky had urged Pound to join him, William Carlos Williams, and Charles Reznikoff as partners in The Objectivists Press. By the next month, however, the organization's name had been changed to The Objectivist Press.

Bill's book: The first publication of The Objectivist Press was to be *Collected Poems 1921–1931* of William Carlos Williams, with a preface by Wallace Stevens.

Duns: Duns Scotus. See "A"–8, p. 46.

"went over. . . .": This and the next quotation are from Canto I.

And out of respect: "A"–8, p. 44.

yr. ABC: ABC of Economics. Gallup A34.

63. ALS–4.

Apr. 12/34 151 Remsen St N.Y.C.

Dear E: Having been in hospital for a week, after fugally knocking himself out, & now reduced to 96 lbs. avoirdupois, tho' out of hospital, Serly asks me to give you the following information, & begs you to let him know what you intend to do about it:
1. He will probably r'cv. a 3 mos. leave of absence from the orchestra in add. to his regular vacation. Which wd. mean 9 months in Urope.
2. Will probably visit Rapallo again, but only for the company, not because of the recitals. Sees no use in getting performed by chamber ensemble.
3. Sailing May 17 & cd. meet you either in Paris or London around May 25
4. Any possibilities of yr. being either place?
5. Cd. you put ⟨over⟩ his Mozart orchestration (or) and Violo [*sic*] Concerto with B.B.C? Espec. interested in this point—i.e. he is. ([Leopold] Stowk[owsk]i—or rather Phila. Summer Concerts will again do the Mozart this summer, of course).
His address
2216 Delancey St Phila. Pa.

For the rest, have been sick myself tho working on a C[ivil]. W[orks]. A[dministration]. job, now transferred to Dep't of Pub. Welfare, N.Y.C.—6 hrs of continual insult to the intelligence, 2 hrs travel, 1 hr. "lunch." 9 hrs a day, & then 1–3 hrs of The Obj[ectivist]. Press. when I get home. Municipal salary $19 a week. Other salary $0. Which leaves very little time for writing, but I've done some. No use bothering you since you'll probably only answer Douglas. Might as well wait till A–8 is down on paper.

C.H.D[ouglas].'s leaning to the Nazi side of anti-Semitism in Soc. Credit not very reassuring—in spite of the fact that I'd betray & immolate most of my people for 1 Serly etc etc

May have to resign Sec'y⟨ship⟩ of Obj. Press if burden of work continues, & the effort spent on the press does not repay in the way of enough sales allowing us to continue. It's a ha-a-rd job, & besides there may be necessity for direct action in another field (in add. to poetry)—and aside from publishing—I'm afraid there is now only I'm holding back. You were right last summer about staying clear of becoming an office boy—besides peeple dun't appreciate.

Yrs

Z

My best regards to D[orothy]. P[ound]. and your mother & father.

Soc. Credit: The London journal of the Social Credit Movement.

64. TLS–4.

6[–7] May [1934] Rapallo

Deer ZZZZ

WAAL, waaal, whood choose deh jews/ an teh think I got one a cuttin stone on my roof!!!

Wall I sez, sez EZ/ serve yeh god damn well right IF YOU dont wake up and start/ a anti=bankshit movement right inside the buggarin sanhedrim.

This here bolSHAVik bizniz looks a bit phonier effery day. . . and Mr Pelley's dope about Bizmark sounds all right.

Wit iz this Xtn. economics?

I spose Mr Pelley will be annoyed wiff me fer askin if all bankers iz jooz? just like Moike [Gold] iz. but still. Also the exact econ. bearing of causing Nic. Romanoff ter rize from the grave. . . escapes me.

But as light on the American mind, I am deelighted wiff th paper.

If I dont git a anti-bank regiment out the Rabinical college before July 4. I sure am going SHIRT (colour not yet decided// what about the drawers . . . any suggestions.

⟨Teebor [Serly] out of horsp. yet wot ells??
are them shirts to be cut down from K[u]K[lux]K[lan] knighties? or has someone so airplane silk for sale?? ==

anyhow Pelley is a stout felly. & obv. onnerstans the murkn mind.

==

I notice they admire A[lexander]. Hamilton which is as it shd. be. ==
as he was circumcied or had one ball shaved. at the least waal wall
thank you fer the paper. I shall subscribe.

greetings to Bill [Williams]. he ain't been kosherd yet. E⟩

NeXXX day/

Note from pore ole Bzl/ [Bunting] all of a tetter cause he has taken the trouble to try to tell you sumfin or other.

Evidently thinks you've a weaker head than I think you have.

At any rate you had orter be glad he takes thet much interest.

I thought the Apol[linaire]/ less of a g/d/ bore in print than in typescript, but that don't mean that I bothered to read thru it.

cheerio/

Seriously, yew hebes better wake up to econ///why don't the rabinical college start delousing the Am/ Univ. system the suppression of history etc.

Speakin to you aza anti-semite??
If you don't want to be confused with yr/ ancestral race and pogromd . . . it wd/ be well to modernize / cease the interuterine mode of life/ come forth by day etc.

If it aint done moderate/ I mean if NO truth is disseminated among the mildly kulchud like Possum Elyot/ it will be disseminated by the K.K.K. etc. in fanatical zestuous ZZZeal.

⟨Voila⟩

E.P. with two pronged fork of terror and cajolery.

Pussnly/ I think Marx wd. have PROCEDED. I don't know of his ever having suppressed or dodged any facts or any sound logic.

He cdn't. possibly have thought the same answer applied ~~to~~ unmodified to two ~~different~~ equations requiring DIFFERENT answers.

As fer class war// BALLZ. yes, class wars occur.

But class/ how the hell do you divide / working man
son of working man
grandson of working man.

and WHERE. ?????

~~or same man~~

Noble and peasant / noble and serf/ coming from opposite ends, with centuries of tradition/ == clash. YES. hell yes/ and hAS been, and Louis fat noze wuz deheaded.

But bugwahsee = what workingman becomes at first opporchoonity. etc.

I shall tell Pelley there haz been non=yitt bankers and financiers. Tho I dunt spose he will fank me/ any more that M. Gold does///

EZ P

Pelley: William Dudley Pelley, American fascist. Founder of the Christian Party and the Silvershirts of America. Editor of the journal *Liberation.* Zukofsky, it seems, had sent Pound the issue for 10 February 1934.
Bizmark: In "The Mystery of the Civil War and Lincoln's Death," *Liberation* 5:25 (10 February 1934), Pelley wrote, "According to Bismarck, the awful Civil War in America was fomented by a Jewish Conspiracy, and Abraham Lincoln, the hero and national saint of the United States, was killed by the same Hidden Hand which killed six Romanov czars, ten kings, and scores of ministers only to bleed nations." See also Canto 48: "Bismarck/ blamed american civil war on the jews; / particularly on the Rothschild. . . ."
Romanoff: Czar Nicholas II. See the above quotation from "The Mystery of the Civil War and Lincoln's Death."
paper: Liberation.
Louis: Louis XVI.

65. ALS–2.

May 23/34 151 Remsen St Brooklyn, N.Y.

Dear E: You better sign E. Pound instead of Ezra—writing to Mr. Pelley.
I was just keeping you in touch. I didn't expect you to write him.
You won't get a anti-bank regiment out of the Rabinical college—why

shd. they? That's the trouble with both you & the Rabbis in this matter. —You see, I hope, that I'm not included.

Anti-bank is only "½" of the problem. The other half—well, I'll let Serly handle yr. economics behind such statements as

"But class / how the hell do you
divide / working man
son of "
grandson of "
&

But bugwahsee = what working man becomes at first opporchoonity."

But show these statements (yrs) to him (Serly)

Yes, Marx wd. have Proceeded. In fact, he did.

As ever
Yours

Z

P.S. Better use my B'klyn address—writing to me—since I'm no longer rcving mail at The Obj[ectivist]. Press orifice.

66. ALS–4.

Feb 17/35 149 East 37 St New York

Dear E: Thanks for writing to Cowden of Michigan University about me, but I'm ⟨not⟩ trying. Too late for me to be trying again in the suburbs. It'll be New York or a large town in the East or hanging on to the present relief job—damn it—or dying.

You can, if it won't hurt your own name, try and get me published with Faber & Faber. Serly off to Europe with my final arrangement and additions to 55 Poems—a most commendable typescript for you to look at. Time fucks it, and if I keep my MSS. in my drawer or my drawers, I might as well shut up altogether.

The dread Tibor [Serly] is also bringing you part of Reisman's scenario of Ulysses, & synopsis—my part in the matter wuz confined to verbal suggestion on what Reisman already had written, occasional additions to the script in like manner, and collaboration on the ⟨short⟩ synopsis which is not for us but the dumb producer. If you have any ideas as to marketing the scenario, there's no reason why you shdn't get a commision when & if, any money comes in. In fact, we'd insist on it. Shall be writing to Joyce as soon as the complete script is typed, to see if it pleases him & to let him handle the business end as he wishes, if he does. We'll send you the rest of the script as soon as it's off the typewriter. Also ~~a~~ ⟨Reisman's⟩ short Scenario of Lorine Niedecker's "Domestic & Unavoidable" to show you we got a young man here who can be as good as Cocteau & the Surréaliste scenarists if luck favors him.

Glad you agreed with me as to the value of Lorine Niedecker's work and are printing it in Westminster.

Pleased also with your choice of my work for the same ampholgy. Enclosure should have probably gone into Westminster, if it reached you in time. No place now to print it in 'Murka. Do you think Mr. Eliot would see it? And Random House continues to print beeyutiful volumes of shit by Spender and Auden.

If you consent, think it opportune etc, to try my 55 on Faber & Faber, you need not worry about an introduction—I don't want it—you can write a blurb for the dust-proof jacket if it jets out of you.

Noo Yok at a standstill. Haven't heart from Bill Willyums in moneths.

O yuss, I may attempt Houghton Mifflin on their $1000 fellowships—& may have to, probably, will have to ask you to recommend me. Unless you think it's ⟨as⟩ useless for me to try 'em as the Gug[genheim] in times past.

If you can, & it comes your way, see the new Russian release Chapayev—it's the first they've ⟨had⟩ something new to film since China Express, & more real as narrative than Eisenstein, in as much as the montage is not pointed at one.

May Serly bring you a none too surly, curly, Spring! Good weather to you and to D[orothy]. P[ound]. for remembering me in her letter to the Magyar.

Yrs

Z

Cowden: Roy William Cowden, Professor of English at the University of Michigan. He was chairman of the Hopwood Committee, which oversaw distribution of the Avery Hopwood awards for creative writing. Zukofsky would have had to enroll as a graduate student at Michigan to be eligible.

55 Poems: 55 Poems (Prairie City, Illinois: The Press of James A. Decker, 1941). *All,* pp. 9–80.

Reisman: Jerry Reisman, Zukofsky's young friend. The screenplay is now in the Zukofsky Collection at the Humanities Research Center, the University of Texas at Austin.

Niedecker: Wisconsin poet with whom Zukofsky carried on a long correspondence. "Domestic and Unavoidable" is a dramatic fragment. It appeared in *The Westminster Review* 24:1 (Spring-Summer 1935), pp. 27–28. This issue was edited by Pound, John Drummond, and T. C. Wilson.

young man: Reisman. Pound's reply of 6 March 1935 indicates that Pound thought Zukofsky referred to Niedecker.

my work: "Home For Aged Bomb Throwers–U.S.S.R.," "A Junction," "Song–3/4 time," and "American Bank-Note Factory." All but the latter poem appear in *All,* pp. 52 and 65–68.

enclosure: Enclosure lacking.

Chapayev: A 1934 film by Sergei and George Vassiliev about a Red Army unit and its heroic commander during the Russian Civil War.

China Express: A 1929 silent film directed by Ilya Trauberg. It is set on a speeding train. The drama consists of third-class Chinese passengers rising in revolt against corrupt first-class passengers.

Magyar: Tibor Serly.

67. TLS–2.

6 March 1935 Rapallo

Dear Z/

It so happens that even the U.S.A. is not at a stand still/

If you will glue your eye onto the bottom of yr/ own piss pot of course you cant see the choochoo cars going by.

I am not an expert on cinema/ I cert/ will NOT mix myself with Joyce's affairs/

I am getting an english opinyun on yr/ damn poems/ but I know what it will be/ and damn it I told you so, when you were here.

If you are too god damn dumb to read what is being printed/ and insist on sticking in 1927. . thass thaaat.

Amurikuh allus is 15 years late/ so is Dean Gauss.

The next anthology will be econ/ conscious and L/Z won't be in it.

People read books because the author tells em something. If his knowledge of life is less than their own the author is a BORE.

Surrealism ⟨meaning the yester year frog variety⟩ is a painter's show/ what fahrtin literature has it got⟨?⟩

Being too DUMB to read Cavalcanti, there was a little dabble/ like Sitwell's collecting Victorian mantlepiece ornaments.

I can't even advise N[ew]/E[nglish]/ W[eekly]/ to print you.

If I started advising Mairet on the basis of personal friendship I wd/ be no better than the Bloomsbuggars themselves.

I think it wd/ be BAD EDITING to print you in England. Be careful or you'll fall back into racial characteristics, and cease to be L/Z at all.

yaaaas, "every man gets more like his father as he gets older."

Most americans miss the boat/ but it is more irritatin' to see 'em catch it; and then step off.

e:e:cummings is more awake than you are. In fact apart from cummings and ole Bill/[Williams] thass thaaat.

cummings is the youngest american writer, pretty nearly.

I don't think yr/ Niedecker is so hot/ thought he was a lady ANYhow. . Lorine . . .?? It got by, because I printed one tadpole on each recommendation of qualified critics/ (i;e; more or less. . qualified.)

I can't hold the boat FOR you.

Tibor [Serly] is goin' good. Local press excellent/ hall full. He wuz nuts to say 75 people/ 160 at least. I wasn't countin. I don't, cause if they shd/ ever come for the tax I got to be iggurunt.

Tax collector stopped me yesterday, but that wuz to explain that he had tried to steer two people to the concert, and being Canadian they couldn't understand how they cd/ pay at the door.

J/HEEZUSS, you aint even caught up with Jules Romains//

and so on.

E.P.

english opinyun: Probably John Drummond's.

Gauss: Christian Frederick Gauss, Dean of the College at Princeton University from 1925 to 1945. Pound was displeased with Gauss's *A Primer for Tomorrow* (New York and London: Scribner's, 1934).

Sitwell: Edith Sitwell, British poet.

Mairet: Philip Mairet, of the *New English Weekly.* A. R. Orage, the original editor, died on 6 November 1934, and Mairet replaced him.

68. ALS–7.

March 15/35 149 East 37 St New York

Dear E: Well, let's have Drummond's opinyun (I suppose you mean Drummond) of "55"—if this doesn't make you sore. I mean your last hasn't concentrated on any particular shortcoming of L.Z. but is merely in the nature of general browbeating. Maybe it's time Sonny bawled out papa, since once upon a time Sonny seems to have had a certain insight into him. Frankly, Sonny has been not a little worried about you for some time. That is, getting back to racial characteristics—sobriety, financial outlook, hoariness etc—or getting away from racial characteristics and using my social sense acquired after 31 years of assimilation—you can't I think afford to depend entirely on an audience composed of the good will of Mr. Cummings & old Doc Bill [Williams] & the quiet, honorable faithfulness of L.Z., who may out of concern tell a coupla' things to you he won't reveal to the pig public—be it Mr. [M]Ike Gold or Gore ham Munson. That is you're not very clear, in fact very vague as to what is happening "even in the U.S.A." And you're not being read in the U.S.A. for reasons you ought to be able to find out for yrself. ⟨And⟩ I'm not going to tell the U.S.A., ⟨even⟩ if my word doesn't spead further than the leetle maggiezeens, that in Mr. Pound's last "Cantos" I have found nothing to move the cockles of my heart or the network of my brain, outside of 5 lines (perfect lines) given over to Hathor & her box and some musical metaphysics of the dark Cavalcanti. It is alright to condense the virtues of Thos. Jeff. & J.Q [Adams], but one can't stop there economically. No one in the U.S.A. is interested in the Boss's reclamation of the marshes—& quite a number here are aware of the fact that Rome when it was caving in did something like it—some time before 1935 A.D. No one in the U.S.A. will be interested in the after-dinner wish fulfillment & table talk of an Irish senator. There must be something that's bogged yr. erstwhile intelligence that makes L.Z. worry over the future of the—whatever—Cantos in process—when he considers the achievements (not the shortcomings) of the last "XI."

"The next anthology will be econ/conscious and L/Z won't be in it." That statement shd. read: The next anthology will be "econ/conscious" and will have nothing in it most probably, if the econ/consc. L.Z. is omitted. Just a pointer for the editor's concern.

Nobody asked you to print me in the N[ew]/E[nglish]/W[eekly] on the basis of personal friendship or otherwise. In fact, the only excuse for my appearing in the N/E/W, wd. be personal friendship—I don't at all like the rest of the company. In fact, I think they're a lot of damned obstructors whom the intelligent public can well do without. Besides, I'd make so little money on it, I can very well afford remaining honest on the quiet. $10 more a year won't improve the quality of my work or intelligence.

What do you mean it we [*sic*] be "Bad Editing to print me in England ⟨etc.⟩"? If you think the English wd. assume I'm writing Yiddisch, say so. Mr. Bunting, an Englishman, doesn't seem to think so. If you can't do it, say so. If it wd. hurt yr. finances to do it, you know I wdn't want to do it. I don't give a damn where I'm printed—if there's any possible printer—I do give somewhat of a damn about having a volume out that wd. be available to the growing young & a few of the elders who still seem to know what poetry & reading are about. If it's impossible to have that done, there are worse things that can & have happened to me—I can still go on, & my new output needn't be affected by it.

Yes, E.E.C[ummings]. is the "youngest American writer"—I refer to his recent printed output. He seemed young <u>for a reason</u> in 1927 or 1928 when <u>I</u> first prodded <u>you</u> about him.

There's no use wasting yr. time calling me down about surrealisme—if you had read <u>Mantis, An Interpretation</u>, you'd have found out I think pretty much as you do about surrealisme—but you haven't read it. Nor have I swallowed Miss Niedecker's mental stubborness. However, her output has <u>some</u> validity, <u>some</u> spark of energy, which the solipsistic daze=maze of Mr. Kummings hath not.

So I haven't caught up with that best seller Jules Romains—in 1928, it was Tailhade I hadn't caught up with—and it was I shdn't go on with "A"—& now you tell me to go on "wif it"—sometimes people change their minds for the better.

About the Joyce scenario—I sent you the first 40 pp. because I knew that you had written some intelligent sentences on the cinema—I didn't send it to you because I want you to squabble with Mr. Joyce. I thought you might read it, as a matter of intelligent human interest—and that, perhaps, if you know of a producer—you do seem to know some people—we might all make something on it. You can't do anything about it—alright. No need to get angry—I understand. You don't want to read the rest of the scenario—you haven't the time, alright. You do, as a matter of wasting yr. time? Alright, if you ask for it—I'll send it. Otherwise I can live a day on what I might spend for the postage.

If you think I have dementia praecox, that I have rotted—

All this, sire, hurts Sonny more'n shd hurt you. You have evidently itched for a bout with the Manhattan Mauler, & if the end of it is yr. quietus, please get up, convalesce, & ponder a while: it won't hurt you.

Damn it, you can hold the boat for me—but not if it's going to sink everybody in it.

Performance of Serly's Viola Concerto in Rapallo more cheering—a sign of some kind of intelligent activity & I notice you end yr. letter and so on—ye-ah ye-ah choochoos & octogenerians' boyhood daydreams realized.

My best whether you give a damn or don't—& to D[orothy]. P[ound]. & the kinsfolk

Z

P.S. I forget—let's have Drummond's opinyun if you still have it. You can about gage what the success of being printed means to me, if I can travel so fast away from it in space of a letter.

Hathor: Canto 39. "When Hathor was bound in that box / afloat on the sea wave. . . ."

Cavalcanti: Most of Canto 36 is a translation of Guido Cavalcanti's canzone, "Donna mi Prega."

reclamation: Canto 41. "Having drained off the muck by Vada / From the marshes, by Circeo, where no one else would have drained it."

senator: William Butler Yeats, quoted in Canto 41: " 'Sure they want war,' said Bill Yeats, / 'They want all the young gals fer themselves.' "

Mantis: All, pp. 74–80.

Tailhade: Laurent Tailhade. See Pound's letter of 24 December 1928.

choochoos: "A"–6, p. 27. "Septuagenarian actor's personal locomotive / For retired estate which his boy day dreams realized."

69. ALS–2.

Apr. 8, 1935 149 East 37 St New York

Dear E: Well, Mr. Drummond is entitled to an opinion, especially an unbiassed one. Would you be kind enough to return the bee-yu-tiful MS of "55"—the lady who typed it for me had a fondness for it. And maybe, maybe, The Objectivist Press, the advisory board now no longer flaunted on its dust-proof jackets, will publish it eventually. This Talmudist shall not be mortified, in any case.

I refuse to argue vis a tergo and to discuss (?) viva voce, one wd. need a vacation. But maybe you don't know Sonny is now bounden feature and continuity writer and special researchist for WNYC, the Municipal Broadcasting Station of the City of New York, and that in May when the Serly-Joyce songs are broadcast over the civic air by Judith Litante, Sonny may even take care of the press releases connected with that program, etc etc.

And you say "What the hell do you know, or have to say? Man's matter has got to be gathered by perception/etc waal, advice no use to them as don't want it." Whereas my sober eye noticeth that in the new eleven Cantos you write about the audience in black at the Matthew Passion, matter handled in "A", and that you write about certain matters in a vein similar to "A" (you might look up "Active"[Anthology]—pg 139—"Played polo / and they-they- the very old stutterers" etc.) I believe in the same Canto.

So-o-o! unless Dame Philoserfy misleads me, we must have both gathered our matter by perception—or we are both "strictly local American product / Emerson, Whittier"—transcendental . .

And I think I have damned the Rabbis and Talmud sufficiently in "The" and the beginning of "A"–4 for you not to spit on my suit of Canadian tweed, and that I have writ of the Wailing Wall as something pertaining to "economic extinctions" (Active Anthology, p. 126) all this, over 5 years ago, so maybe you haven't paid attention to Sonny's latest de⟨-e-e-⟩velopment, and maybe he's not entirely a rejeck. But—

Goink on from here. I am applying for a Houghton Mifflin Fellowship, which wd. net me $1000 if I get it—and I am applying specifically for to finish a novella—parts enclosed, if you can find time to look at 'em with one eye closed—or you needn't look at 'em—** but if the Houghton outfit write you asking for a character—please say one word for Sonny—and a good one. Be a good papa, I have not yet gone the way of consummate righteousness, and God has not yet exceeded you in my estimate, so (Cross My Heart) my best to you ever,

Amen,

Z

**Fortunately (?) I haven't a duplicate copy—I'll send it some time when you're freer.

the lady: Possibly Celia Thaew, later Mrs. Zukofsky.

Serly-Joyce songs: Probably "Four Songs from 'Chamber Music'," composed by Serly in 1926.

you say: In a letter of 23 March 1935 to Zukofsky.

eleven Cantos: Eleven New Cantos: XXXI–XLI (New York: Farrar & Rinehart, 1934).

Matthew Passion: Referred to in "A"–1 and in Canto 35.

"Played polo": See "A"–6 (p. 30) and Canto 35, "Oh yes, there are nobles, still interested in polo / said the whoring countess of course there were nobles."

"strictly local . . . .": Quoted from Pound's letter of 23 March 1935.

p. 126: "A"–4, p. 18, "Speech bewailing a Wall, / Night of economic extinctions / Death's encomium–"

novella: Unidentified. Celia Zukofsky's *A Bibliography of Louis Zukofsky* (Los Angeles: Black Sparrow Press, 1969) does not record any work on a novella in 1935.

70. TLS–3.

28 May [1935] Rapallo

You bloody buggaring fool/
Have you not even sense enough to USE A WORD with a meaning and let the meaning adhere to the word.

A commodity is a material thing or substance/ it has a certain durability.

If you don't dissociate ideas, and keep ONE LABLE for ONE thing or category, you will always be in a gormy mess.

Labour may transmute material, it may put value into it, or make it serviceable.
I suppose it comes of being a damn foreigner and not having bothered to learn english.

Call me a liberal and I'll knock yr/ constipated block off.

Commoditas, latin = advantage, benefit. ⟨all right⟩

But commodity in english, and in econ/ used to mean WARES. not underwear.

In Italian it is clear, <u>lavoro</u> non è <u>mercé</u>.

The workman can't store it/ it is not a product, that he can put on shelf for a month. It is not something he can dig up and keep.

God damn Talmudic footling
instead of tryin' to think.

a man who is any good; TIRES to learn/ tries to see the what the other bloke means instead of frittin round hunting for loophole
to back up his own ignorance.

Also, idiotic to insist on saying the PART of what you think which CANT get over/ instead of looking to see what CAN.
also/
idiocy not to try to measure the interval between external world and yr/ private ~~money~~ ⟨monkey⟩ garden.
I am fed up with half/gooks who don't know their private world has a relation to anything outside it.
After all you LIVE in the fkn (or rather the onanizing) country and daren't leave it.

N[ew]/⟨Masses⟩ is quite right/ my poetry and my econ/ are NOT
separate or opposed.
essential unity/

The unwillingness to LOOK at your work, is stronger in YOU than in anyone else.
that is the rub.

Don't embrace social credit/ LEARN a little about human relations; and don't try to kid me that monetary system don't affect 'em.
soc/ credit me yarse. . . plenty of thinking men continue to think
, dozen live men thinking econ/ without swallowing soc/ cr/ lock stock and barrel UNTHOUGHT about.

There is plenty of REAL work to be done/ and interesting jobs to do.

Your're worse than blind Joyce.

Plenty of intellectual ACTIVITY, without even mentioning me an Bill[Williams]. I frequently write without mention of either.

You cant buy foreign books, cause you wd/ have to pay in MONEY and you are too hog lazy to think what it (money) is.

and that condition will git more so/ until several people start thinking what M. is.

Anybody worth a 1.25 ⟨lire in⟩ postage, tries to IMPROVE on verbal formulations of any correspondent.

different activity
from running back like any pink tea pseudo bolo/ to what Charlie [Marx] SAID in the 1880,

---

All right, you get an article on a ~~magry~~ ⟨magyr⟩ printed in London, on the strength of having seen some mss/ and heard something done on abbreviated instruments in a bathing village in Italy.

for the prupose of boostin the Tibor [Serly]. . . and not as a contribution to science.

I thought I HAD been advising the Le[a]g[ue]/ ⟨of⟩ Am[erican]/ Writers for the past year and a haff. (ain't they the people that have been writing to me?? and several lamenting on how hard it is to get any one to think unless I write 'em personal letters

I shd/ have been better employed on Fenollosa, during the past 25 minutes or whatever. how many hours per day . . etc. are you worth.

EP

[handwritten postscript]
⟨you are merely becoming a bore from lack of mental intake & digestion⟩

an article: "Tibor Serly, Composer," *New English Weekly* 6:24 (28 March 1935), p. 495. Gallup C1173.

magyr: Tibor Serly.

Am[erican]/ Writers: Zukofsky to Pound, 11 May 1935, "I forgot to say what you can do for yrself: the League of American Writers having been formed at the recent American Writers Congress and a united front of writers being its intention you can join or criticize, or in one way or another help put 'em straight." Malcolm Cowley discusses the origin and political character of the League in his chapter, "Assembly on the Left," in *The Dream of the Golden Mountain: Remembering the 1930s* (New York: Viking, 1980).

Fenollosa: Perhaps a reference to the reprint of *The Chinese Written Character as a Medium for Poetry* that was to be published the following year. Gallup B36.

71. ALS–4.

June 7/35 111 East 36 St New York

Dear E: Have you not even sense enough to know that a definition is worthless if it is so general as to include nothing? If it does not particularize, have the possibilities of suggestion for use. —What the hell good has Fenollosa brought to you anyway, what will it mean if you continue to read him without getting anything out of him?

"A commodity is a material thing or substance / it has a certain durability"—E.P. May 28/35. I.e. taking you at your word, the moon, Mars, an extinct crater, man's shit—not fertilizer because labor has been put into it, and it has social value. Unmined coal is a material thing, but not a commodity. When the miner digs it up, it has a use value because so much labor power has been expended digging it up for a social need. Yes, what is the use of my trying to rehash what "Charlie" said in the first chapter of "Das Kapital" when you've never (evidently) taken the trouble to read it, having started with the chapter on the working day, and stopped there, without knowing why each fact, each incident, in that chapter has been set down. There's more material fact and more imaginative poetic handling of fact in that first chapter of Marx than has been guessed at in your economic heaven. I tried to handle the matter in my song 3/4 time, & maybe I've made a gormy mess of it—but you can still read Charlie and find out for yourself why labor is the basic commodity (if that word is to have any consequential meaning at all) and how the products of labor are just the manifestations, and money yr. capitalistic juggling, of that commodity. (That money shd. be just a medium of exchange is another matter, but you write as if it is to-day, when you know perfectly well it isn't. Marx put it: Commodity-Money-Commodity (what exchange shd. be): Money-Commodity-Money (what ⟨the⟩ exchanges are).

What do you think labor is aside from what you say it does—"transmute material"—just automatic exhilaration in the best of all possible—to-day—economic worlds?

And why'n hell do you think the U.S. Supreme court has decided against the codes? Because labor sells itself under the capitalistic system (despite unionization, despite liberal reforms) in the market, and the capitalist wants a "free" market to buy in. If yr. Cantos—those that are solid—are not opposed to yr. economics, God must have helped you to include such facts as there has been no restriction on child labor since Marx recorded the slavery of poor little buggers in dark England in the 1840's. Or maybe I'm worth that 1.25 lire in postage because I've been helpful enough to read more into yr. verbal formulations than you intended to put into 'em. "lavoro non è merce" "In Eye-talian" you say "it is clear"—yes—labor is not merchandise ("Wares" is too glossy! ! !) Your Italian fascist is clear enough in his noble predatory philorsophy—frank enough—but can you you, not dizzy with the sweet sound of the Wop tongue, afford to be that frank in English. Has the sound of another tongue merely become a source of hazy analogy to you? Or has English been so natural to you that you no longer bother to weigh each word you handle, translate etc. The damn foreigner you say I am has more respect for English than you have.

Yr. English language (private pauperty!)! It's like your "call me a liberal and I'll knock yr / constipated block off," like the line in a Fascist play we've heard about—"when I hear of culture, I cock my gun!"

Well, there's no use calling you a liberal—as you say. The next war will show your stand, will show whether you've been a liberal or not.

Question—

You've written about the Boss's reclamation of the marshes, you've said nothing about the Soviets doing the same, because that's only an incident in a larger undertaking? —Which you haven't mentioned either. You have gassed a great deal about the banks. What have you said about the fate of private banking in the U.S.S.R.?

Yes, there are plenty of things you can do, and in a bathing village in Italy. But forgetting Kung's advice to the old guy on the road pretending to be receiving wisdom, You seem to think you are the Messiah. Your last is filled with spit-fire similitudes of the proverbial wise irate old man. Who's put his Talmudic foot into it? "Blind Joyce" knew 15 years ago what a prig Stephen [Dedalus] was and set it down frankly. James Joyce is not interested in economics. He at least knows what he wishes to ignore and is frank about it.

Why ask me what I'm worth, how many hrs. of yr. day etc when you can probably guess my answer. Not a minute of yr. time if you can produce anything to equal in value the first Canto or the opening of the XXXeth; maybe a good deal more of yr. time than you can imagine I'm worth, if you continue to say the same things, after de Gourmont, you said 20 years ago, having forgotten by now what they meant.

Thanks for having returned "55".

And a new life to you,

Z

P.S. You can't have been advising The League of Am. Writers because it's in the process of being formed now.

song 3/4 time: Song 27 of *29 Songs*. Song 27 begins with a quotation from *Das Kapital. All,* pp. 65–68.
codes: On 27 May 1935, the Supreme Court had ruled the National Recovery Administration's codes unconstitutional.
Kung's advice: Canto 13: "You old fool, come out of it, / Get up and do something useful."
the XXXeth: Canto 30 begins: "Compleynt, compleynt I hearde upon a day, / Artemis singing, Artemis, Artemis / Agaynst Pity lifted her wail: / Pity causeth the forests to fail, / Pity slayeth my nymphs, / Pity spareth so many an evil thing."
de Gourmont: Pound's appreciation of Remy de Gourmont was recorded in "Remy de Gourmont" [Part I], *The Fortnight Review* 98 (N.S.): 588 (1 December 1915), pp. 1159–1166 and "Remy de Gourmont" [Part II], *Poetry* 7:4 (January 1916), pp. 197–202. Gallup C213 and C214. The essay was reprinted in *Instigations* and in *Literary Essays on Ezra Pound.*
"55": The manuscript of Zukofsky's *55 Poems.*

72. TLS–3. Enclosure.

7 January 1936 Rapallo

Dear Zuk

I have read with pleasure A.8 and will tell the Rev. [T.S.] Eliot to print it/

BUT he will probably find that Duns Scotus didn't swallow the 39 articles, or invent some god damn irrelevant reason for NOT.

//

Send me a few Noo Masses/ if you have to spare.

Am not disputing whether Amerigo Vespuci or Columbus discovered america/

I want to KNOW if any american reds/ have the sense to see MATTER in ACTION, or know WHY I share what I believe to be yr/ statement on the subject.

ANYone who can understand the phrase "BY MEANS OF" (a preliminary to "IN PROPORTION TO")⟨??⟩

AND what do I mean by "COMMUNIZE THE PRODUCT"
⟨if⟩ and why is that contrary to communism?
WHY is the only communism that American reds will accept precisely the non-marxian, anti-leninite abstraction IN VACUO?

why is every concrete proposal for beating the usurer considered treachery to the working man by all yr/ damn friends?

I suppose there is no use telling you that there is a LEFT as well as a right in Italy, and that a STRUGGLE persists.

CAN any of yr/ Noo Asses stand UP to the enclosed 8 questions.
When you go up against a responsible cabinet minister who is getting things DONE, you have to have something BRIEFER than a reference to Thos Aquinas or asking him if he has read vol. 37 of the Encyclopedia.

If you had EMPHASIZED the Gold bug/ whatever, instead of sending me the Chartres, it might have enlightened me more effectively.
better late than never. BUT even what Gladstone said in 1887 is NOT enough for 1936.
The ECONOMIC means TO an end functions IN 1936.
a Rasputin wd. be useless in Washington or London/ ⟨different kind suited to different kind⟩
some other osmosis of governing asses must be effected.
It is the lack of precisely the MATTER IN ACTION, and cap/acity of dealing with same, that causes me NOT to sign of dotted line of Mike Gold's dictatorship.
do yoi GIT me.

Things have NOT stayed where they were at time of yr/ incursion into Rapallo.
Even Frankie at Atlanta knew more than he did in 1933.
(impossible as that may seem)

WHAT is the red dictrorship of the DIMINISHING working class doing to get REAL issues into the next election?

What about ⟨E.P.⟩ McGrady? he has good initials.
I heerd he told the owners thaty couldn't do THAT any more.
A gleam of hope or soap?

Why does the reds so hate all EFFECTIVE measures? or all concrete proposals for communizing ~~the~~ AMERICAN ~~plenty~~ ⟨consumable & usable goods.⟩ (~~which~~ ⟨American Plant⟩ is further along than the rhooshun, and the amurkn LAND which is more abundant than Italy's?)
⟨They⟩ Git the MEANS all collywobbled up with the END or PURPOSE of la rivoluzione continua.

An bigod/ your sphincter loosened up WHEN you got into action. no matter WHAT action/
⟨you⟩ come out of yr/ mouse hole and mixed with the vulgar, and
THEN the damn poEM proceded.
Q.E.D.

Ez P

[The following enclosure is a copy in Zukofsky's handwriting.]

Volitionist economics

Which of the following statements do you agree with?
1. It is an outrage that the state shd. run into debt to individuals by the act and in the act of creating real wealth.
2. Several nations recognize the necessity of distributing purchasing power. They do actually distribute it. The question is whether it shd. be distributed favor to corporations; as reward for not having a job; or impartially and per capita.
3. A country can have one currency for internal use, and another good both for home and foreign use.
4. If money is regarded as certificate of work done, taxes are no longer necessary.

5. It is possible to concentrate all taxation onto the actual paper money of a country (or onto one sort of its money).
6. You can issue valid paper money against any commodity up to the amount of that commodity that people WANT.
7. Some of the commonest failures of clarity among economists are due to using one word to signify two or more different concepts: such as, Demand, meaning sometimes want and sometimes power to buy; authoritative, meaning also responsibility.
8. It is an outrage that the owner of one commodity can not exchange it with someone possessing another, without being impeded or taxed by a third party holding a monopoly over some third substance or controlling some convention regardless of what it be called.

Answer to E. Pound
Via Marsala, 12/5. Rapallo,
Italy.

Duns Scotus: "A"–8, p. 46. "Whether it was 'impossible for matter to think?' / Duns Scotus posed." The quotation is from Friedrich Engels' *On Historical Materialism* (New York: New York Labor News Company, 1928), p. 5. "Materialism is the natural-born son of Great Britain. Already the British schoolman, Duns Scotus, asked, 'whether it was impossible for matter to think?' " The passage is itself a quotation from Marx and Engels' *Die Heilige Familie* (Frankfurt a.M., 1845), p. 201.
39 articles: The Church of England's 39 Articles of Belief.
Goldbug: In a letter of 25 December 1935, Zukofsky had called Pound's attention to Henry Adams's "The New York Gold Conspiracy."
the Chartres: Henry Adams's *Mont St. Michel and Chartres.*
Gladstone: William Ewart Gladstone, four times Prime Minister of Great Britain. I have not been able to determine whether Pound had any specific statement by Gladstone in mind.
Rasputin: A Russian monk who gained great influence over the family of Czar Nicholas II.
Frankie: Franklin Delano Roosevelt defended the New Deal in a speech at Atlanta, Georgia, on 29 November 1935.
McGrady: Pound seems to have mistaken the middle initial of Roosevelt's Assistant Secretary of Labor, Edward F. McGrady.

73. ALS–5.

Mar. 12/36 111 E. 36 St New York

Dear E: Next week's (Mar. 17) New Masses came out to-day with yr. letter to R.C. Summerville, written in 1934, under the head of Ezra Pound, Silvershirt. R.C.S.'s answer included.

Damn stupid thing for them to have printed it: but if you will yump before you look, what do you expect? You shd. have investigated who Summerville was before you wasted yr. time to write him. If I remember rightly now I did warn you by sending you Pelley's rotten organ, but you didn't take it as warning I guess, & went purblind. New Masses readers—and they include most anybody these days who is interested in literary magazines—will ⟨probably⟩ not read H. Ward's review, in same number, of de Kruif's book and the quotes from it, "honest, cantankerous etc E.P.," or at least not collate that fact with yr. letter. If you're dead set on completely losing whatever readers you still have in America, keep it up. ⟨Not to mention the cry of anti-semitism that'll be raised all over the country against you. Even decent Jews will miss yr "And" "or Aryan"⟩ So much for high class lithography.

Especially annoying to me, since I'm still hunting for some one in C[ommunist]. P[arty]. to answer yr. Volit[ionist]. Econ[omics]. questions. Typical of some of the nitwits on New Masses to steal thunder and substitute a fart.

V.J. Jerome too busy on agitprop & Communist, to handle yr. questions himself, in the meantime has probably misplaced yr. questions so I can't get at 'em immediately, & the copy I made has been sent on to an economist who's also busy & ain't answered. I have, of course, no more respect for this kind of inaction than I have for yr. inability to see that the questions in the form you put 'em are not just questions but full of the cantankerousness of a cantankerous manifesto, let alone program. You expect people to answer you & you don't present the problem but bark at 'em.

Anyhow, Jerome has asked me to broach the matter to Anna Rochester, Labor Research Ass., 80 E. 11 St, N.Y.C. Her new volume Rulers of America may interest you. Why not send her the questions yrself and ask her to communicate with me for League of Am. Writers mag., at once—while I persist in trying to get hold of the lost copy. Understand that Comrade Rochester is a Daughter of the Am. Rev., & a descendant of the founder of Rochester, N.Y. Maybe they go back to the Lord (R.)

For the rest, I must be deafer than dumb, because yr. cussing blows past me.

It ain't important whether E.P. or L.Z. read Lenin's S[tate] & R[evolution], first. The point is, having read it how can you find Social Credit, Vol[itionist]. Ec[onomics]., & Mussolini compatible with it. I'll send a copy, first chance I get to pick it up, however. Might be profitable for you, too, to re-read it. Sure Lenin knew how to handle the banks, after the revolution. Gesell's schwundgeld didn't get that far.

Thanks for the bibliog. of Por etc, but I guess my salary doesn't afford ordering all the mags. from Italy. Instead of cussing me out abstractly for 4 pages, you'd be much more effective as propagandist, if you think there's any use propagandizing me, by summarizing Por etc in so many sentences. I have examples of excellent insight on the part of E.P. stated with extreme precision & concision—but they go back a number of years. No time?

And what the hell makes you say I think you're a liar (you must be getting soft.). If I did, do you think I'd bother, or wd. have eight or 10 years ago? And all this curry-spun-dense.

But I do think you're too damn gullible, have been for the last five years. You really believe that Mussolini means the "prolet. (and fas.) revolution." And Hamilton Fish attacks ⟨F.D.⟩R. for being a Communist. Two examples merely of clairvoyance.

And you're sure the real bolshie when he said "ca appartient à lux" in referring to the ⟨difference between⟩ "one party systems" of Italy and Russia, wasn't being the slightest bit ironic & honest at the same time & avoiding what to him wd. have been futile discussion since he probably didn't have yr. welfare at heart (I can't blame him). What the hell for are you bringing up the business of one party system as the real truth etc about Amer. democracy, pseudo two-parties etc at this late date—I used to hear it when I wuz five and listening to Socialist stump speakers in Manhattan where I was born. We all know it's one party, the question ⟨today⟩ is which the Fascist or the Communist. Lenin who died in 1924, knew this, so you can't claim him for yr. own. I never heard of him supporting The Boss.

He ⟨(Lenin)⟩ must have also known about Douglas. Did he call him to Russia? Presume he knew about Douglas, since he knew about DeLeon whom few people on the continent knew. And he did evaluate DeLeon.

Why should I in Marx's holy name get in touch with Stalin for you, you're asking the questions, not me.

You're letter to Tibor [Serly] shows more wisdom (I think) tho he seems to disagree with you about wut's might possibly still yet be done in Europe. And if you'd come here you'd really find out: no reason at all why you cdn't fare as well as Gertie [Stein] & Possum [Eliot] did on a tour, seein' as you have more bizness intelligence than both of 'em put together when you don't want to put yr. foot into it.
Etc——

Yrs

Z

letter: "Ezra Pound, Silvershirt," *New Masses* 18:12 (17 March 1936), pp. 15–16. Gallup C1306. Pound wrote, in part, "That S/[ilver] S/[hirts] should attack financial tyranny BY WHOMEVER exercised. i.e., whether by international jew or by local aryan" and "That the plot, conscious and unconscious, manipulated by jews AND others to prevent American education from educating americans should be exposed and foiled."

Summerville: Robert C. Summerville, an official of The Silvershirt Legion.

organ: Liberation, one of the various names Pelley used for his magazine.

review: "The Hunger-Fighters' Next Battle," by Harold Ward, *New Masses* 18:12 (17 March 1936), pp. 25–26. "Paul de Kruif, romantic herald of the great names and honorable achievements of medical science, was challenged by 'honest, cantankerous, deep-seeing Ezra Pound' to look that society full in the face, to submerge his complacent ego in the cleansing waters of direct contact with its myriad horrors." De Kruif's book was *Why Keep Them Alive?*

V. J. Jerome: Zukofsky to Pound, 18 January 1936, "I am sending yr. 8 questions to V. J. Jerome, editor of The Communist, party organ, and asking him to answer 'em for League of American Writers magazine. I don't know whether he will, he's a very busy man, head of the agit-prop (propaganda) outfit of the party. . . ."

Rochester: American Marxist, author of *Rulers of America: A Study of Finance Capital* (New York: International Publishers, 1936).

Lord (R.): John Wilmot, second Earl of Rochester (1647–1680), English poet.

schwundgeld: "Shrinking money." Gesell proposed that owners of paper money be required, every month, to affix a stamp on each note equal to one percent of the note's face value. Silvio Gesell (1862–1930) was a German economist much admired by Pound.

Por: Odon Por, an Italian propagandist for Fascism.

Fish: Republican Representative from New York.

bolshie: Unidentified.

DeLeon: Daniel DeLeon (1852–1914), American socialist and author.

73. TCS.

30 May [1936] Rapallo

Been reading Uncle Joe [Stalin] with pleasure/ also seen Partisan Rev[iew]/ crabbing the venerable doc. Williams/ and IF Dreiser and [Kenneth] Burke are what they WANT as instigation, theyd better resign. Am sending you an essay, which OUGHT to be paid for. But I doubt if such apes as Mike G[old]/ wd. even print it.

However it prob/ says more re M[arx]/ism or Americanism than the Part/ rev. has managed to.

30 May XIV

Of course if you CANT print it, that will show that "they" are all sapheads, and that you have withered on the stalk. No question of conversion, I have been THERE all the time but objects like [Horace] Gregory cant LOCATE anyone's position.

EP

reading Uncle Joe: Stalin's *Foundations of Leninism,* tenth anniversary edition (New York: International Publishers, 1934). Zukofsky had sent Pound a copy on 9 May 1936.

Partisan Rev.: Williams's answers to a questionnaire sent him by the editors of *Partisan Review,* and the answers of a number of other writers, including Kenneth Burke and Theodore Dreiser, were published in the April 1936 issue. In the May issue, the editors printed a letter from a reader that took Williams to task for his allegiance to "the official myths of liberalism and democracy." The editors followed the letter with their own blast: "Needless to say, the editorial position of *Partisan Review* is utterly opposed to the direction of thought shown in Mr. Williams' contribution."

an essay: "That So Very American Flavor." Never published, the essay berates New York Communists for being ignorant of modern economic developments. (MS. Beinecke).

Gregory: The May issue of *Partisan Review* contained a review by Horace Gregory of C. Day Lewis's *A Time to Dance.*

74. TLS–2.

25 June [1936] Rapallo

Dear Z/

Remembering yr/ remarks re/ yr/ father. I shd. like his opinion on Leviticus' chap. 25.

Neschec and Tarbit.

/

in all communist efforts to obscure jewish question, or in all jewish internationalism we have no clear statement re/ whether the jew IF he enters a community of nations proposes to treat the goyim as his own law tells him to treat his own people.

"inter IPSOS prohibeat".

I shd/ also like from YOU a clear statement as to whether communism proposes to have ANY ethics.

say you get dictatorship of the proletariat" (marvelous word, meaning whereof long lost in propagandist licherchoor)

WHAT if ANY ethical

discriminations are to be made⟨?⟩

or is the subject to remain undigested (on principle?

This is private communique.

I su/goddam/spose Coughlin/ the Communists the Farm boober party etc; will waste next 5 months attacking each other instead of attacking tweedelDUMB Farley/ and TweedelDun Hoover and co.

HELL/ASS

I see Coug/ has started. I shd/ like to think yr/ two paladins were clear enough in the head to overlook that and mass the attack on money monopoly. NESCHEC etc.

yr

E

Neschec and Tarbit: In "What is Money For?" (1939) Pound says, "The tendency to 'gnaw into' has been recognized and stigmatized from the time of the law of Moses and he called it *neschek*." The essay is reprinted in *Selected Prose*. See also Zukofsky's reply of 11 July 1936.

Coughlin: Father Charles E. Coughlin, who in his radio speeches and publications attacked Communists, President Roosevelt, labor unions, and private banking.

Farm boober party: In the spring of 1936, the leaders of the Minnesota Farmer-Labor Party attempted to organize a national Third Party movement. By June the attempt had failed.

Farley: James A. Farley, President Roosevelt's Postmaster General.

two paladins: Probably Earl Browder and V. J. Jerome. Zukofsky to Pound, 10 June 1936, "I've sent you the address of Earl Browder (BROWDER) Sec'y of the U.S. Communist Party & V.J. Jerome, Editor of The Communist, Nat'l Organ of the U.S. Com. Party. Your only response has been the shutting of both eyes. I'll give you the address again: both are at Workers Center, 35 East 12th St., N.Y.C. You can contact one or both as you please."

75. ALS–7.

July 11/36 111 E 36 St N.Y.

Dear E: Neschec & (not "Tarbit," you goy!) Marbis (or Marbit or Marbith as it is writ. in Eng.—I have never been able to fathom why the Hebrew s is transformed into a lisp when rendered into English.). Meaning: respectively biting (like a snake's bite)—Neschec; and increase (with connotation of accretion, pathological?)—Marbis.

My father's opinion seems to be merely literal explanation of text of all of Leviticus, 25; his natural & sweet conscience troubling him wherever he runs across an explicit difference, or what may possibly be interpreted as an implicit difference, btwn the rights of yid & goy. All that follows is his opinion, (not mine which is naturally that of Shagetz, my interest in the whole matter being confined to common ownership of ⟨farm⟩land & unfortified cities by the people—evidently the bastard hierarchy wuz in control of the fortified cities—& which offers resemblances to rights guaranteed by Soviet Const.).

Dada (my father) saze: obviously, line 36, re- usury applies to thy brother, the Jew. And so does 37. But obviously neither 36 nor 37 implies that a jew shd. take interest from a goy. He calls attention to the fact that the law as expressed in Leviticus 25, ⟨verses⟩ 36 & 37 is paramount, & that belief in it compels that no true adherant of the faith take interest of anyone with impunity. And that is the absolute sense of the passage as fur as ethics is concerned. Nevertheless, he calls attention ⟨to⟩ the fact (a very distant one to him who goes to the synagogue 3 times a day, & still works as a presser at an average weekly wage of $7 a week at age of over 70) that under the diaspora the absolute carrying ⟨out⟩ of the law has not been possible. The Jews get around it among 'emselves by the lender charging a "fair rate" after making out a written agreement with the borrower, making the former a contractural partner in the enterprise to which the loan is put—hence the permissible rake off, the assumption being the borrower wd. not be able to carry on any bizness or living without the loan. Without said written agreement, no lender may ⟨now⟩ charge interest. Pawpaw also assumes that all goyim are to-day aware of this under the present state of things, forced-on-people circumvention of the law, and that therefore similar agreement is made out for loans to goyim. And as far as he is concerned, my father asserts it is a crime to make any distinction.

Obviously whatever sense there is in his "interpretation" is historical, & not Messianic, absolute etc (except the fact that he's an honest man, that you're an honest man etc). Where he's Messianic he's as antiquated as you sunk in an absolute which has no useful relation to the present, or a bettering of the present. Strikes me in trying to isolate the root-idea of the reprehensibility of usury—which is what you seem to be doing?—you forget that even roots grow in a soil, & that soil changes with the times. You're both suffering from cart-before-the-horseness. Serves you right for not making any effort to understand Marx's criticism of Proudhon: "the economic forms in which men produce, consume, exchange are transitory and historical . . . Why does M. Proudhon talk about universal reason . . is he not implicitly & necessarily admitting that he is incapable of understanding economic development . . What is society, whatever its forms may be? The product of men's reciprocal activity. Are men free to choose this or that form of society for themselves? By no means. Assume particular stages of development in production, commerce & consumption & you will have a corresponding social order . . civil society. Presuppose a particular civil society, & you will get particular conditions which are only the official expression of civil society. M. Proudhon will never understand this because he thinks he is doing something great by appealing from the State to society—that is to say from the official summary of society to official society."

On the face of it, it ought to strike anybody with a little common sense that the contradictions in Leviticus 25—such ⟨as⟩ verse 10 against verse 44—"proclaim liberty thruout all the land" and "they shall be yr. bondmen forever, but over the children of Israel etc"—are the results of different tempers operating under different conditions, & with different motives, & probably at different times—i.e. if you want to be mythical at all verse 10 is nearer to having been produced in the golden age, whereas 44 must have been an interpolation of the age of iron.

It is ridiculous to speak of "communist efforts to obscure the Jewish question" when they obviously understand all the nationalist ramifications of it—ranging from sponsorship of Biro-bidfan to opposition of Jewish fascists in Palestine. "Jewish internationalism"—there ain't no such thing & exists only in yr. mind tainted by Nazi bigotry—or some other infernal silliness beyond yr. sensible control. Might as well speak of Italian internationalism or French or whatever. Bankers internationalism is another matter—but that ain't confined to nations or dispersed nations: that exists, & that's what you want to wipe out. Neither is there any such thing as Soviet Internationalism—There is ⟨against bankers internationalism⟩ communist internationalism—the struggle of the workers of the world all engaged in the present stage of workers' national struggles all over the world against the imperialist oppressors of the world who operate in different nations so as to affect all the nations of the world. If you think a Jewish banker or a jewish worker is now affected by sumpn which has faded into a book like Leviticus written 3000 yrs ago, you're just wasting yr. time.

Ethics: There is enough ethics in Communist Manifesto: Capital is not a personal, it is a social "power," & realizing the consequences of that statement is what that statement ⟨the Manifesto⟩ is about. Chap II of Manifesto is all ethics, if you're willing to read. The "free development of each is the condition for the free development of all" is as good as Confucious tho not "received from the sky." In fact, that's the only ethic on which any decent civilization can continue. Marx's "different people are not equal one to another" "but to make the exploitation by one man of many impossible" is enough ethical basis to start any decent govt. now. If you really understood Marx "equal right . . . bourgeoise right . . . presupposes inequality" you wdn't ask if communism proposes to have Any ethics. As for practical day to day working out of ethics under dictatorship of proletariat you can follow up news in U.S.S.R by reading the newspapers: if a drunk or scatterbrain whether railroad engineer or gov't official endangers the lives of the workers he is "liquidated." They recently liquidated a troup of educators working on basis of "new" educational psychology, intelligent tests, segregation of pupils into fit & unfit, psychoanalysis etc.

Can say this much for Amurkn Com. ethics—they don't attack Father Couglin for being a Catholic except in so far as the church is out for gain, & the Rev. Father himself has silver interests which he's trying to safeguard, nurse etc.

Etc——Yrs.

Z.

P.S. My father saze he will consult the local rabbi for his interpretation of Nesech etc—& if there's any further low-down, this shagetz who has ⟨as⟩ much love for the subtleties (if!) of the local Rabbi as for the lacunae of yr. goishe kopf ain't averse to lettin' you have it.

As ever

Z

Shagetz: Leo Rosten's *The Joys of Yiddish* defines a "Shaygets" as a young, male Gentile. But see Zukofsky's letter of 15 April 1940, in which he defines it as an anti-Semitic Jew.

Marx's criticism: Zukofsky quotes from *Karl Marx and Friedrich Engels: Correspondence* (New York, International Publishers, 1934), p. 7. The letter is to P. V. Annenkov, dated 28 December 1846.

Biro-bidfan: Birobidzhan, capital of the Soviet Far Eastern province where the Soviet government encouraged Jewish settlement between 1928 and 1936.

Manifesto: The quotations from Marx, beginning "different people. . . ," "but to make. . ." and "equal right. . . ." are used in "A"–8, p. 45.

76. ALS–3.

July 16/36 111 E. 36 St N.Y.

Dear Ez: There will be no end to it: my father consulted the Rabbis. They confirm his opinion, but nacherally dread the act of making a distinction between Jew and Goy in matter of usury, not from point of view of natural generosity (as my father) but from anticipation of anti-semitism such distinction may provoke. But as you know not all rabbis are better bizness men than my father.

My father has also dug up a commentary on Leviticus, 25,—the gist of which is (wish I had as little to go thru as you!): The Talmud says that a right modesty is the way a good jew disseminates the reason of the faith; also, that the Torah was given to mankind on one of the lowest mountains (Sinai)—God himself behaving according to just principle; that the Torah is like water which flows down but not up a run (i.e. to the people). It flows down to the people, for the people, (by the nipples I suppose).

The Talmud also says that it is a worse evil to cheat you goyim than our own jews, because then (if we do) you will be in a position to slander our faith & our God. Shd. you ⟨az goy⟩ by any chance give me as yid, more money than is coming to me in a transaction, az result of an oversight on your part, I must refund. Whether you find out your error or don't, I must refund. (So don't embarrass us, because we'll never get over it, if we're inclined to embezzlement, our sins will be on our children's heads & children's children unto etc, for the Lord Gord is a zealous Gott etc). And if we are honest, God will reward us double.

Example of Jacob returning ⟨to Pharoah⟩ the silver found in the grain in Egypt: az precedent.

Solomon also urged God to accept the prayers of goyim in the Temple, whether they were worthy or not, so that the goyim wd. not speak against the true faith. —Even in that time the same fears, the same mess. All of which proves (?) that even a chew is not always a "chew."

Tibor [Serly] sailing tomorrow & not sure whether you will be in Rapallo or Siena when he lands, discusses his quandry with me as tho expecting my written guarantee that you will be in one place or the udder. ⟨etc⟩—as ever

Z

77. TLS–1.

23 July [1936] Rapallo

Dear Zuk

AZ to reezults. If it is any satisfaction to you, I had news ⟨yester p.m.⟩ from head of one of the small worker's parties in Eng/ that was sympathetic to germany that they have dropped antisemitism. Three letters from yr/ aged friend in a week after some preliminary work.

AND lemme say that fer six months that bloke has been putting out some of the best (i,e; most active and cutting) anti semitic stuff I have seen.

This is OFF the main line of argument. BUT yet it AINT so off, as it indicates dropping of irrelevant fuss, for fundamentals.

I don't suppose you ever deign to speak to a fellow N. Yorker, but if you ever did get mixed with someone who denied the authorship of the Yiddisher Charlestown BAND, etc/ you might as well have this item.

That pore fool Basil has got to London, having gone to Canaries for QUIET. ‹don't print›

2 Doughty St. W.C.1

And you can look up my Lenin in N[ew].E[nglish].W[eekly]. four numbers July 2;9,16 and today.

a) leavin this machine fer the summer.

E

head: Graham Seton Hutchison, leader of the minuscule National Workers' Party.
Yiddisher: Published in *An "Objectivists" Anthology*. Gallup B29.
Basil: Basil Bunting had been living in the Canary Islands. He departed for England just before the outbreak of the Spanish Civil War on 18 July 1936.
my Lenin: "Atrophy of the Leninists." Gallup C1346, C1349, C1350 and C1353.

78. TLS–2.

nex day or whenzdy 24 March [1937] Rapallo

⟨Z⟩

Waaaal; I hav read it/ an Olga [Rudge] has read it, an I know a helluva lot of peepul who never WILL read it, and it is heavy, and it has some good stuff in it, as on P/ 20/25/33

And it don't show that Marx knew anything about money/ AND I xxpekk the only way to make didactic poesy is to KNOW fer sure.

Anyhow poetry can NOT consist in trying to anchor knowing to what some bloke KNEW.

And Marx was far from an entire man. Lenin knew his own limitiation/ Trotsk the iggurunt ape, with no literary or plastic sensibility tried to blubb about art and letters.. waaal whazza use/ a iggurunt professor is no more a poet or critic than a learned professor.
However A.8 ain't CRAP. and that is a distinction.

But it wd. be better poesy if you weren't trying to argue the reader into thinking you know more than you do know.

and as fer Auden getting printed/ NATURALLY blokes git printed where they have friends etc/

Rupe Brook wuz printed.

As you are too goddam lazy to circulate, and as Miss Millay gets printed/ and as the boob Zabel is NOT pleased to get three cantos fer pore ole [H]Arriet[Monroe]'s arse rag . . . what do you eexxxxxxpkk ov Amurikah.

Whoever does print it wont git their money back

I pint out ALSO that both Arriet and the Dial mutilated Propertius (the one) and Mauberly the other.

so dont go to gittin prosecution cx/

I wuzza going to giv/ it to [Gerhart] Münch last night and fergot/ but he haz xxpresst interest/

⟨He⟩ having just set the gol dumbest lot of stuff (Goethe's f[a]ust, repeated by a half/living goy/hun Midnight mass/

all simple and dull and no discoverable technique in the writing)

for 4000 more or less instruments choRuss, orgum etc.

waaal I hope to gorrr he git zit played.

Wer bist du/ ?

I am the whoosis,

Ver bist do, wo pisst du etc.

I am the whassis. etc.

hoodo in the dark. and so fort/ Der Menchs, Das Weip/

der Münch / undsoWeiter.

Waaal; me Japs izza movin.

More tdone dtamm you, I gann stdill hear deh
ZZingerzz.

However the boy CAN play the pyanny. I and I spose he knows some contrapunto.

What's Serly'ssymph/ sound like?

an wot iz ole Bull [Williams] a snoozin? etc?

yrz. EZ

have read it: "A"–8.
Trotsk: See Leon Trotsky's *Literature and Revolution.*
Brook: Rupert Brooke (1887–1915), British poet.
Miss Millay: Edna St. Vincent Millay, American poet. Winner of the Pulitzer Prize for Poetry in 1923.
Zabel: Morton Dauwen Zabel, editor-in-chief of *Poetry.*
arse rag: Poetry.
Propertius: The March 1919 issue of *Poetry* contained only four sections of *Homage to Sextus Propertius.*
Mauberly The September 1920 issue of *The Dial* printed the first six poems of Part I of *Hugh Selwyn Mauberley.*
Münch: German pianist and conductor. Münch was a frequent summer visitor to Rapallo. He often participated in the summer concerts organized by Pound.
Japs: Katue Kitasono's *Vou* group. In a letter to Kitasono of 11 March 1937, Pound thanked him for sending their poems. Paige, *Letters,* p. 292.
Serly'ssymph/: Symphony No. 1, by Tibor Serly. Eugene Ormandy conducted the Philadelphia Orchestra in its New York premiere at Carnegie Hall, 26 January 1937.

79. ALS–4.

1 Apr. 1937 111 E. 36 St N.Y

Dear Ez: Lessee, I woke up this morning, after dreaming the lonza leggiera had just made its way thru my door—only it did more like a great Dane and wuz yellow without spots. No anagoge intended, tho the theosophists can record it. Anyhow, yr. letter wuz downstairs. ⟨And you can record that.⟩

No, I don't have a "prosecution cx."

Naturally, I didn't expect yr. reading A–8 to settle any controversy, so I'm quite settled & have gone on with it for 10 lines more. Glad to have the numbers of some of the pp. you liked.

In re- yr query as to Serly's symph. One wd. say it is *lovely* as to someone who had done something sufficiently competent and clear. It does not, however, come up to the dynamics one might expect from it, from listening to the piano score. Gives one the feeling of a concerto with the solo part omitted. More a work of chamber music than a symphony—i.e. of the order of something that had been done before and yet valid enough to-day. I can't say that his melody gives one the feeling of an inevitable source, of moving in a straight line without constructions stopping it, but the various groups of instruments carry thru their parts polyphonically, are *heard* over & against each other, and that effect is enhanced naturally by the visual execution of the players. I.e.⟨as⟩I⟨heard⟩ it there is enough order & absence of shoddy in the score to force the players not to slop all over 'emselves. And this is a layman's opinion. I expected fire and got something more like regimentation, but it was always enjoyable—the disappointment changing almost immediately into the pleasant surprise that the terrible Tibor had ordered hisself. My fears are for the future—I shd. like to hear his work for wind instruments before I decide as to what he has done—i.e. I can't say the symph. is invention. In fact, his Viola Concerto, has more gism. All of which I've told him, & I think he wuz prepared for it, tho' a little surprised that one shd. tell him. Nacherally we needn't repeat it to him. The trouble is—& I told him that too—that he wants to go over with his audience, as success, and he tries to make it easy for 'em (or at least he says he does, pieces together early work with "new experiment" in rhythms, which *don't* strike me as being as new as the best in Harlem, & not at all consecutive mechanism of Stravinsky). He shd. forget his pooblic & give what is in him, if it is, even at cost of success. At that, the audience I'm sure wd. prefer being hit on the head by power, rather than exposed to something more comme il faut. He's on the whole too good to fool anybody & not clever enough to sweep 'em up with a "popular" work. And why 'n hell he gives a thought to the latter end beats me: there is enough of an audience willing to listen to serious *modern* work. That he didn't get Gugg[enheim]. again this year is proof that his bizness tactics, at least, is wrong. Wish you had heard symph. & if yr. opinion confirmed mine, you cd. tell him to forget compromise & write exactly what he feels he shd. be writing.

You on Munsch's new score in the great Wagnerian tradition, the night we descended the mountang into Rapallo.

What iz Japs which you say "izza movin"?

Bill [Williams] has said some analytical things on A–8 worth having as analysis of prosody. He spoke over the air recently & read from his poems, youthful as ever, with a voice almost as pleasant as the President's—even if a bit nervous. He shd. exploit it. And the radio is the nearest I've got to him in six months.

Yes Basil [Bunting] wrote me about the mess. Easy enough to understand why he feels as etc. But the worst of it is he's prob. so in the dumps, he won't even write. Maybe if he cd. be published—

The Townsman, London Mag., wrote me & I offered to review Polite Essays. But I don't want to do anything else without pay. I did send two short pomes. Az fer A–8, if I can't get paid for it, I don't care to have it printed yet—want to try Am. publisher first etc, so unless you know of anyone, mag or what that'll pay don't please bother to circulate it to edtrs. etc.—The more of yr. friends 'll read it, the better tho, I appreciate that since it ain't anything to skim, & my respects to those who have troubled to read it.

Just got the card you wrote before yr. letter: what I say on pg 32 is that if the bloomink workers would issue it, there wd. be a revolution, & there Ain't no preventive—nuthin didactic about that, chust statement history seems to support.

Thanks for asking Faber to send Cantos etc.

As ever,

Z.

lonza leggiera: Inferno, Canto 1, 11. 31–32. "Ed ecco, quasi al cominciar de l'erta / una lonza leggiera. . . ." Charles Singleton's translation: "And behold, near the beginning of the steep, a leopard light-footed. . . ."

the mess: Pound to Zukofsky, 23 March 1937, "Las' I heard of Bzl his wif had left and took the chillens. It wuz preyin on his cerebrum/ why? some folks iz never satisfied."

Townsman: A London literary magazine edited by Ronald Duncan. Zukofsky's poems were not published. Pound did, however, manage to place two poems by Katue Kitasono in the first issue.

Polite Essays: Published by Faber in February 1937. Gallup A42.

the card: Pound to Zukofsky, 23 March 1937, "Re/ P:32 The answer is if the bloomink workers WOULD only issue it, but they keep on refusing to think an issue wd. be of any use."

what I say: "A"–8, p. 89. "Preventives for this ease?/ Friends, let two fingers salute./ If these banks' moneys come out of nothing/ And take out of all/ Will No Thing–No Man–/ Resign to the people's issue of nothing,/ Or must he devolve upon all?" In a letter of 8 March 1937 to Pound, Zukofsky had written, "There is a passage on pg. 32 (of the enclosed MS) meant to answer another in yr. Canto XLVI." There are two passages in Canto 46 that Zukofsky could have meant: "The bank makes it *ex nihil*" and "Bank creates it ex nihil."

80. ALS–3. Enclosure.

Dec. 7/37 41 W. 11 st N.Y.C.

Dear E: Murkin contract for your 5th Decade, O.K., will be glad to get copy in time.

I thought you didn't like Trotsky. So why recommend me Partisan Rev[iew].? In any case, I doubt if they'll put forth more than one issue. The day of the little magazine is definitely over. Nobuddy sees even a commercial venture like Globe anywhere around—not even in Brentano's which has damn near everything—not to mention Partisan. Seein' as you might appreciate a fact, if you can see it—were here to see it—the battle as far as the mag. field is concerned is between Universities old style & the newly "enlightened" factions in 'em. Old Nick & his ilk & the trustees will support Harpers etc, & the younger professors concerned with economick etc will make a go of Science & Society, Marxist Quarterly, New Masses. Lost on the fringe of things the younger litterati who don't know nuthin & have less guts & less conviction will hang on to corrup the latter (New Masses or Daily Worker etc) or break away if they can't make pin money & form cliques etc which will come to naught anyway.

What concerns yr. erst. son are the facts, Communism. Not how to make a leettle beezness of an idea. The leetle politick of the small ticks etc too petty to go into, & even the successes of a Gregory (Horace) who has had "A"–8 since June 7, & has not answered 7 letters asking for its return & appropriated ⟨the⟩ return postage to boot, not disturbing enough to despair about when one knows he too etc can't last in face of the movement, & that the people will read poesy after the Revolution.

Wdn't even mention it except for the pass-the-buck, I-should-worry-attitude of the elders of yr. generation which since 1933 say have publickly not winked an eye at the good work—what you know—to be the only good work of the young not so young anymore. If that has caused the rise of the Cambridge, Oxford, Blooms buggery "communists," aryio-kikes (sic) etc, you know who's to blame—or shd. know.

What I need, & I wdn't mention it except that you persist in recommending me gristle, not even a bone, like Partisan Rev. is a Reputable Bourgeois Publisher. And a thunk & a wunk of an eye & a push—balls, as you know, unfinished intention toward life, IF, has nothing to do with it.

However, I shdn't kick beink still on W[orks]P[rogress]A[dministration] in even a responsible position while it lasts, since I am now outlining the economic, political background of American Design (useful arts)—and with a chance to read & study history. Before me, Basil [Bunting] who is probably starving shd. be taken care of.

I would send you "A Test of Poetry" which now is finished, if I cd. have another copy typed, but the rent, as you say, must be paid first. So I will myself go the rounds of the publishers with the unique copy I have.

The "POINT of the Fufth" Decad, Usura etc nacherally one can't escape your intention, but Ef I thought XLV were as inevitable as XXX on which in your blood it is founded—

What interests me about XLIX is not the ivory fishpond, but the fact that you have used words and sounds, cadence & beat ⟨& pause⟩ like strokes of the chinese characters, that it is a development of technique 20 years after Cathay, the outgrowth but not at all like Cathay (whatever its beauties)—and I told you since prob. no more than 3 people in Europe will verify you, & no one here but yr. erst son, since I've already tried it on all the smart people & they just have to be told.

And there's a comprehensive woman here, techincal [*sic*] supervisor of the project (Index of Am. Design, Fed. Art.) & expert textile designer one Ruth Reeves who says she knows you, & who has read "A"–8 with intelligent liveliness, so add a fifth reader for yrs. trewly—and as for a close, conclusions. I enclose the latest angle of incidence.

An epic New Year & to all there.

etc

Z.

contract: Here and in his reference to *Partisan Review,* Zukofsky seems to be responding to a Pound letter that has not survived. *The Fifth Decad of Cantos* was published by Farrar & Rinehart in November 1937. Gallup A43b.

Globe: A travel magazine based in St. Paul, Minnesota. In a letter of 24 July 1937, Pound had recommended it to Zukofsky as a source of income. There is no evidence, however, that Zukofsky ever submitted any articles. Pound published several items in *Globe* in 1937 and 1938.

Nick: Nicholas Murray Butler.

Science & Society: Science & Society: A Marxian Quarterly began publication in the fall of 1936. It was based in New York.

Marxist Quarterly: This periodical published three numbers in 1937 and then expired.

aryio-kikes: Pound to Zukofsky, 29 November 1937, "And say aint we got keplol levy/ or Levy and all the aryio-kikes." Allusion unidentified.

Design: The Index of American Design, a survey of American decorative arts and crafts, conducted by the Federal Art Project.

A Test: Published in 1948 (New York: The Objectivist Press).

"POINT. . . .": Pound to Zukofsky, 29 November 1937, "The point of that Fifth is the Usura."

fishpond: Canto 49 has come to be known as "The Seven Lakes Canto." Zukofsky singled out the last seven lines of this watery canto for praise in his statement printed in Charles Norman's *The Case of Ezra Pound* (New York: The Bodley Press, 1948). The statement was reprinted as "Work/Sundown" in *Prepositions* (pp. 165–166).

latest angle: A poem titled "Anew: I." This poem, minus the title, became the third poem in *Anew* (Prairie City, Illinois: The Press of James A. Decker, 1946). *All,* p. 86.

81. TLS–1.

10 Lug. [1938] Rapallo

Dear Zuk

Hope you and BZL [Bunting] will accept dedication, at present am being taxed by the damn brit/ fisc/ and also paying fer proove corrections in EXCESS. So you will have to wait fer Laughlin's emission of KULCH. ⟨to see same⟩

wotter you know about Khazars? Bloke has just writ me that "only a small percentage of jews are semites". "Khazars converted between 200 and 1000 de notre ere"

wot abahat it?

neat alibi fer blokes who don't wanna be reeeesponsible fer Mike Gold's mentality/ and would eggs/plain a lot.

Do you pussnly favour being a sem/ or a Tartar?

Undboubtedly the neschekers are gittin UN=pupular. A nice anti=neschek boom wd/ conduce to the amenities/ I mean FROM a semetic source (whether Khazars be included or knot)
I suspect address on the env/ is out of date/ but dunno where a later one is.

my kurryspondent favours the lean long headed jew as vs/ the Khazar. waaaal . . zamatter of act/ all the good ones I have known WERE thin. But blime!!

EP

dedication: Pound dedicated *Guide to Kulchur* (first published in America as *Culture*) to Zukofsky and Bunting.
Laughlin's: James Laughlin, founder of New Directions. *Culture* was the first New Directions publication of Pound.
Khazars: An ancient people who, according to the Eleventh Edition of *The Encyclopaedia Britannica,* inhabited "the territory between the Caucusus, the Volga and the Don, with the outlying province of the Crimea." They ceased to exist as a separate entity in the 11th century. According to *The Jewish Encyclopedia* (Funk & Wagnalls, 1903), "large numbers" of them converted to Judaism in the 7th and 8th centuries, "the chazhans of the Chazars . . . took great interest in and protected their coreligionists, the Jews."
Bloke: Unidentified.
neschekers: See Pound's letter of 25 June 1936 and Zukofsky's letter of 11 July 1936.

82. ALS–3.

July 23/38 41 West 11 St New York

Dear Ez: Can't guess what <u>Kulchah</u> is about, but if you want to dedicate yr. book to a communist (me) and a British-conservative-antifascist-imperialist (Basil [Bunting]), I won't sue you for libel, and I suppose you know Basil. So dedicate.

From what news I can gather about Italy—the height of its contemp. culture seems to be the concerts at Rapallo—I got nuthn against music.

But how, why, shd. I know about Khazars, & why shd. they bother you? Are you sure your correspondent ain't kiddin you and doesn't mean the Hebrew word Chazir (= swine)? Basil is the authority on the Tartars, when I get in touch with him again, I'll refer yr. query to him. Maybe

Jewish Encyclopedia has a convenient article—I remember one on Chinese Jews. But "pussnly" I don't give a damn whether I'm a Semite or a Tartar. Mike Gold's real name being Granich & his parents hailing from Roumania is ultimately probably one of yr. pure Latins, if not a gypsy. Fat & lean jews—well a chazir iz a chazir—Smollett says they sewed up the guts of the poultry in London, thus fattening 'em & then sold 'em to the people.

Basil wuz here for 2 months, trying to get job as navigator on yacht, or wut else, & now has gone for west coast on chance that there might be a job there for an extra in the movies. I hope he lands one. Things probably not so hopeful there either.

Yes, my address as you see is still the same.

Wuz gonna write you about it—but I enclose the program instead—the singers ain't much to brag about but they attempt something at least.

Hope you put all this to good uses

as ever, yrs

Z

Smollett: Tobias George Smollett (1721–1771), British novelist. In Smollett's *The Expedition of Humphry Clinker* (1771), Matthew Bramble observes that in London "the poultry is all rotten, in consequence of a fever, occasioned by the infamous practice of sewing up the gut, that they may be the sooner fattened in coops, in consequence of this cruel retention."
program: Enclosure lacking.

83. ALS-2.

Nov. 14/38 41 W. 11 St N.Y.C.

Dear Ez: [James] L[aughlin] IV sent "Culture," so I hope you haven't gone thru the trouble of reminding him. I have read up to p. 162, and will continue. It is hard, however, after your mention of Hitler on p. 134 to continue without going back to yr. Digest of The Analects. There are things—oh, maybe a hundred, between that chapter and where I stopped that gave pleasure, coming from right reason, but I remember only "Man is an over-complicated organism. If he is doomed to extinction he will die out for want of simplicity." Yes, the Analects have endured. And if I weren't concerned, & didn't appreciate yr. dedication, I wouldn't be writing this letter.

It may interest you that Jerry [Reisman] here saw a relation btwn the Gaudier on the jacket & the frontispiece, before seeing p. 346. Or rather he probably hasn't seen it yet. —I mean if you're interested in public reaction to yr. method.

I go back—to-day—to the German terror. If the Duce is the great man you say he is on p. 105, you can affect another meeting that might save the mug of Central Europe AND Italy in the eyes of the world?

On the other hand, Jerry says you should also meet Fermi in Rome.

I'd rather have sent "A"–9 than this, but things don't* go too fast in the desert. But you'll get it—what's fit to see—in time, I hope.

Yrs

Z.

*"Shdnt.", I should have said.

Hitler: "Form-sense 1910 to 1914. 15 or so years later [Wyndham] Lewis discovered Hitler. I hand it to him as a superior perception." *Guide to Kulchur,* p. 134.

Digest: Chapter 1, Section 1, Part 1, of *Guide to Kulchur.*

"Man is. . . .": Guide to Kulchur, p. 135.

the Gaudier: The Gaudier profile drawing of Pound used on his stationery.

frontispiece: The profile of Salustio Malatesta impressed in wax.

p. 346: Pound praises a London architect named Ricards, "a man with a true sense of form, that is in three dimensions and hollow. His buildings were magnificent until finished. Their structure was the work of genius and their final encrustation the tin-horn ornament of the never sufficiently damned 1900. AND at this same time Gaudier was out of employment and wd. willingly have made architectural odds and ends."

p. 105: "Mussolini a great man, demonstrably in his effects on event, unadvertisedly so in the swiftness of mind, in the speed with which his real emotion is shown in his face, so that only a crooked man cd. misinterpret his meaning and his basic intention."

Fermi: Enrico Fermi, Italian physicist. He emigrated to the United States in 1939.

desert: Pound's dedication: "To Louis Zukofsky and Basil Bunting[,] strugglers in the desert[.]"

84. ALS–4.

Jan 18/39 41 W. 11 St N.Y.C.

Dear E: Yours of Jan 7th here.

As I said more or less in my last—your letter which offended Basil [Bunting] because he feels I'm a very Jewish Jew, which I don't feel, was written to me. It was none of his business to take it upon himself etc, but I admire him for having done it, whatever reservations I may have as to the usefulness of his action. He thinks it may lead you to think again. Frankly, I don't.

There is no use calling anybody names, when the time and one's health demand acting on one's own conviction as best as one can under handicaps—there is no use, the way I'm made up, reasoning with your convictions as they are now. If I'm good enough, I'll reach more fruitful ground. In your case, the best I can do is shut up. That does not mean I don't respect yr. integrity. I've gone on respecting it ever since you got yourself drowned in the batter of credit economics—at a loss ⟨to myself⟩ of every practical & helpful contact in U.S. & Europe. I don't regret it. From point of practical politics, I'm not ready and never will be to attack you before the public. Can't help it, if I start with a feeling like integrity. There are some things that are personal, & one can't build right, on them, as if they were not.

I don't doubt that to yourself, you are "serious character" "wanting to see the ROOT." All I say is you don't see it. Blame my stupidity or your own, but as I've said time & time again there's no use our arguing once an impasse has been reached. I can't see the use in it, in view of your Fascist position, yr. reaction to the events in Spain, your statements about Hitler etc etc, your unwillingness to see what Russia's position really is. Yr. articles in Brit[ish].-It[alian]. Bulletin, N[ew].E[nglish].W[eekly]., etc, are not worth one's time looking at, let alone worth intelligent discussion. I cannot see—tho I have made every attempt to understand social credit—that any good can come out of thinking that involves itself in a mess of "incarnation" etc such as Douglas has recently involved himself. Obviously, these things affect you. I can't take 'em seriously, except as symptoms of the rest of the mess. I agree with you, burning down an orphanage in Germany & sending ⟨the⟩ naked kids to the Dutch border under military escort is only a <u>symptom</u>, but you don't <u>know</u> the root.

You tell me my "quote" from Marx is merely a blurred bit from Aristotle. If you took the trouble to read M., he'd tell you so himself. And if you took the trouble to read, you'd see that he faces the problem of money & defines its nature etc etc, & that the metaphysics he uses as thin disguise is just one huge piece of irony. But you won't read, so let it go at that. As for yr. anti-semitism I believe you're no more anti- than Marx himself, tho' the cluttered mess of the rest of yr. economic & political thinking makes it appear so. Naturally I can't give you "Data on jewish participation in drive toward monetary health"—it happens that the jews who think about such things understand the ROOT problem, & that one jew in Holland doesn't.

No use going on in this vein. I sent you Anew 6 the last time, not because the Marx "quote" in the Postscript was intended to impress you as Torah any more than the rest of it. The intention of the postscript is merely to say that such & such things enter the human intelligence & complex of feeling in the process of writing a poem. To clinch what I've been saying, I enclose the first two stanzas of a canzone—knowing what you know about poetry is more than most of us know I'm not ashamed to send you uncompleted work, if you care to be bothered. The local small fry would no doubt accuse me of being a fascist for having lived with the Guido as basis day in & day out for the last two years. You will probably see how far gone I am on the Marx side of it, & attribute all my faults to the influence of his unenlightened use of language. But no matter if there's any poetry in ⟨it⟩, you'll still see it, I believe. Some insight a man never loses. —But let's not correspond about politics etc.

As ever,

Z.

your letter: In a letter to Zukofsky of 2 December 1938, Pound suggested that the Rothschilds (rather than Hitler) were at fault for the persecution of the Jews in Germany. Bunting saw the letter and wrote an angry retort to Pound.

my "quote": Notes for poem 29 of *Anew* (but numbered "6" in the version Zukofsky sent to Pound–probably in December 1938). *All,* p. 114.

"Data. . . .": Requested by Pound in a letter of 7 January 1939.

one jew: Pound to Zukofsky, 2 December 1938, "so far as known, only ONE Jew, Ernst Loeb is working for monetary decency. He is in Holland and I suppose will get about as much 'hand' from the local sanhedrin as Spinoza had."

Anew 6: Ultimately collected as "Anew 29" in *All.*

canzone: Enclosure lacking. Probably the first two stanzas of "A"–9, First Half.

Guido: Guido Cavalcanti, whose "Donna mi Prega" serves as a basis for "A"–9.

85. TLS–2.

22 March [1940] Rapallo

Dear Zuk

If I dont answer yr/ letter ⟨arrived yester⟩ now and partially gord knows when I will get time to answer even less of it.

I am glad you are having a rebirth or spring freshet. The Catullus is good / am not sure of "girl" in line So Long, girl, etc . . . sounds literary not real speech but by very small margin. / dearie; wd. come nearer London.

I have never heard "girl" alone in vocative. "my girl," dialect ⟨or old Victorian⟩
question of vocative accent/ believe some phoney gk/ words in the 17th declension shift an accent/ hence the wrong reading of Sappho's ⟨ποικιλοθρον⟩

(gord I didn't KNOW any grammar, but preferred the right accent, and don't yet know which declension it is, or if Dazzi invented it. HOWever.

Lay off it, you ass, Catullus
Its finish', na poo, its over, damn you, it is OVER it was good while it lasted, and it stopped being, damn it you had her, she liked it
⟨etc⟩
Now she dont want it. (good line)
so long, sis, Catty can take it.
you'll miss him at fucking time /
what is the good of you anyhow? ⟨to suffer yrself⟩
who'll notice yr/ undies?

and so forth

The canzone seems to me harmless undergrad/ exercise.

Mebbe if you an th kumrad an ole Ez and ⟨Boozle B[unting]⟩ keep AT it, we'll evolve ⟨in ano Rez 24 years⟩ a style of the period that will give the Catullian certainty/ estlin [Cummings] clicked in his "Dirge".

//

Weelll mebbe just as well I didn't see yr/ proposal re/ Jeff. It is O.K. as a proposal to what I spose a awarding commytea may be//

danger of its being a smoke screen to keep pea/roozer's mind off of Jefferson's main content or "message"??
BUT anything that gets him into the gnus IZ good.

///

Thank god I've finally found a quotation from Chas. Mordecai Marx on Rothschild etc/ that will stop off Bull Bublle WillieYams [Williams] from tellin the woild I am an anti=semite.

If Karl weren't I aint. If YOU had had a better hand at quotin' ⟨Marx⟩ you might have got me into the ranks sooner. I sure am with the late lamented on THAT point.

⟨Re housepitality.⟩

Thanks fer the invite? answer in the affirmative. will Celia [Zukofsky] egg-spect me to dine wiff me hat on so as to seem like the Zewkorfsky homestead? ⟨its ok by me⟩

Who was J.R. Drake? a admiral pirate? I have been unable to read yr/ encyclopedic whatiz on poesy/ it may be O.K. fer them that dont know the answer; but when I read I want to learn something I DO NOT KNOW, not to be bored to death by being told what I learned in 1897.

The test of peotry IZ: 1. can EZ read it? 2/ can he read it with approval and/or pleasure?

an' as Kreymborg learned about chess/ when you see a good move? NO, dont make it, look fer a better one.

deewotedly yrn.

Ez Pound

⟨ang-sax
geo-man pierat⟩

yr/ letter: Of 23 February 1940, enclosing a translation of Catullus VIII. *All,* pp. 97–98.

Sappho's ⟨ποικιλοθρον⟩: This is the first word of Sappho's ode to Aphrodite. See Edgar Lobel and Denys Page, *Poetarum Lesbiorum Fragmenta* (Oxford: Oxford University Press, 1955). There is no connection between the Catullus poem and Sappho's ode. Pound's consideration of the use of the vocative case in the former caused him to recall the Sappho ode, whose first word is a vocative. Pound's remark about the "wrong reading" refers to the fact that some editions of Sappho printed ποικιλοφρον rather than ποικιλοθον'. There is of course no "17th declension." For an extensive commentary on the word and the poem, see Denys Page, *Sappho and Alcaeus: An Introduction to the Study of Ancient Lesbian Poetry* (Oxford: Oxford University Press, corrected edition 1959), pp. 3–18. Pound also quotes the first line of the ode in Canto 76. In the third chapter of *ABC of Reading* he says, "I know of no better ode than the POIKILOTHRON. So far as I know, Catullus is the only man who has ever mastered the lady's metre."

Dazzi: Torquato Manlio Dazzi, Italian librarian, translator, and friend of Pound.

canzone: Zukofsky's "A foin lass bodders," a parody of Cavalcanti's "Donna mi Prega."

kumrad: E. E. Cummings.

"Dirge": Cummings' "flotsam and jetsam." E. E. Cummings, *Complete Poems 1913–1962* (New York and London: Harcourt Brace Jovanovich 1980), p. 492. In "A Visiting Card," Pound remarks that in this poem Cummings "achieves a Catullian ferocity." *Selected Prose: 1909–1965,* ed. William Cookson (New York: New Directions, 1973; London: Faber & Faber, 1973), p. 324.

yr/ proposal: In a letter of 3 January 1940, Zukofsky had asked Pound to write a letter of recommendation to Philip M. Hayden of Columbia University. Zukofsky hoped to obtain a "William Bayard Cutting Traveling Fellowship" or "as an alternative, the Columbia University Fellowship, for 1940–41." Zukofsky did not specify what he intended to do with the fellowship, but nevertheless asked Pound to state in the letter of recommendation that "I am fit to do research." In a letter of 23 February 1940, Zukofsky revealed to Pound that his research would be a "revision" of his study of Jefferson's style, a project first conceived in 1930. The title of the study, *How Jefferson Used Words*, appears in the list of abandoned works in "A"–12, p. 257.

the invite: Zukofsky to Pound, 23 February 1940, "Celia & I hope you will see fit, when and if you come to U.S. again, to accept the horsepitality of our 'ome."

Drake: Zukofsky to Pound, 23 February 1940, "Our windows overlook the Bronx River which still runs for a mile and a half or so thru the old haunts of Joseph Rodman Drake." Drake (1795–1820) was an American poet. Portions of his poem "Bronx" are quoted in poem 15 of *Anew*. Some of the vocabulary of "Bronx" is also woven into "A"–11.

whatiz: The manuscript (or parts of it) of *A Test of Poetry*.

Kreymborg: Alfred Kreymborg was an ardent amateur chess player. In his essay "Small Magazines" Pound remarks, "I cannot see that Kreymborg has ever understood language. He is an excellent chess player. Chess is a highly conventionalized game. Each piece moves in a certain, set, determined way. Words do not function in this manner." *The English Journal* 19:9 (November 1930), p. 701. Gallup C787.

86. ALS–4.

Apr. 15/40 1088 E. 180 St New York

Dear Ez: It does me good your liking the Catullus. "And admit it's over" better than "Admit what's over," I had thought of your correction before you wrote, so I'm accepting it now. "Vocative accent" or whatever of "so long, girl" is O.K. tho, good American speech, in any case, good New York.

I enclose the first canzone of the two which will make up "A"–9—which canzone I suspect you'll have a number of objections to, as I have,—if you like it at all. Personally, I've worked too hard and too long at it to dislike it. I suppose it's a sublime failure, or as Jerry [Reisman] says after the movie formula—"Any resemblance to things living or dead is purely coincidental."

I don't suppose anyone'll be anxious to print the canzone—& 2 years actual labor on it plus 7 years thought (?) and study won't, in any case, be rewarded with even nominal compensation. So, since Celia [Zukofsky] can and has offered to mimeograph it, I'll have run off 55 copies, about 30 for friends, and, maybe if someone'll handle 'em, the rest for sale at the prohibitive price of $5. I'm bothering you with the business end of it, because my intention is to get out ⟨the canzone in a⟩ a brochure entitled First Half of "A"–9 to include (in the following order): your text of Donna Mi Prega; Extracts from Marx—Capital Chap. 1–13 & Value, Price & Profit; several notes from modern physicists; your two translations of Guido's canzone; my undergraduate version, part of which you've seen, & Jerry[Reisman]'s; a note on the mathematical analogy to the form of the poem; the canzone as enclosed, & a prose restatement about the same length as the canzone. —And, so, I'd like your permission to include your material along with mine—and if there are any sales of the brochure I'm willing to divide the net income. I hope you'll take time off to answer this part of my letter, even if it's jest a postcard.

You say mebbe if you & Boozle B[unting] & me & the kumrad keep at it, we'll evolve a style of the period. For the record & guidance' sake who'z the kumrad? Enclosed canzone not towards a style of the period. Mebbe the one following will be easier, because the subject won't be Marx, but even so I doubt if it'll fulfill your wish—& mine. However, I've set my mind to it—so I'm not promising Catullian certainty tho the subject will be love. When I'm thru, however, I'll have had enough of "complexity" &

intend to swing entirely—if that is possible—the contrary way. So don't give up hope.

Jerry says " 'you'll miss him at fucking time'?? SHIT! ! !—who'll look up your cunt"? !

Anti-semitism, Marx etc. When a jew says it, it's different: among us we call him a shagetz & let it go at that. Nobody's accusing either you or Bill [Williams] of the crime—but if both of you avoided mention of jew, jews, in your writings, the atmosphere would be less charged all around. I prefer, even knowing the ⟨pure⟩ motives behind your impassions to retreat to the safety of my own home. When Marx, in connection with transformation of money into capital (Chapter 4, Kapital) laces it into "inwardly circumcised Jews," he follows this particular parable with one on the Trinity: I suspect not as palliative, but for further airing of information.

Basil [Bunting] writes of the tremendous display of energy on the part of the English people—"One thinks of . . Rome in Hannibal's time; military genius, superior wealth & the command of the seas were all helpless against it. And yet nearly all the Roman leaders were mediocrities or worse." —I wunner what the war in Scandinavia will show.

I agree with your amendment of Mr. Voorhis' bill H.R. 8080. Naturally. But I can't see the Republican "leadership" being taken in, ⟨in peacetime⟩; and certainly not Mr. Morgenthau, who if he cares for his people—both the Jews and the 'Murkns should resign right now. —Maybe Mr. Voorhis is quite sure there'll be a war? In which isn't he seeing a bit eye to eye with Mr. Col. House Wells? But I certainly have no objection to the banks being taken over.

Anyhow, I hope the intn'l. situation don't prevent yr. visit. You don't have to eat with yr. hat on. If you do, we'll all probably bolt our food, thinking you're in a hurry. But maybe I ought to invite my father to see you wid a hat on, so'z he can say I have one god-fearing friend, tho' he'd probably be too moved with pleasure to utter a word.

O yuss, I saw Dean Pegram of the Graduate faculties of Columbia in re- Cutting etc, & one of the questions he asked was how do I happen to know E.P., with a view I suppose to tracking down the extent of our mutual stability—So maybe he thinks a little more highly of you now.

Yrs

Z.

first canzone: First Half of "A"–9.
the kumrad: E. E. Cummings.
Voorhis' bill: Introduced 23 January 1940. "National Credit for Defense Act—Provides for the issuance of currency (which shall be legal tender but shall not be eligible as cash reserves for banks) equal to the difference between appropriations for the Military and Naval Establishments and the net increase in revenue resulting from wartime taxes which shall equal as nearly as possible the anticipated rate of final consumption of all supplies used by the armed forces. At the conclusion of the war such wartime taxes shall be repealed and any balance of unexpended currency issued hereunder shall be divided pro rata among all citizens 21 years of age." The bill did not become law.
Morgenthau: Henry Morgenthau, Secretary of the Treasury.
Mr. Col. House Wells: Benjamin Sumner Welles, American diplomat. He was Undersecretary of State and a close friend of President Roosevelt. In February and March of 1940, Roosevelt sent Welles to Rome, Berlin, Paris, and London. Welles' ostensible mission was to attempt to arrange a peace. But according to *The Dictionary of National Biography,* "the more immediate aim of the trip was to lure Mussolini away from Hitler." Colonel Edward House was Woodrow Wilson's friend and chief advisor.
Cutting: The William Bayard Cutting Traveling Fellowship.

87. ALS–2.

May 7/51 30 Willow St Brooklyn 2, N.Y.

Dear E: Since I don't know why neither you nor Dorothy answered me a few years ago, I don't want to intrude. Maybe I intruded then by seeming to ask something for myself—and one shouldn't bother friends. Basil [Bunting] has been urging me to write to you, says I have the pride of the devil. I wouldn't know, never having met him—my "orthodoxy" precedes the Hellenistic invention. Nor do I believe what others say that you won't write to a Jew—it does not jibe with your verse on Jeremiah and Micah. Life is bitter and one speaks out of one's blood at times—I understand that. As to my one public statement as to what happened to you—I don't think you need doubt the quality of its affection.

What's there to say? I'm still as thin as I was. You used to approve of thin Jews, and I enjoyed your humor then; I've met a few paunchy ones not worse than myself. I don't feel righteous, and Basil in urging me regrets the quality of some people you're thrust back on. Be that as it is—I am not concerned with names he mentions. Also, if you have heard, as Basil says he heard, that I refused some letters of yours to me for publication because I wanted money that's not true. It will do you no good, I suppose, to know that I offered all your letters to a publisher, provided all royalties go to you and you do the selection—do you no good because without influence such an offer had no effect.

I don't want to go into all this—because it's painful to me, as all the stupid attacks on you during the war were painful to me—dour worms then and after that all spring green.

I wish I could help—I'm no richer than when you knew me. But there may be something I can do to make up for that? If it'll do you any good to hear from me, it will do me good to hear from you.

Life of assistant professor who began as trap-door spider (you will remember your remark about spider) leads to silence—too much of it.

Perhaps you'll find some interest in the enclosures. Only reason for sending them. Basil thought if one can make poetry out of Plato, perhaps he ought to read him again. The double canzone—if you're interested at all, maybe you ought to begin with page 2 "An eye to action; that's recent; then, if you can go to the end, glance back at the first half of pome which you saw 12 years ago—just for look at gyrations of the whole form. I hope "A"–11, after Perch' io non spero, will be less crabbed. You will recognize the Spinoza in A–9: there are no judges who will.

Contacts? Practically none—except occasional correspondence with about three people we once knew (of) in common. Read Edward Dahlberg's Flea of Sodom—especially "The Rational Tree"—we won't dispute about metaphor—the man's good.

You know my wishes. All the best

Yrs

Z

a few years ago: After eight years of mutual silence, Zukofsky wrote Pound on 18 June 1948, requesting his permission to quote from Pound's poetry in *A Test of Poetry*. Pound did not reply.

your verse: Canto 74: " 'Thou shalt purchase the field with money.'/ signed Jeremiah." This is Pound's paraphrase of *Jeremiah* 32:44, "Men shall buy fields for money. . . ." See also Canto 78: "Each one in the name," and Canto 84: "Saith Michah: / Each in the name of. . . ." *Micah* 4:5, "For all people will walk everyone in the name of his God. . . ."

public statement: Zukofsky's statement in Charles Norman's *The Case of Ezra Pound* (New York: The Bodley Press, 1948). Reprinted in *Prepositions* (pp. 165–166) as "Work/Sundown."

a publisher: Unidentified.

enclosures: Enclosures lacking. The "Plato" poetry may have been part of "A"–12. See "A"–12, p. 177.

double canzone: "A"–9.

Perch' io: Guido Cavalcanti's *ballata* beginning "Perch' io non spero," which serves as a framework for "A"–11.

Flea of Sodom: One of the essays in Edward Dahlberg's *The Flea of Sodom* (New York: New Directions, 1950) is "The Rational Tree." In it Dahlberg praises certain customs, rites, and institutions of the ancient Mediterranean world. His remarks often resemble some of Pound's statements in *The Cantos.* For example, Dahlberg points to the quality of a culture's bread as an important index of its vitality: "The first sign of a tepid theogony is a mealy, pinchbeck loaf of bread. False bread and a rabble literature and town go together" (p. 88 of *The Flea of Sodom*).

88. ALS–2.

June 23/54 LOUIS ZUKOFSKY 30 WILLOW STREET
BROOKLYN 1, N.Y.

Dear E: Thanks for writing. I'm writing supt. Barring the unforeseen I should be able to make it Sat or Sun July 10 or 11. I don't suppose pass covers yr. well-wishing family Celia & Paul, aged 10 & pretty good fiddler—in case they get as far as the entrance with me and would rather see you than wait for me? I'll mention possibility to supt. in this writing—so you don't have to bother, unless you prefer seeing me alone—company being heavy—let me know.

[. . . .]

Yrs

Oddysseus etc

supt.: Dr. Winfred Overholser, superintendent at St. Elizabeths Hospital.

Paul: The only child of Louis and Celia Zukofsky. He was already well advanced in his career as a violinist. The Zukofskys visited on 11 July 1954. See David Gordon, "Zuk and Ez at St. Liz," *Paideuma* 7:3 (Winter 1978), pp. 581–584.

89. TL–3.

11[–12] LUG/ [1954] [St. Elizabeths]

impression at p/ 15.

I now divide poetry into what I CAN read and what I cannot. I hv/ read thus far and expect to read to the end. I note that you have got OUT of influence of E.P. and Possum [Eliot]/

NO longer the trace of linguistic parasitism that I noted with surprise on rereading some early Zuk. about 1942.

more Ez/ in it than I had thought.

BUT up to p. 15, I note NONE of that. Zuk on his own. not ALWAYS comprehensible. whether rereading wd/ make it clear I dunno.

alzo not smart elik, as dear Mt kumminkz IS at times.
and TOO bloody often.

** time come to cut away a lot of rubble, of them we once COULD work with/

they being about all (or ALL) there wuz opposing the slicks and sewage in genral.

poem 22. YES, Catullus, translated. good.
is bit a misprint for bite?
CAN yu do TEN Catullus poems?

as incorrigible IMpressario, grampaw sees a chance.

24/ not clear re/ boundaries?? for rhyme or wot T hell?
3 lines O.K.

of course there is the better known "pa's in jail"

fambly named French is EXporting its kids at all cost/ as YU say How the HELL keep Paulito from catchin' the murkn virus GORRRRnoze.

haow can yu keepPUM down on deh fram? that is NOTHING to it.

He'll make a CAREER, o.k. that is easy. Has Basil [Bunting] seen the volumette? He has never mentioned it to me.

2/ damn all I think yu have got yr/ own idiom /

is Zadkine as good as that? have yu a foto of it?

What do yu make of Lekakis? Or if yu haven't made,
go as from me to his studio
57 W. 28th. phone for to be sure MU 9–5391
prenom/ Michael.

*** damn if I see what yu wd/ lose by a rewrite making EVERY line comprehensible.
You've got the slush OUT,
squeezed out/
now what happens if you put in enough grammar etc. to make the stuff TOTALLY intelligible?

vide The Classic Anthology
compiled by Confucius/
whose name the goddam hAAAAAvids
have tried to obliterat / and damn near have TOtally on the dust jacket.

even the "there" who has never seen p. 61

wdn't it be clearer with a comma?
there,

I'd putt one after Jerry,
alZo
and ov curse the Bhloody NOTES shd/hv/ page refs/

****** ____
12 Lug/ AND my prophetik soul / foreseeing: every time that brat gits a thousand $ bukks fer playin Weiniawski, Zuk will be beatin' his breast and crying: why did I beget this cocatrice.
Only practical suggestion is that yu begin distinguishing between infantilism and MUSIC FER ADULTS.

BUT Paolito is young yet, let him have a few games of tiddledeewinks and other suitable, to his age, relaxations.

no use pretending I know all about a score from looking at it without instruments to test. Question of whether C[elia Zukofsky]/ jams one LINERARR statement against another, or merely puts in chords?

No time yester to use ~~min~~ my alledged mind, AND wd/ take helluva lot of work on my part/ why dont that mutt Serley try out some of it? mebbe he has?

definitely the chop Antheil hadn't the Kulch ⟨or GUTZZ⟩ to tackle in 1927. My amateur impression is that the play is too long for a libretto and that a good deal of the speech COULD be brot into more lyric shape/

Metastasio'd.

BUT I haven't worked on it. AND my doin muzik is vurry elephant climbing tree/

again mere theory / but believe third note in a chord is often horsefeathers, a cushion.

pop/ kulch/ raDIO / Weekend / how they tune banJO in Ky/
wich eggsplanes quite a lot/ NOT wohltempiert.
THAT wd/ be a nice title / kumminkz rather:
"wohltempierte banJo,"

p/ 15: Zukofsky had presented Pound with a copy of *Anew* (Prairie City, Illinois: The Press of James A. Decker, 1946). The poem on p. 15 of this edition is poem 9, "For you I have emptied the meaning[.]" *All,* p. 89.

kumminkz: E. E. Cummings.

22: Poem 22 of *Anew*. *All,* pp. 97–98.

24: Poem 24 of *Anew*. *All,* p. 98.

"pa's in jail": Unidentified.

French: William and Gloria French, friends of Pound.

Paulito: Paul Zukofsky.

Zadkine: Poem 25 of *Anew* is "for Zadkine." It is a response to the sculpture "La Prisonnière" (1943) by Ossip Zadkine. *All,* p. 99.

Lekakis: Michael Lekakis, American sculptor.

Classic Anthology: The Classic Anthology Defined by Confucius (Cambridge, Mass.: Harvard University Press, 1954). Gallup A69.

"there": Pound's emendations apply to poem 43 of *Anew* (*All,* p. 112). Zukofsky did not adopt them.

Weiniawski: Henryk Wieniawski (1835–1880) Polish composer and violinist. His *Violin Concerto Number Two* is his most performed work.

a score: Celia Zukofsky often set her husband's poems to music. But the piece under discussion is probably her setting of *Pericles,* eventually published with *Bottom: On Shakespeare.*

90. TL–1.

24 or [2]5 Sep[t. 1955] [St. Elizabeths]

Dear Zuk

The statement that NO jew will ever do anything useful, cannot be sustained / Del Mar did a whale of a LOT that was and is useful.

It might be asked: under what circs/ will a jew do anything useful to anyone but himself,

OR to anyone but himself when not considering the ultimate utility in reflex.

Enthusiast re/ Spirit Romance, yester. spurs me to reflection that I may have IMPROVED the bloody bk/ when preparing for TO reprint.

The floppin' of Oppen / has bred two versions/

Zuk/ may have had further data / since his first report on same.

Bro/ Freedman has dug up a few savory morsels.

The endeavour to distract me from my own concerns / might seem to stem from the venerable Stag without whom no southern regional "movement" wd/ ever have stuck out its touseled and maggoty head.

Now take the case of dear Ruthie / the gal woiks on her technique/ but why the HELL shd/ a damn goy be eggspected to act as wet nurse/

perfectly willing under Hippocratic oath to OPERATE but surely some goddam Kazar shd/ take that bloned head under his wing/

surely them bonnie blue eyes shd/ FIND some sheltering rock in the weary muck heap of N[ew York].?

The N. is sometimes altered/ and van Buren Autobiog has footone New Pork (due to printer)

but the XOIROS ought to be allowed to eat his acorns in peace.

did yu ever DO anything with yr/ wife's muZika fer Peric[les]?

Covici keeps sending me Vick[ing]/ bks/ why dont you coalesce wiff him??

Del Mar: Alexander Del Mar (1836–1926), American author of works on currency and monetary reform.
Enthusiast: Unidentified.
Spirit Romance: See Pound's "post-postscript" in the New Directions printing, in which he notes that To Publishers had not been able to publish the complete, revised version of *The Spirit of Romance.*
floppin': The collapse of To Publishers.
Freedman: Benjamin Freedman, author of the booklet *Facts are Facts* (Union, New Jersey: Christian Educational Association, 1955). Freedman argues that modern Jews are descended from the Khazars. He also vaguely refers to a global Jewish conspiracy.
Stag: Sidney Mttron Hirsch, one of the founding members of the "Fugitive" group of Southern poets. Apparently Hirsch sent one or two visitors to Pound, thus rousing his ire.
Ruthie: Jeanne Ruth, an aspiring poet who visited Pound at St. Elizabeths.
Kazar: See Pound's letter of 10 July 1938.
van Buren Autobiog: Annual Report of the American Historical Association for the Year 1918, Two Volumes. Volume 2, The Autobiography of Martin Van Buren, p. 99, fn. 1.
XOIROS: "Young pig."
Covici: Pascal Covici, then a senior editor at Viking.

91. ALS–3.

Sept 27/55 30 Willow St Brooklyn 1, N.Y.

Dear E: Glad you wrote. Wish the news were more to glad this earth—about yourself, that is. If I don't write it's becuz I don't wish to interrupt Chinese etc, focus as you said.

"Useful"? alwus comes down "to whom"? I'm probably irreclaimable you would say—And I'll agree—in respects. Ain't in my nature to circulate tho heaven nose Id like to unite others in friendship, taking Baruch [Spinoza] to heart on honesty etc.

Not up on some of yr. current abbreviations—If I'm to try—these questions:

Do you imply there's a possibility of Spirit of Romance reprint, accdg. to To version—which I believe if memory doesn't fail was revised. But only part appeared. I haven't heard from Oppen these 20 years or more. Rexroth said he was in Mexico, summer of '54.

Who is Bro Freedman, & what has he dug up?

Nacherally, if I can foster reprint of Spirit R.—i.e. help someone who wants to reprint it to compare versions etc I'll do it.

Who is the venerable Stag that steered the soup? And bodders you?

Who is "dear Ruthie"—would talk to her, if you think it's worth—I'm not gallant.

"N." = N[ew]. D[irections].?

Vicks = Viking? of which Covici is editor? I
once tried ↗ but to no avail.

Got all to do I can—I mean all I can do to keep 106 lbs walking, 100 infants to wet nurse in my engineering kawledge.

Thought I'd see you this summer, but the doctors took care of that: Celia [Zukofsky] got an aristocratic ulcer—not easy to get rid of, so she faces the year's ratrace from Sept to June with a solid 88 lbs.

I got together ⟨unprinted or unvulumetted⟩ short poems of 10 years or more. Jonathan Williams wants to, depending on funds. And Robert Creeley wants to serialize my Shakespeare—part 2—which should appear in Black Mountain Review No. 6. (You may have seen No 5 includin a bit of A–12). In which case, a bit of the Pericles music will appear with it. No, I never did do more with it. I know the answers. Who's there to get in touch with then?

The Black Mountain boys have character & integrity; head and feelings. In any case, the worst one could say is if it all turns to fish—it shouldn't—it smells fresh now. No pay—but I'm glad to work with them.

Greetings from the Mrs. & Paul [Zukofsky] & to D[orothy]P[ound]

Z

Who's pubn. Van Buren—again, can't make out the allusions!

kawledge: Zukofsky taught English at the Polytechnic Institute of Brooklyn.

Williams: American poet and publisher. He published Zukofsky's *Some Time* in 1956.

Creeley: American poet. *Black Mountain Review* 2:6 (Spring 1956) featured "Song of Degrees" from *Bottom,* including Celia Zukofsky's "Gower Chorus" from Act I of *Pericles.*

92. ALS–3.

Oct 1/56 30 Willow St Brooklyn 1, N.Y.

Dear Ez, You shouldn't have done it. Breaks my heart thinking of you typing out all those addresses. Thanks no end—a fadder's thanks and sighs.

And don't worry we won't make any faux pas and mention your name where we shouldn't—seein az Paolo [Paul Zukofsky] reveres you more 'n than the Ineffable.

All the names useful, of course—and the slants on 'em makes me think back 30 years as if it were today. —And, if it delights you, I suppose you know that you & Paul are the only two friends who could ever get me to "work" against my natural piety—or mulishness.

Just got a note from Marion Cummings, from Silver Lake N.H, saying she and Estlin [Cummings] will be back in N.Y. by Nov 30 and attend. Haven't seen them since 1948 I guess when my awlmost still-born Test wrung commicerations from Estlin, contributor—when Paul saw the signature—he was not quite 5—he asked, Is the man's name 3-3 Cummings? What followed was tea for us 3 at the Cs. —No, this a case where I kept the address. But thanks all the same for thinking along the same lines.

And while we're thinking P[aul]. sent an announcement to Basil [Bunting] —but the perennial question? Where is he? Do you know? Has not answered to several letters since I saw you last.

Wonder if Tate 108 Perry is Allen? Who is a fiddler—or was—I understand and liked "Ferdinand" (my novella) but was disconcerted by Anew (which, of course, E.P. liked)—and just said "Please!" when he saw some of it in his mail pre-publication.

We had sent an announcement to H[arvey]. Breit—who some weeks ago expressed benevolence for Jon. W[illia]ms.' forthcoming posies—i.e. his list inc. L.Z. He knows of me I guess.

New ViYoler has given the young one such pleasure I shall not hear the end of it till I file your letter out of his sight—

⟨C[elia Zukofsky]. says you want to know which sup. Always practical! It's the N.Y. Times Sunday Book Review—"In & Out of Books" column

(Wd. have saved but surely thought you'd get a copy. Will know better in future))

Now Papa is a noivous wreck—This Papa—

Thanks for encouraging his Italian

Yrs

Z

addresses: Addresses of people Pound believed might be interested in receiving tickets to Paul Zukofsky's Carnegie Hall debut. The letter and list do not appear to have survived.

Marion Cummings: The wife of E. E. Cummings.

Test: A Test of Poetry (New York: The Objectivist Press, 1948).

"Ferdinand": First published in 1950 in *The Quarterly Review of Literature.*

Breit: Harvey Breit, American novelist and literary critic. One of the authors of the "In and Out of Books" column in *The New York Times Book Review.*

his list: Jonathan Williams published Zukofsky's *Some Time* in 1956.

Book Review: In *The New York Times Book Review,* 23 September 1956, p. 8. Breit wrote, "The poet who resides in St. Elizabeth's Hospital in Washington, D.C., was born in 1885 and last year New Directions, Ezra Pound's publishers, planned to celebrate Mr. Pound's seventieth birthday by bringing out a small brochure of salutations and tributes. The miniature pamphlet has only just come out, perhaps because Mr. Pound is even more controversial in literature than Mr. Dulles is in politics." Breit went on to quote Ernest Hemingway's suggestion that Pound be allowed to return to Italy. He also mentioned a statement by Giovanni Papini, urging Pound's release, that appeared in the *Corriere Della Sera.*

93. TCS.

23 Giug [1959] [Rapallo?]

[Ford Madox] Ford used to speak well of the Rabbi Hillel (must have been after 1930) spose he ever read him or more than a few quotes?
anything of interest accessible?
Yu evr writ crit of Marianne [Moore]?
or in fact shown any interest in life of
the mind, for past 20 years?

EP

Hillel: Hillel lived in the first century B.C. His sayings are preserved in the Talmud. In an undated note to Pound, Zukofsky referred him to the *New*

Edition of the Babylonian Talmud, ed. Michael Levy Rodkinson (New York: New Talmud Publishing Company, 1900).

94. TCS.

10 Sept [1959] Hot. Ital. Rapallo

Mass of literary Criticism in letters of L.Z. to E.P. wd/ make one vol or 6 if well selected.
came on some here, also poems possibly inedit.
Any practical use to L.Z.?

E.P.

Were Joyce's six lines italian translation of Jas Stephens "Stephen's Green" ever printed?

What does one do with possibly unique typescript
of same? ask Marianne [Moore] if yu dunt kno

or better. Forrest Reid 818 Hanshaw Rd
F. READ Ithaca, N.Y.

Stephens: James Stephens (1882–1950), Irish novelist and poet. Joyce's translation had already been published in Stuart Gilbert's edition of *Letters of James Joyce* (New York: Viking, 1957; London: Faber & Faber, 1957); p. 319.
Read: Forrest Read, American scholar and editor of *Pound/Joyce: The Letters of Ezra Pound to James Joyce, with Pound's Essays on Joyce* (New York: New Directions, 1967; London: Faber & Faber, 1968).

95. ALS–2. On air letter form.

Sept 29/59 135 Willow Street Brooklyn 1, N.Y.

Dear Ez, Thanks for inquiry. I don't getcha exactly. If you mean you would like to select from "mass of literary criticism in letters of L.Z. to E.P. (and) also poems possibly inedit." nothing would please me more and if you know of a publisher let him pay you and give one a bonus ⟨For musick which we're still supporting⟩ if there's anything left. If there isn't, your labor will be your gift to me.

On the udder hand, if you mean you have some clutter on hand you want to dispose of, but think I might be interested in looking at it first, send it back if the shipping costs are no burden.

I don't know if Joyce's Stephens translation was ever printed, and since I don't know who F. Read, Ithaca, N.Y. is—I'd rather not write him. Hasn't Joyce an executor? And wouldn't that be your answer?

One goes on az wuz trying not to be distracted from one's own job by all the daily nuisance of yearning a living etc and there's isn't much news except the work done or going on. Bill [Williams] you have heard has come out of it—it was trying on top of one's own aches. And so at the head of the year 5720 health and all good to you and D[orothy]. P[ound].

Yrs

Z

Bill: William Carlos Williams underwent a serious operation in August 1959.

96. ALS–4. On air letter form

Dec 15/63

NEW ADDRESS (I guess)
160 COLUMBIA HEIGHTS
Brooklyn 1, N.Y.
U.S.A.

Dear Ez, Mainly to wish you and D[orothy Pound]. & all a Happy New Year & a plenitude of 'em to follow—having just run into Desmond O'Grady and heard you'd wake him in the morning with 'now Zuk used to say'—which almost proves there is a theosophy? Need I say it's more than memory here too—& if I don't write it's not that I won't get an answer—but you shouldn't after all be bothered—& I've got to the age where I too have stopped writing letters and the lag of no one answering has become habitual.

One thing I must say—even if I put my foot into it—if the rumors are true about the 'Cantos being all wrong,' as you feel it today, only the guy who wrote

To confess wrong without losing rightness

Charity etc
like a rush light
has a right to say it. But you shouldn't "tell 'em" as you once told me. And anyway when I can't read myself, happens too, I can still read ol' Ez—even the "curriculum" tho one's time is bogged (⟨still "workin' "⟩ o what the hell,) becomes so much one hopes some day to find time for (& bull leaf me I feel agèd most of the time) & for the rest the song carries along, yours, always right. So stop saying such things.

I met the ⟨good⟩ O'Grady at Havahd—at last I was invited to read—60 in January—that lag even longer than you predicted: so you see you were right there too.

Texas U. will be sending you Bottom: on Shakespeare. Hope you can enjoy some of it. And if those letters of mine you offered me some years ago are still around, please sell 'em to Texas for a price and buy comforts or what—since the exhumers will be exhuming anyway & they have all my other MSS. there, these might as well be there. ⟨Take care of yourself Ever⟩

⟨P.S. (or under thought) I understand Mary de R[achewiltz]. has been receiving my Catullus translations in Origin—sometimes wonder what you* might think of 'em if you ⟨can⟩ read 'em.⟩ ⟨*Don't matter what anyone else thinks—even the praise. Still obstinate you see

Z⟩

⟨You'll be glad to hear the kid, ⟨taller than I am now⟩ was in Genoa, Paganini Concours—& won a prize u[nd].s[o].w[eiter].—It's a helluva a "career" tho—wuss than poetry with allee scheisse.⟩

O'Grady: Irish poet and friend of Pound's. Pound lived in O'Grady's Rome apartment for a short time after his return to Italy. See his "Ezra Pound: A Personal Memoir," *Agenda* 17:3–4; 18:1 (Autumn, Winter, Spring 1979/80), pp. 285–299.

rumors: Zukofsky had perhaps heard of Pound's 1963 interview, published in the Italian journal *Epoca,* in which he denigrated his achievements. Gallup C1895.

To confess wrong: From Canto 116. First published in the Summer/Fall 1962 issue of *The Paris Review*. Gallup C1886.

Havahd: Zukofsky read there on 15 December 1963–the date of this letter.

Catullus: Origin, Second Series, in which appeared Catullus IV, XI, XXXI, XXXVII and LXI.

the kid: Paul Zukofsky.

Concurs: This competition is recalled in "A"–19.

Biographical Notes

ALDINGTON, RICHARD (1892–1962). British novelist and poet. He and Pound met in London in 1912 and became literary allies. An important Imagist, he was represented in *Des Imagistes* (1914). His marriage to H.D. in 1913 ended in separation (1918) and eventual divorce (1938). Aldington's experiences as a soldier in World War I are referred to in Canto 16. By the late 1920s relations between Pound and Aldington had cooled somewhat, and although Pound sent Zukofsky a copy of Aldington's *Remy de Gourmont* (1928), it was clearly intended to teach Zukofsky about Gourmont rather than about Aldington.

ANTHEIL, GEORGE (1900–1959). American composer. He first met Pound in Paris in 1923. Pound championed his avant-garde music in *Antheil and the Treatise on Harmony* (1924). Antheil assisted Pound with his opera *Le Testament de Villon,* and he participated in its 1926 premiere. After 1930, however, Pound lost interest in Antheil's development. Zukofsky attended performances of Antheil's work in New York, including a 1927 presentation of the *Ballet Mécanique*. In the fourth number of *The Exile* Pound printed a Zukofsky poem inspired by the concerts: "Critique of Antheil." Pound recalls Antheil in Canto 84.

BLACKMUR, RICHARD P. (1904–1965). American literary critic and poet. Blackmur began corresponding with Pound in 1924. In *The Saturday Review of Literature* for 20 April 1927, Blackmur said of Pound, "All his work exemplifies a fresh use of language: words used with an amazing aptness and pertinence." Blackmur became managing editor of *Hound & Horn* (1929–1930). It was in *Hound & Horn* that Blackmur's major assessment of Pound—was published in 1934. In this essay Blackmur qualified his earlier admiration: "For Mr. Pound is at his best a maker of great verse rather than a great poet. When you look into him, deeply as you can, you will not find any extraordinary revelation of life, nor any bottomless fund of feeling; nor will you find any mode of life formulated, any collection of established feelings, composed or mastered in new form."

BONI, ALBERT. American publisher. In 1913 Albert Boni, in partnership with his brother Charles, opened the Washington Square Book Shop in New York. It quickly became a gathering place for Greenwich Village writers. From the shop the brothers began publishing *The Glebe,* edited by Alfred Kreymborg. The brothers Boni also published Pound's anthology, *Des Ima-*

gistes, in 1914. They went into partnership with Horace Liveright in 1916, forming the firm of Boni & Liveright. The partnership dissolved in 1918. The brothers departed from the company, and Liveright continued publishing as Boni & Liveright.

BRYHER, WINIFRED (1894–1983). Born in Margate, England, the daughter of shipping magnate Sir John Ellerman. Baptized Annie Winifred Ellerman, she took the name Bryher from one of the Scilly Isles, where in her childhood she had spent holidays. Bryher met Hilda Doolittle in 1918, and their intimate friendship lasted until H.D.'s death. She was twice married, first to Robert McAlmon.

BUNTING, BASIL (1900–1985). British poet. Born near Newcastle, England. He first met Pound in Paris in 1922 at the Cafe du Dôme. Pound introduced him to Ford Madox Ford, who employed Bunting as a subeditor on *the transatlantic review.* In 1929–1930 Bunting visited America, where he met Zukofsky. From 1930 to 1933 Bunting lived in Rapallo. His first volume of poetry, *Redimiculum Matellarum* (Milan, 1930) was published with Pound's help. Zukofsky reviewed it in *Poetry.* Pound also edited Bunting's *Villon.* Zukofsky printed section three of "Attis: Or, Something Missing" in the "Objectivists" number of *Poetry.* In "Mr. Ezra Pound," *The New English Weekly* (26 May 1932), Bunting called Pound "one of the most consummate masters of the technique of versification that our literature has ever seen." From 1933 to 1936 Bunting lived in the Canary Islands, and Bunting continued to correspond with Pound and Zukofsky. During World War II he served in the British army. After the war, Bunting spent time in Iran as a correspondent for the London *Times.* In 1953 he returned to England, where he lived for the rest of his life. It was only with the publication of *Briggflats* in 1966 that Bunting began to receive recognition as an important poet. In 1978 the Oxford University Press published his *Collected Poems.* Bunting is mentioned in Cantos 74, 77, 81, and 110.

BUTLER, NICHOLAS MURRAY (1862–1947). President of Columbia University 1901–1945. Butler was also president of the Carnegie Endowment for International Peace 1925–1945. In 1928 Pound wrote Butler suggesting that the Endowment should look into munitions manufacture and other possible causes of modern war. Pound received only a polite acknowledgment. In Pound's *Exile* article "Peace" (reprinted in *Selected Prose*), Pound implies that Butler was deliberately or ignorantly blocking the avowed aims of the Endowment and the intentions of Carnegie. In a letter to Felix Schelling (April 1934), Pound wrote, "But can you, a man with a decent culture, lie down in peace with Nic Butler as titular head of the country's intellectual life? The man who, apart from all his obvious grossness, has sabotaged the Carnegie Fund."

CANBY, HENRY SEIDEL (1878–1961). American literary critic. Editor of *The Saturday Review of Literature* (1924–1936). Chairman of the board of judges of the Book-of-the-Month Club (1926–1958). Author of numerous works of criticism about American literature. Pound's first recorded association with Canby occurred in 1921, when Canby printed Pound's article, "Parisian Literature," in the *Literary Review* of *The New York Evening Post.* In a 1921 letter to Ford Madox Ford, Pound reported that he was "inclined to regard his [Canby's] character with disfavour." In subsequent references to Canby, Pound consistently treated him as an obstructor of genuine literary merit. In a 1945 editorial in *The Saturday Review of Literature,* Canby argued that Pound's poetic achievements were no alibi for treason, and that Pound was a traitor "to the cause of humanity and civilization."

CARNEVALI, EMANUEL (1897–1945?). Italian poet. He emigrated to the United States some time before World War I and settled in New York City. Harriet Monroe published his work in *Poetry.* For a short time he was associate editor of the magazine. He fell ill with *encephalitis lethargica,* a condition which prevented him from working at any gainful employment. He returned to Italy and passed the rest of his days at a hospital in Bazzano. Carnevali received financial support from his friends, including William Carlos Williams and Pound. Pound published two Carnevali poems in *Profile* and found small translation jobs for the invalid. In an undated letter from Carnevali to Williams at the Poetry Center of the State University of New York at Buffalo, Carnevali writes that he has undertaken the task of translating the first 30 cantos and has gotten to number 8. See *The Autobiography of Emanuel Carnevali: Compiled & Prefaced by Kay Boyle* (New York: Horizon Press, 1967).

CHAMBERS, WHITTAKER (1901–1961). Chambers entered Columbia University in the fall of 1920. His faculty adviser–and Zukofsky's–was Mark Van Doren. Zukofsky and Chambers were both members of the Columbia circle of student poets; both published in the student literary magazines. In one of these magazines Chambers published an allegedly atheistic playlet. The university authorities asked him to leave the university. Chambers did so, but he and Zukofsky continued to be friends. Chambers joined the Communist Party in 1925, and it was he who arranged an interview with Party officials when Zukofsky expressed an interest in forming closer ties to the Party. The interview was unsatisfactory on both sides, and though Zukofsky and Chambers' friendship lasted through the 1920s, Chambers' activities for the Party removed him from his old circle of friends during the 1930s. After Chambers' allegations about Alger Hiss caused a sensation, the FBI interviewed Zukofsky about his friendship with Chambers. It is likely that the literary friend Chambers mentions in *Witness* (p. 207) is Zukofsky.

COVICI, PASCAL (1888–1964). American publisher and editor. In 1922 Covici opened a book shop in Chicago, and in the same year began to publish independently. Samuel Putnam was his editor and publicity manager. In *Paris Was Our Mistress,* Putnam claims that it was he who suggested to Covici and to Pound that Covici should take over publication of *The Exile.* In 1928 Covici moved to New York and joined in a partnership with Donald Friede to found the firm of Covici-Friede. The firm went bankrupt in 1938. Covici then joined the Viking Press as an editor, where he had a distinguished career.

CREELEY, ROBERT (b. 1926). American poet. From the early years of his career Creeley has greatly admired Zukofsky's work. Besides publishing Zukofsky in *The Black Mountain Review,* Creeley has in reviews and occasional pieces spoken of the importance of Zukofsky for himself and for other poets in his generation. See his memoir, "For L.Z.," in *Louis Zukofsky: Man and Poet,* ed. Carroll F. Terrell Orono, Maine: The National Poetry Foundation, 1979), pp. 75–77. Creeley wrote the introduction to the Doubleday/*Paris Review* edition of "*A*" 1–12 in 1967.

CROSBY, HARRY (1898–1929). Poet, publisher. Descendant of a patrician Boston family, Crosby turned away from the careers that were marked out for one of his station and plunged into the avant-garde literary life of Paris in the 1920s. His poetry was receiving wide circulation in notable little magazines of the day at the time of his death. Pound contributed an afterword to Crosby's posthumous book of poems, *Torchbearer* (1931). The definitive biography of Crosby is Geoffrey Wolff's *Black Sun* (New York: Random House, 1976).

CUMMINGS, EDWARD ESTLIN (1894–1962). American poet. Cummings lived in Paris from 1921 to 1923, and it was there that he and Pound first met. Pound included work by Cummings in *Profile* (1932) and in *Active Anthology* (1933). Pound thought very highly of *Eimi,* praising it in an article for *The New English Weekly,* "E. E. Cummings Alive" (20 December 1934). In a letter of 11 September 1939 to Wyndham Lewis, Pound said Cummings "is the one writer in America whose mind is active." Cummings is mentioned in Cantos 74, 80, and 89. Cummings' response to Pound was cryptic, though favorable. He discusses Pound briefly in *We Moderns* (New York: The Gotham Book Mart, 1940) and in Charles Norman's *The Case of Ezra Pound* (1948). Zukofsky first wrote to Cummings in 1928. He tried to enlist Cummings as an American supporter of *The Exile,* and mentioned his review of Cummings's play, *Him* (the review is reprinted in *Prepositions*). Cummings is quoted in "A"–1 and in "A"–18. Selections from Cummings are also used in *A Test of Poetry* (1948).

CUNARD, NANCY (1896–1965). English poet and publisher. She first met Pound around 1914 in London. Cunard made a reputation for herself as a poet in the 1920s, especially with her long poem *Parallax* (1925). In 1928 she purchased the types and press that William Bird had used for his Three Mountains imprint. For the next three years she published—under the name of Hours Press—books by Aldington, Aragon, Norman Douglas, Samuel Beckett, Robert Graves, John Rodker, George Moore, and others. In 1930 she published Pound's *A Draft of XXX Cantos*. Pound also contributed to her anthology *Negro* (1934). Cunard objected to Pound's defense of Fascism; she herself was anti-Fascist. Pound mentions Cunard and her black lover, Henry Crowder, in Canto 80 ("Nancy where art thou?") and Canto 84 ("H. Crowder").

DAHLBERG, EDWARD (1900–1977). American novelist and essayist. Dahlberg first made his name with his fictionalized autobiography, *Bottom Dogs* (1929). Writing to Herbert Read in 1955 he said, "Please see, that like Pound, the attempt is not to instruct, but to astonish, and that the conclusions are wild and as predatory as Esau. The *Cantos* are the result of outside speculation, and not of the inward man." Dahlberg did have a close friendship with Zukofsky during the late 1940s and early 1950s. Dahlberg tried to find publishers for Zukofsky's writings. His epitaph for their friendship is contained in a letter of 1958 to Isabelle Gardner, "Speaking of writers, I broke my connection with Louis Zukofsky, who I had aided very greatly. I once asked him to do me a kindness, to see a writer, not a poet or a man of letters, but a gifted man who has shown the connection between Dadaism and modern nihilism, and you know he wouldn't do it because this author is absolutely deaf and would be too burdensome for L.Z.! At one time I fought with Bill Williams over L.Z., and the latter said I was interfering in his friendship with Williams!" Paul Zukofsky states that Dahlberg was, in fact, of little help to his father, and he takes strong exception to Dahlberg's statement.

DEL MAR, ALEXANDER (1836–1926). American historian. His major works are *A History of the Precious Metals from the Earliest Times to the Present* (1880); *The Science of Money* (1885); *Money and Civilization* (1886); *The History of Money in America from the Earliest Times to the Establishment of the Constitution* (1899), and *History of Monetary Systems* (1896). This latter work is quoted from extensively in Canto 97. See Daniel Pearlman, "Alexander Del Mar in the *Cantos*," *Paideuma* 1:2 (Winter 1972), pp. 161–180. Pound thought Del Mar's investigations were important enough to reprint in the Square Dollars series he edited from St. Elizabeths. The two titles published were *Barbara Villiers: A History of Monetary Crimes* and *Roman and Moslem Moneys* (1956).

DOOLITTLE, HILDA (1886–1961). American poet and novelist. Born in Pennsylvania, she met Pound in the spring of 1905. The affection between them resulted in an engagement, but this was finally broken off in 1908. In 1911 she traveled to Europe. In London she became acquainted with many of Pound's friends, including Richard Aldington. She and Aldington married in 1913. Meanwhile, Pound had dubbed her "H.D., *Imagiste*," the signature he supplied for a group of her poems published in *Poetry* in January 1913. Pound and H.D. retained a lifelong affection for each other.

DOUGLAS, CLIFFORD HUGH (1879–1952). British economist. Douglas originated the theory of Social Credit, which holds that maldistribution of wealth due to insufficient purchasing power is the reason for economic depressions and wars. Assisted by A. R. Orage, Douglas expressed his views in *The New Age*. Pound first met Douglas in the offices of that periodical in 1918. Pound took up the fight for Social Credit; it became a crucial component in his own economic theory. Pound urged Zukofsky to admit the value of Social Credit and to work with Gorham Munson's Social Credit magazine, *New Democracy*. Zukofsky, however, thought Marxian economic analysis was more cogent.

DRUMMOND, JOHN. British author. A friend of Pound, he lived in Rapallo during the 1930s. He helped Pound with the proof corrections and made the index for *Guide to Kulchur*. He also translated *Carta da Visità* (1942) as *A Visiting Card* (1952). Other translations by Drummond are: *America, Roosevelt and the Causes of the Present War* (1951) and *Gold and Labour* (1952). The selections from the Cantos published in *Active Anthology* (1933) were made by Drummond, who also annotated them. Along with Pound and T. C. Wilson, Drummond selected the poetry of modern English and American poets for the Spring/Summer 1935 issue of *The Westminster Magazine*.

DUNNING, RALPH CHEEVER (1878–1930). American poet. Born in Detroit, Dunning moved to Paris around 1905 and made it his home until his death. Pound probably met Dunning in Paris after World War I. Pound persuaded the reticent Dunning to submit his poem "The Four Winds" to *Poetry* and to the *transatlantic review*, both of which published portions of it in 1924 and 1925. His next major publication, *Rococo* (1926), was greeted with derision by almost every reviewer. Pound, however, called him "one of the four or five poets of our time" and praised the beauty and musicality of Dunning's verses.

ELIOT, THOMAS STEARNS (1888–1965). American poet. He and Pound met in London in 1914, where Pound dubbed him "The Possum." During the period of Eliot's editorship of *The Criterion*, Eliot published Pound and those authors Pound recommended, though hardly to the extent that Pound desired. Eliot published poems by Zukofsky in *The Criterion* in April 1929 and "The Cantos of Ezra Pound (one section of a long essay)" in April 1931. Zukofsky and Eliot did not meet until Zukofsky called on Eliot in London in 1957. Pound attended the memorial service for Eliot in Westminster Abbey in 1965. Eliot is mentioned in Cantos 46, 65, 77, 80, 81, 74, 94, and 102.

ERSKINE, JOHN (1879–1951). American novelist and teacher. He was a professor of English and American literature at Columbia from 1909 to 1937. Zukofsky includes a portrait of Erskine lecturing in 11. 173–180 of "Poem Beginning 'The.' " It was Erskine who introduced the Great Books program into Columbia's curriculum in 1919, a method carried on by one of his students, Mortimer Adler. Erskine was also an excellent pianist, appearing with several major symphony orchestras. He became president of the Juilliard School of Music from 1927 to 1938. In 1930 and 1931 Erskine collaborated with George Antheil on an opera, *Helen Retires,* for which Erskine wrote the libretto. Erskine was also a novelist; his most popular work was his first, *The Private Life of Helen of Troy* (1925).

FENOLLOSA, ERNEST (1853–1908). American Far Eastern art and literature specialist, appointed Imperial Commissioner of Art in Tokyo. Pound first met his widow in London in 1913. She entrusted Fenollosa's literary remains to Pound, asking him to edit and publish them. The major work resulting from his efforts was *The Chinese Written Character as a Medium for Poetry.* It was first published in four numbers of *The Little Review* (September-December 1919). Other items in the Fenollosa archive included notes on Far Eastern literature and translations of Chinese poetry and Noh plays. Pound published various portions of this material. The Chinese poetry was transformed under Pound's hand into *Cathay* (1915).

FORD, CHARLES HENRI (b. 1913). American poet, novelist, painter, and editor. His first literary venture was the founding of a little magazine in Columbus, Mississippi: *Blues: A Magazine of New Rhythms,* which he edited with the help of Parker Tyler and Kathleen Tankersley Young. Ezra Pound contributed "Program 1929" to their March 1929 number. Ford founded the magazine *View* in 1940, and edited it until its cessation in 1947. Zukofsky published an essay on the painter Dometer Guczul in the fall 1943 issue.

FORD, FORD MADOX (1873–1939). British novelist and poet. In 1908 he founded *The English Review,* which published Conrad, Hardy, and James, as well as such younger talents as Lawrence, Wyndham Lewis, and Pound (whom Ford first met in early 1909). Pound paid tribute to Ford's poetry in "The Prose Tradition in Verse" in 1914 (reprinted in *Literary Essays*). In the 1920s Ford lived in Paris and edited *the transatlantic review.* In the 1930s he divided his time between France and the United States. One of his later projects was the founding of a literary society in New York, "The Friends of William Carlos Williams," of which Zukofsky was a member. Ford is recalled in Cantos 74, 80, 82, 98, 100, and 104. Brita Lindberg-Seyersted's *Pound/Ford: The Story of a Literary Friendship* (New Directions, 1982; Faber & Faber, 1982) gives a complete picture of the Pound/Ford relationship and prints their letters.

FOSTER, JEANNE ROBERT (1884–1970). American poet and editor. Foster was a close friend of John Butler Yeats and John Quinn. From 1910 to 1922 she served as a literary editor for *The Review of Reviews;* she was also the American editor of Ford Madox Ford's *the transatlantic review.* She traveled to Paris in 1921, where she and Pound met for the first time. In the late 1920s Foster moved to Schenectady and lost contact with her literary acquaintances. Pound was briefly in touch with Foster in 1939.

FROBENIUS, LEO (1873–1938). German anthropologist and archaeologist. Pound refers to Frobenius often in the Cantos and in *Guide to Kulchur*. Pound thought his *Erlebte Erdteile* (seven volumes, 1925–1929) more important than Frazer's *The Golden Bough*. He was indebted to Frobenius for the concepts of *Paideuma* and *Sagetrieb*. In April 1937 Frobenius came to the United States to attend the opening of an exhibition (at the Museum of Modern Art in New York) of 200 prehistoric cave drawings from his collection. During his stay in the U.S. he lectured on "Rock Pictures of Africa and Europe." Zukofsky reported to Pound in a letter of 17 June 1937 that he and William Carlos Williams had attended one of Frobenius's lectures.

GESELL, SILVIO (1862–1930). German economist. Author of *The Natural Economic Order* (1934–1936). Pound's monetary theories were influenced by Gesell. Pound found Gesell's proposals regarding stamp scrip and *Schwundgeld* especially attractive. The Austrian town of Wörgl used this system with apparent success, and Pound pointed to this experiment as an example both of the soundness of Gesell's thinking and the fear it aroused in the hearts of financiers. Pound treated Gesell at length in his 1935 essay "The Individual in His Milieu: A Study of Relations and Gesell" (reprinted in *Selected Prose*). Gesell is mentioned in Cantos 74 and 80.

GOLD, MICHAEL (1893–1967). American novelist and editor. Born Itzok Granich on New York's Lower East Side. He joined the American Communist Party in 1915 and remained an active member until his death. Gold became editor of *The New Masses* in 1928 and wrote a regular column for *The Daily Worker* in the 1930s. Pound's respect for Gold disappeared in the 1930s as the rift between their political beliefs widened. Zukofsky, though from the same background as Gold (they were born on the same street), thought Gold too ready to subordinate art to politics. Gold appears briefly in "A"–1 under the name of "Carat."

GOULD, JOE (1889–1957). American author and Bohemian. While living in New York in 1917 Gould decided to give up gainful employment and live in Greenwich Village on the charity of others while he composed, or ostensibly composed, his "Oral History," a massive compilation of his thoughts, observations, and quotations overheard in the streets, bars, and houses of Manhattan. In the early 1920s Gould became acquainted with E. E. Cummings, and Cummings told Pound about Gould. From 1929 to 1931 portions of the "Oral History" appeared in *The Dial, The Exile, Broom,* and *Pagany*. These seem to have been the only fragments of the "Oral History" that Gould actually wrote down.

GOURMONT, REMY DE (1858–1915). French poet and essayist. During the 1890s and the early years of the twentieth century Gourmont produced numerous critical works. Pound first began reading Gourmont in 1911–1912. When Gourmont died in 1915, Pound wrote two obituaries, the second of which (for *Poetry*) began, "Remy de Gourmont is dead and the world's light is darkened." Pound also edited a de Gourmont number of *The Little Review* in 1919. In 1922 Pound translated de Gourmont's *Physique de l'amour,* which was published as *The Natural Philosophy of Love.* For a complete account of Pound's response to Gourmont, see Richard Sieburth's *Instigations: Ezra Pound and Remy de Gourmont* (1978).

GREGORY, HORACE (1898–1982). American poet. The first of many collections of his poems was *Chelsea Rooming House* (1930). He was a professor of English at Sarah Lawrence College from 1934 to 1960. In "The Search for a Frontier" (*The New Republic,* 26 July 1933), Gregory gave a mixed review of *A Draft of XXX Cantos.* This lukewarm reception to the Cantos was confirmed in *A History of American Poetry 1900–1940* (1946), which Gregory co-authored with his wife, the poet Marya Zaturenska. Their view of Pound was, "It would seem that Pound in the years after 1920 had exhausted the wealth and abused the fine temper of his poetic gifts."

HARMSWORTH, DESMOND (b. 1903). British poet and painter. Though in the late 1920s and early 1930s Harmsworth was known as a newspaperman and publisher, his subsequent career was as a painter. He continued to publish poems, but gained his primary fame as the portraitist of Norman Douglas, James Joyce, Osbert Sitwell, and others. *How to Read* (1931) was the only Pound volume published by Harmsworth.

HILLYER, ROBERT (1895–1961). American poet and critic. Professor of English at Harvard University (1919–1945). His *Collected Verse* won the Pulitzer Prize in 1933. According to James Laughlin, one of the reasons he left Harvard to visit Pound in 1933 was "to get away from Robert Hillyer." Hillyer became one of the most bitter opponents of the awarding of the Bollingen Prize to Pound. In "Treason's Strange Fruit" and "Poetry's New Priesthood" (published in *The Saturday Review of Literature,* 11 June 1949 and 18 June 1949, respectively), Hillyer condemned the Bollingen Prize committee, the award to Pound, Pound, and Pound's poetry.

JOSEPHSON, MATTHEW (1899–1978). American biographer and historian. In the early 1920s Josephson lived in Paris and Berlin, where he became allied with the Dadaists. He helped edit the small magazines *Secession* and *Broom.* In the mid-1920s, however, Josephson broke with the Dadaists and Surrealists and became convinced that his mission was to promote the idea of the socially conscious writer. His 1928 "Open Letter to Mr. Ezra Pound" in *Transition* prompted Pound to write William Carlos Williams to inquire about Josephson and the reason for his attack. During the 1930s Josephson leaned to the literary left, as indicated by his *The Robber Barons* (1934) and *The Politicos* (1938).

KAHN, OTTO (1867–1934). American financier and patron of the arts. Born Mannheim, Germany. Emigrated to the United States in 1893 and became a partner with the New York investment banking house of Kuhn, Loeb & Company. He became a senior partner in 1920. Kahn supported a variety of artistic projects and artists, including the Metropolitan Opera, the Provincetown Playhouse, Hart Crane, and *The Little Review*. Pound urged Kahn in 1931 to become a sort of liaison officer between the governing class and the intellectual leaders of mankind. In addition, Pound wrote Kahn about the obstacles to progress in the United States and urged him to do something about them.

KIRSTEIN, LINCOLN (b. 1907). American author and ballet promoter. Founded and edited *Hound & Horn* (1927–1934). In "Crane and Carlsen: A Memoir," *Raritan* 1:3 (Winter 1982), Kirstein recalls the founding of *Hound & Horn*. He notes that "Pound wrote us almost weekly tyrannical letters, called us 'Bitch & Bugle,' considered he controlled the quarterly, and quarreled with us when we bridled at his demands for the publication of Ralph Cheever Dunning, Louis Zukofsky, and Adrian Stokes."

KITASONO, KATUE (d. 1978). Japanese poet. Editor of the Tokyo literary magazine *Vou*. An admirer of Pound's works, he published between 1936 and 1940 translations of some of Pound's poetry, an abridged translation of *ABC of Reading*, and a translation of "Mediaevalism" from a copy of *Guido Cavalcanti Rime* sent him by Pound. A group of poets connected with Kitasono became known as the *Vou* group, and Pound wrote an introduction to a collection of their poems translated into English. Ronald Duncan published them in the first issue of his magazine *Townsman*. In his introduction Pound said, "I know that nowhere in Europe is there any such vortex of poetic alertness. Tokio takes over, where Paris stopped." In *Guide to Kulchur* Pound included a statement on poetics by Kitasono. In "For a New Paideuma" (*The Criterion*, January 1938) Pound remarked, "I know of no group of poets in Europe or America as alert as Mr. Kitasono's Tokio friends." The essay is reprinted in *Selected Prose*.

KREYMBORG, ALFRED (1883–1966). American poet. Editor of the little magazine *Glebe* (1913–1914) and *Others* (1915–1919). *Glebe* introduced to the United States the poetry of Pound and his fellow Imagists. In 1921 Kreymborg met Pound for the first time, in Paris, an incident recounted in his autobiography, *Troubadour* (1925). With Harold Loeb, Kreymborg founded and edited the little magazine *Broom* in Rome in the same year, 1921. In 1922 Kreymborg returned to the United States, where he lived for the rest of his life, writing poems, drama, and criticism. In 1927, with Paul Rosenfeld, Lewis Mumford, and Van Wyck Brooks, he founded the *American Caravan* series of American writing, volumes of which appeared in 1927, 1928, 1929, 1931, and 1936.

KRUIF, PAUL HENRY DE (1890–1971). American microbiologist and author. De Kruif became famous for his numerous books detailing medical advances in the nineteenth and twentieth centuries, the most popular of these being *Microbe Hunters* (1926). A lively and considerable correspondence passed between de Kruif and Pound in the 1930s. Pound reviewed de Kruif's

Hunger Fighters in *The New English Weekly* for 22 February 1934, calling it, "a just record of heroisms that have solved vital problems of food production."

LAUGHLIN, JAMES (b. 1914). American publisher and author. Laughlin and Zukofsky first met in Rapallo. In 1936 Laughlin founded New Directions. Zukofsky's poem "Mantis" was printed in Laughlin's anthology *New Directions in Prose and Poetry* (New Directions, 1936). Laughlin sketches his relations with Pound in *A Memoir of Ezra Pound* (1982).

LÉGER, FERNAND (1881–1955). French painter. Pound recalls an encounter with Léger in Paris in his "D'Artagnan Twenty Years After" (*The Criterion,* July 1937). " 'We' London 1911–1914 were subsequent to a great deal of Paris. For example Fernand Leger in 1902 was doing the kind of drawing which Gaudier did in 1911. I can not believe that any great number of people in England, the U.S.A. or even in Paris know this. I know it only by accident, having lived a few doors from Leger and having by sheer chance turned over a soiled bit of paper amid a heap of his sketches, saying at once: 'My God, Fernand, I didn't know you could do that!' To which the rich slow voice: *Oh voui, mais je pouvais pas PEINDRE.*" The essay is reprinted in *Selected Prose.*

LEWIS, PERCY WYNDHAM (1886–1957). British painter, novelist, and essayist. He attended Rugby and the Slade School of Art. He met Pound in 1909. As one of the leading Vorticists he was primarily responsible for the publication of the two numbers of *BLAST*. After Pound moved to Paris he and Lewis did not collaborate further, but remained lifelong friends. Their relationship is documented most fully in *Pound/Lewis: The Letters of Ezra Pound and Wyndham Lewis,* ed. Timothy Materer (New York: New Directions, 1985; Faber & Faber, 1985). Pound himself recalled Lewis and the *BLAST* period in "D'Artagnan Twenty Years After," *The Criterion* (July 1937). (Reprinted in *Selected Prose.*) Pound also mentions Lewis in Cantos 16, 80, and 115.

LIVERIGHT, HORACE (1886–1933). American publisher. Liveright joined with Albert Boni to form the firm of Boni & Liveright in 1916. Boni departed from the firm in 1918 and Liveright carried on until 1930. Boni and Liveright published Pound's anonymous translation of Edouard Estaunié's *The Call of the Road* in 1923, and his *Personae* in 1926. In a letter to Liveright of 23 March 1928, Pound recommended Louis Zukofsky as a translator of German books. In September 1929 Pound asked Liveright if he would consider bringing out an American edition of *The Cantos,* but Liveright declined. Liveright is mentioned in Canto 80.

LOWELL, AMY (1874–1925). American poet, a descendant of James Russell Lowell. In 1913 she associated herself with the Imagists, and was represented by one poem in *Des Imagistes* (1914). According to Pound, she took over the Imagist movement and converted it into a less vital and rigorous "Amygism." In 1919 Lowell wrote to Florence Ayscough, "Poor Ezra, he had a future once, but he has played his cards so badly that I think he has barely a past now." Her 1925 collection of verse, *What's O'Clock,* won the Pulitzer Prize in 1926. Pound mentions her in Canto 77.

MAGARET, HELENE (b. 1906). American poet and biographer. Her first volume of poetry, *The Trumpeting Crane,* was published by Farrar and Rhinehart in 1934. Pound's assessment of her is contained in a letter to Mary Barnard of 13 August 1934, "Or take Helene Magaret–don't seem to *go on.*"

MCALMON, ROBERT (1896–1956). American writer and publisher. William Carlos Williams and McAlmon founded the little magazine *Contact.* Shortly thereafter, McAlmon met and married Winifred Bryher, whose father, Sir John Ellerman, provided the funds that enabled McAlmon to begin his Contact Publishing Company in Paris in 1923. In 1929 McAlmon suspended Contact Publishing and left Paris. He traveled widely in Europe and North America, and then settled permanently in Albuquerque, New Meixco, taking a position in his family's hardware store. Pound noted in his 1934 "Date Line" (reprinted in *Literary Essays*), "America is now teeming with printed books written by imitators of McAlmon, inferior to the original." McAlmon's *Being Geniuses Together* (1938) is a memoir of life in Paris in the 1920s.

MCKENZIE, DONAL. American poet. McKenzie was one of the editors of *The Morada* (extant 1929–1930). Pound wrote to Harriet Monroe, on 29 October 1931, "Did I or did I not suggest tempering Zukofsky with McKenzie? Zuk to provide the good sense and McKenzie the conviction of the value of the new group." Pound's regard for McKenzie seems to have waned rapidly. Perhaps Pound saw McKenzie's essay, "T(h)inker Pound and Other Italian Legends," *The Left* (Autumn 1931), in which McKenzie says, "Pound is an incurable Romantic Liberal, toasting his toes at the better Fascisti fires, and trying to rationalize about a system of which he really enjoys the fruits."

MACLEISH, ARCHIBALD (1892–1982). American poet. MacLeish went abroad between 1923 and 1928 and lived in Paris most of the time, where he became acquainted with Ezra Pound. His poem *Conquistador* (1932) won the Pulitzer Prize. His *Collected Poems 1917–1952* (1953) won for him a second Pulitzer Prize, the Bollingen Prize, and the National Book Award. He was also awarded the Presidential Medal of Freedom. During the 1950s MacLeish was persistent in his attempts to free Pound from St. Elizabeths, and was primarily responsible for Pound's release.

MACLEOD, JOSEPH GORDON. British poet. His only book of verse was *The Ecliptic* (London: Faber and Faber, 1930). On 28 March 1936 Pound wrote to him, congratulating him on Faber's rejection of another volume of poems (*Letters,* pp. 279–280). Pound mentions him in Canto 114: "There was a thoughtful man named Macleod."

MACLEOD, NORMAN (1906–1985). American poet, novelist, and editor. Editor of *The Morada* (1929–1930). American editor of *Front* (1930). Macleod published his poetry in *Transition, This Quarter, The New Review,* and other magazines. His first book of poems, *Horizons of Death,* appeared in 1934.

MANGAN, SHERRY (1904–1961). American poet, novelist, editor, and journalist. From 1930 to 1933 he assisted Richard Johns with *Pagany.* He corresponded regularly with Pound during the late 1920s and early 1930s. In the January-March 1931 issue of *Pagany,* Pound commented, "In choosing Sherry Mangan as its critical spokesman, if he was chosen, *Pagany* could not have done better." Mangan published a highly favorable review of Pound's *Guido Cavalcanti Rime* in the March 1933 issue of *Poetry.*

MOCKEL, ALBERT (1866–1945). Belgian-born French poet, critic, and editor. Mockel edited a little magazine, *La Wallonie,* in Liège from 1885 to 1892. In his October 1918 *Little Review* essay, "Albert Mockel and 'La Wallonie,' " Pound praised the quality of the magazine and summed up, "There is perhaps no greater pleasure in life, and there can have been no greater enthusiasm than to have been young and to have been part of such a group of writers working in fellowship at the beginning of such a course, of such a series of courses as were implicated in *La Wallonie.*" In December 1929 Zukofsky sent his essay on Pound to Mockel, asking if he would submit it to the editor of the *Mercure de France.* Pound refers to Mockel in Cantos 78 and 80.

MONROE, HARRIET (1860–1936). American editor and poet. Born in Chicago, Monroe's reputation was confined to that city until 1912, when she published the first numbers of *Poetry: A Magazine of Verse.* She engaged the services of Pound as the magazine's foreign correspondent. Pound summed up Monroe's part in the poetry revolution in *Il Mare* (18 March 1933): "The talent of Monroe–conscientious and goodwill, we might even say a maternal instinct towards poetry–in whom critical sense was lacking, but who performed the miracle of extracting the money needed from the pockets of the biggest butchers in Chicago to carry on a review, one might say the bulletin of the union or profession of American poetry, which has lasted for twenty years." In January 1924, *Poetry* published one of Zukofsky's first poems to appear outside of Columbia University's literary magazines, "Of Dying Beauty." Monroe also printed a batch of seven of his poems in the issue for June 1929. Harriet Monroe's autobiography is *A Poet's Life* (1938).

MOORE, MARIANNE (1887–1972). American poet. She edited *The Dial* from 1925 to 1929. In her 1949 essay, "Ezra Pound," she commented, "Ezra Pound is that rarity, an artist who is a preceptor by *example:* a master or 'sage,' whose inexhaustible virtuosity has made and is making his verse and criticism an archive of poetic wisdom." Pound's early essay, "Marianne Moore and Mina Loy," is reprinted in *Selected Prose.*

MÜNCH, GERHART. German pianist, arranger, and composer. Münch frequently visited Rapallo in the 1930s, where he participated in the summer concerts arranged by Pound. Canto 75 features, in Hugh Kenner's words, "a violin part which Gerhart Münch made from Francesco da Milano's lute reduction of Clement Janequin's choral arrangement of perhaps some Provençal tune." When the Zukofsky family visited Pound at St. Elizabeths in 1954, Paul Zukofsky played it for Pound.

MUNSON, GORHAM (1896–1969). American editor and essayist. He edited *Secession* from 1922 to 1924. In 1924 he met A. R. Orage, with whom he became friends. Munson was a frequent lecturer at the New School for Social Research from 1927 on. In 1933 he began editing the Social Credit journal *New Democracy,* to which Pound contributed a number of articles. The journal ceased in 1939.

NIEDECKER, LORINE (1903–1970). American poet. She began corresponding with Zukofsky in 1931, after seeing the "Objectivist" issue of *Poetry*. Zukofsky forwarded her work to Pound, who published it in *The Westminster Magazine.* She did not meet Zukofsky until 1933, when she visited New York. The last meeting between Niedecker and Zukofsky occurred in 1968, when he, Oppen, Rakosi, and Reznikoff were participating in a conference on the Objectivists at the University of Wisconsin at Madison. Her "The Poetry of Louis Zukofsky" in *The Quarterly Review of Literature* (April 1956) was one of the earliest studies of Zukofsky's work.

OPPEN, GEORGE (1908–1984). American poet. He first met Louis Zukofsky, Tibor Serly, and Charles Reznikoff in New York in 1928. In 1929 Oppen and his wife Mary went to France, where they settled for three years. Here they began publishing books under the imprint of the Objectivist Press. They issued *An "Objectivists" Anthology,* William Carlos Williams' *A Novelette and Other Prose,* and Pound's *ABC of Reading.* In late 1930 the Oppens visited Pound at Rapallo. Here they also met Basil Bunting. They returned to New York, where they lived from 1933 to 1937, at first in Brooklyn Heights, not far from Zukofsky. In 1934 Oppen published his first book of poems, *Discrete Series.* Pound's foreword said, "I salute a serious craftsman, a sensibility which is not every man's sensibility and which has not been got out of any other man's books." Oppen resumed writing (in the late 1950s) and publishing poems (in 1962) with *The Materials.* He won the Pulitzer Prize for *Of Being Numerous* (1968). Oppen's career is recounted in Mary Oppen's memoir, *Meaning A Life* (1978).

POR, ODON (b. 1883). Italian journalist and economist. Por wrote *Fascism* (English translation, 1923), an important, early book defending Mussolini and his policies. He served as a propagandist for Fascism throughout the life of the Fascist regime in Italy. Pound translated his essay "Systems of Compensation" in 1937 (Gallup C1409). In 1941 Pound translated his book, *Italy's Policy of Social Economics* (Gallup A49).

POUND, DOROTHY SHAKESPEAR (1886–1973). Wife of Ezra Pound. She met Pound in January 1909, and they were married in London on 20 April 1914. They remained together for the next twenty-one years, until Pound was arrested at the end of World War II. After the war, she came to the United States to be close to her husband and to act as his legal guardian. Their early life is documented in *Ezra Pound and Dorothy Shakespear,* ed. Omar Pound and A. Walton Litz (New York: New Directions, 1984; London: Faber & Faber, 1985).

POUND, HOMER LOOMIS (1858–1942). Ezra Pound's father. He married Isabel Weston in 1883 and was appointed Register of the United States Land Office in Hailey, Idaho. Here Ezra Pound was born on 30 October 1885. In 1889 Homer Pound was appointed assayer at the U.S. Mint in Philadelphia, where he remained until retirement in 1928. In 1929 he and his wife moved to Rapallo, where he died in 1942.

POUND, ISABEL (1860–1948). Ezra Pound's mother. Her father, Harding Weston, was (like the Loomis branch of the Pound family) descended from old New England settlers. Her aunt, Frances Weston, ran the boarding house in New York City that Pound recalls in *Indiscretions* and *The Cantos.* Isabel joined her husband in retirement in Rapallo.

PUTNAM, SAMUEL (1892–1950). American editor, essayist, and translator. In 1930 he started his magazine, *The New Review.* Pound acted as associate editor. Zukofsky was represented in the second number of *The New Review* by "A"-3 and "A"-4. The magazine's last issue (1932) contained a poem by Kay Boyle, "In Defense of Homosexuality," which prompted Pound to resign his editorship. When Putnam returned to the United States in 1933, he published an article in *Mosaic,* "Ezra Pound: Cracker-Barrel Revolutionist," in which he said that Pound "dwells in a murky Hinterland of his own into which only now and then a fancied ray of light flickers." In *Paris Was Our Mistress* (1947), Putnam recalled that "At Ezra's instigation, a literary journal known as *L'Indice* was founded in the vicinity of Rapallo, and in its columns . . . he would hold forth at great length on such writers as Robert McAlmon, Louis Zukofsky, Carl Rakosi, and the American 'Objectives,' long forgotten now. . . ." He also concluded that "Ezra may or may not be convicted of treason, but the *Cantos* will nonetheless remain the masterpiece we always declared them to be, and we still shall read and cherish them even as we lament their author's fate."

RACHEWILTZ, MARY DE (b. 1925). Daughter of Ezra Pound and Olga Rudge. She is a distinguished translator of the works of her father and other poets. Her memoir of her life and her parents is *Discretions* (1971).

RAKOSI, CARL (b. 1903). American poet. Rakosi was represented in *The Exile,* and it was Pound who arranged the first contact between Zukofsky and Rakosi. Zukofsky published Rakosi in the "Objectivists" issue of *Poetry* and in *An "Objectivists" Anthology.* His *Selected Poems* were published by New Directions in 1941.

RASCOE, BURTON (1892–1957). American critic and editor. In 1916 he became chief book reviewer for *The Chicago Tribune,* and his career as a well-known critic was launched. During the 1920s he reviewed for *The New York Tribune* and wrote a syndicated literary column. From 1931 to 1933, he was the literary critic for *The New York Sun.*

REISMAN, JERRY (b. 1913). Zukofsky met Reisman in 1929, when Zukofsky was working part-time as a teacher in the New York public high schools, where Reisman was a student. During the 1930s, according to Zukofsky, Reisman was his "best friend." Zukofsky encouraged him to write, but Reisman's interests were in the sciences and mathematics. It was Reisman who helped Zukofsky with the mathematical and scientific material in "A"–8 and "A"–9. In early 1947, however, the friendship was ended.

REXROTH, KENNETH (1905–1982). American poet. According to Carroll F. Terrell, in *Louis Zukofsky: Man and Poet,* Rexroth and Zukofsky were colleagues at the University of Wisconsin in 1930–1931. There is no mention, however, of Rexroth in Zukofsky's letters to Pound from that period. Zukofsky did include work by Rexroth in the "Objectivists" issue of *Poetry.* Reviewing Zukofsky's *Some Time* in 1957, Rexroth noted that, "Louis Zukofsky is one of the most important poets of my generation," that "In 1930 most qualified judges would have put him in the first rank," and that "Ill-informed critics have often dismissed him as being merely a disciple of Ezra Pound and William Carlos Williams, the latter especially. This is really just an abusive cliché."

REZNIKOFF, CHARLES (1894–1976). American poet. Together with George Oppen and Zukofsky he founded the Objectivist Press, which published his *Jerusalem the Golden* (1934), as well as his *In Memoriam: 1933* (1934), and *Separate Way* (1936).

RIDGE, LOLA (1883–1941). Irish-born American poet. She became an editor for *Others,* and then American editor for *Broom.* During the *Others* era her apartment was a famous gathering place for the members of that group and other writers and artists.

RODKER, JOHN (1894–1955). British novelist, poet, and publisher. In 1919 he founded The Ovid Press, which published titles by Gaudier-Brzeska, Eliot, Lewis, and Pound. In 1928 Rodker published a limited edition of *A Draft of the Cantos 17–27 of Ezra Pound.* In "Pound's Villon on the Radio," *The New Review* (Winter 1931/32), Rodker praised Pound's Villon opera in his review of the two B.B.C. broadcasts it had received. Pound's opinion of Rodker's novel, *Adolphe, 1920,* was very high. Writing to his father on 11 April 1927, Pound said, "As to the Rodker: I rather think he gets more into the 90 pages (that makes the complete nouvelle) than most novelists get into 300." In his 1928 essay, "Dr. Williams' Position" (reprinted in *Literary Essays*), Pound remarked, "The other offspring of *Ulysses,* the only other I have seen possessing any value, is John Rodker's *Adolphe, 1920.*"

RUDGE, OLGA (b. 1895). American concert violinist. Pound heard her play in London in 1920, and noted her in one of his musical reviews (under the name of William Atheling) in *The New Age* for 25 November 1920. By 1923 they had met. Rudge played in concerts of Pound's music in Paris in 1924. In July 1925 Rudge bore him a daughter, Mary. Rudge translated Jean Cocteau's *Le Mystère Laïc,* which appeared in *New Directions 1936.* She was able to visit Pound at St. Elizabeths in 1952. From 1962 until his death, Pound was cared for by Rudge.

SAVIOTTI, GINO. Italian editor, novelist, and literary historian. Saviotti edited the Genoese journal *L'Indice,* for which Pound wrote a number of articles on literary affairs in 1930 and 1931.

SERLY, TIBOR (1900–1978). Hungarian-American violinist and composer. At some point in the late 1920s he became friends with Zukofsky. Through Zukofsky he became acquainted with Pound. During the 1930s Serly made frequent trips to Europe, often visiting Rapallo. Some of his music was performed at the Rapallo concerts. Pound gave Serly the manuscript of his *Ghuidonis Sonata,* which Serly performed for Pound privately during Pound's New York visit in 1939. It was at Serly's home in New York that Zukofsky and Pound met for the second time, in September 1939.

STEVENS, WALLACE (1879–1955). American poet. Zukofsky's appreciation of Stevens is contained in his late essay, "For Wallace Stevens." Stevens wrote the preface to the Objectivist Press edition of Williams's *Collected Poems 1921–1931* (1934).

STOKES, ADRIAN (1902–1971). British writer about art and aesthetics, poet and painter. He became acquainted with Pound in the late 1920s. Among his early works were two which studied a period and artists in whom Pound was also interested: *The Quattro Cento* (1932) and *Stones of Rimini* (1934). Pound reviewed both books favorably in *The Criterion* (the reviews are reprinted in *Ezra Pound and the Visual Arts*).

TATE, ALLEN (1896–1979). American poet. Educated at Vanderbilt University, Tate joined the university's group of poets known as the Fugitives. Tate's early opinion of *The Cantos,* expressed in a 1933 review of *A Draft of XXX Cantos,* was that it might not be a great work, but "it is the repository of the most beautiful verse writing of our age." Later, in his *Sixty American Poets, 1896–1944,* Tate cited Pound as "a great teacher of other poets in the principles of the craft," but Tate also noted that *The Cantos* "have neither form nor progression, and remain a chaotic museum of beautiful fragments."

TAUPIN, RENÉ (1904–1981). Franco-American critic and educator. After writing *L'Influence du symbolisme français sur la poésie Américaine* (*1910–1920*) (1929), Taupin emigrated to the United States, where he made his living as a professor of French. During the 1930s Taupin made trips to Europe, where he became personally acquainted with Pound. Taupin's "La poésie d'Ezra Pound," *Revue Anglo-Américaine* (February 1931), is a highly favorable summary of Pound's career. When Zukofsky arrived in France in 1933, Taupin took him on a week-long tour of Normandy and Brittany.

TITUS, EDWARD (1870–1952). American publisher. In 1926 Titus established the Black Manikin Press in Paris. Among its publications were works by Ralph Cheever Dunning, Mary Butts, and D. H. Lawrence. In 1929 Titus took over the magazine *This Quarter,* which he owned and edited until 1932, when it ceased publication.

TYLER, PARKER (1904–1974). American editor and author. Tyler began his literary career by aiding Charles Henri Ford with the editing of *Blues.* He also collaborated with Ford on a novel about life in Greenwich Village, *The Young and Evil.* Tyler also helped edit *View.*

VAN DOREN, MARK (1894–1972). American poet, critic and educator. Van Doren taught English at Columbia from 1920 to 1959. Among his students was Louis Zukofsky. Zukofsky kept in touch with Van Doren. In *Bottom: On Shakespeare,* Zukofsky thanks Van Doren "for his gift of a facsimile volume of the original First Quartos of Shakespeare's *Poems* and *Pericles,* inscribed 10/7/47."

WILLIAM CARLOS WILLIAMS (1883–1963). American poet. It was Pound who urged Zukofsky to meet Williams; the meeting took place in April 1928, and they became lifelong friends. In addition, Zukofsky helped Williams by editing much of his work, especially *The Descent of Winter* (1928) and *The Wedge* (1944). Zukofsky wrote several essays on Williams; they are collected in *Prepositions.* "A"–17 is a memorial to Williams, written by Zukofsky in March 1963. Williams' essays on Zukofsky are reprinted in *Something to Say: William Carlos Williams on Younger Poets* (New York: New Directions, 1985). Neil Baldwin analyzes the Williams/Zukofsky tie in "Varieties of Influence: The Literary Relationship of William Carlos Williams and Louis Zukofsky," *Credences* 2:1 (Summer 1982).

WINTERS, YVOR (1900–1968). American poet and critic. From 1932 to 1934 he was the Western editor for *Hound & Horn.* In his *In Defense of Reason* (1947), he observed that "Pound at maturity, then, sees life primarily as a matter of remembered impressions, and his art is an art of revery: he is a sensibility without a mind, or with as little mind as is well possible."

YEHOASH. The pen name of Solomon Bloomgarden (1870–1927), Yiddish poet. Born in a town near the Russo-German border, he emigrated to the United States in 1890, settling in New York. A. A. Roback, in *The Story of Yiddish Literature,* comments that "Yehoash was probably the first Yiddish poet to become interested in the poetry of his adopted country." Charles A. Madison, in *Yiddish Literature: Its Scope and Major Writers,* notes that "Yehoash was strongly influenced by English poetry. . . . Were his expressionistic verse composed in English it would have placed him among the leading imagist poets."

ZABEL, MORTON DAUWEN (1901–1964). American editor, educator, and author. He became an associate editor of *Poetry* (1928–1936), and then editor-in-chief (1936–1937). Pound, writing to Ford Madox Ford on 8 June 1937, said "I take it Zabel is sheer SHIT and will do nothing to maintain decent critical standards."

ZUKOFSKY, CELIA THAEW (1913–1980). Wife of Louis Zukofsky and mother of Paul Zukofsky. Born on the Lower East Side of New York City, she first met her future husband in 1933. They married in August 1939. Their son Paul was born in 1943. Her words are woven into many of her husband's poems, and many of the poems are addressed to her. She composed the music for the poems in his *Autobiography* (1970). She also composed the music for *Pericles,* the second volume of *Bottom: On Shakespeare.* The "L.Z. Masque," which she composed, was used by L.Z. for "A"–24. After his death she published a comparative anthology consisting of quotations from his works and the works of other American writers, *American Friends* (1979).

ZUKOFSKY, PAUL (b. 1943). American violinist and conductor. The son of Louis and Celia Zukofsky. He began taking violin lessons at the age of four. At seven he became a pupil of Ivan Galamian. His formal debut recital occurred at Carnegie Hall in 1956. His father's novel, *Little* (1970) is a *roman à clef* (centering on Paul's career) about the Zukofsky family during the years 1945–1968. Ezra Pound appears in it under the name of R. Z. Draykup. Paul had played for Pound when the Zukofskys visited him at St. Elizabeths in 1954. Paul Zukofsky's words and deeds are extensively recorded in *"A"* and in his father's shorter poems.

ZUKOFSKY, PINCHOS (*c.* 1860–1950). Father of Louis Zukofsky. He was born in Lithuania, in the province of Kovno. Emigrating to the United States in 1898, he settled in New York's Lower East Side. Zukofsky summarizes his father's life in "A"–12, pp. 150–156.

Selected Bibliography

Ezra Pound

ABC of Economics. London: Faber and Faber, 1933.

ABC of Reading. London: George Routledge & Sons, 1934.

Active Anthology. London: Faber and Faber, 1933.

The Cantos. New York: New Directions. Rev. ed., third printing, 1972. London: Faber and Faber, 1975.

Cathay. London: Elkin Mathews, 1915.

The Classic Anthology Defined by Confucius. Cambridge, Mass.: Harvard University Press, 1954.

Des Imagistes. New York: Albert and Charles Boni, 1914.

A Draft of XXX Cantos. Paris: Hours Press, 1930. New York: Farrar & Rinehart, 1933.

Eleven New Cantos. New York: Farrar & Rinehart, 1934. London: Faber & Faber, 1935.

Ezra Pound and Music: The Complete Criticism. Ed. R. Murray Schafer. New York: New Directions, 1977. London: Faber and Faber, 1978.

The Fifth Dacad of Cantos. London: Faber and Faber, 1937. New York: Farrar & Rinehart, 1937.

Guide to Kulchur. London: Faber & Faber, 1938. New York: New Directions, 1968.

Guido Cavalcanti Rime. Genoa, Italy: Edizioni Marsano, 1932.

Instigations. New York: Boni and Liveright, 1920.

Literary Essays of Ezra Pound. London: Faber and Faber, 1954. Norfolk, Conn.: New Directions, 1954.

Lustra of Ezra Pound. London: Elkin Mathews, 1916.

'Noh' or Accomplishment. London: Macmillan, 1916 [i.e., 1917].

Pavannes and Divisions. New York: Alfred A. Knopf, 1918.

Personae: The Collected Short Poems of Ezra Pound. New York: Boni & Liveright, 1926.

Personae: The Collected Poems of Ezra Pound. New York: New Directions, 1949. London: Faber and Faber, 1952.

The Pisan Cantos. New York: New Directions, 1948. London: Faber and Faber, 1949.

Poems 1918–21. New York: Boni and Liveright, 1921.

Polite Essays. London: Faber and Faber, 1937. Norfolk, Conn.: New Directions, 1940.
Profile: Milan: Giovanni Scheiwiller, 1932.
Quia Pauper Amavi. London: The Egoist, 1919.
Selected Letters of Ezra Pound. Ed. D. D. Paige. New York: New Directions, 1971. London: Faber and Faber, 1971.
Selected Prose 1909–1965. Ed. William Cookson. New York: New Directions, 1973. London, Faber and Faber, 1973.
The Spirit of Romance. Norfolk, Conn.: New Directions, 1968.
Ta Hio: The Great Learning. Seattle, Washington: University of Washington Book Store, 1928.

Louis Zukofsky

"A." Berkeley, California: The University of California Press, 1978.
All: The Collected Short Poems. New York: W. W. Norton, 1965.
An "Objectivists" Anthology. Le Beausset, Var, France: To Publishers. 1932.
Anew. Prairie City, Illinois: The Press of James A. Decker, 1946.
A Test of Poetry. New York: C.Z. Publications, 1980.
Bottom: On Shakespeare. Austin, Texas: The Ark Press for the Humanities Research Center, the University of Texas, 1963.
Catullus. London and New York: Cape Goliard Press in association with Grossman Publishers, 1969.
55 Poems. Prairie City, Illinois: The Press of James A. Decker, 1941.
First Half of "A"-9. New York: Privately printed, 1940.
It Was. Kyoto, Japan: Origin Press, 1961.
Le Style Apollinaire. Paris: Les Presses Modernes, 1934.
Prepositions: The Collected Critical Essays of Louis Zukofsky. Berkeley, California: The University of California Press, 1981.
Some Time: Stuttgart, Germany: Jonathan Williams, 1956.

Index